Vicar to Dad's Army

Vicar to Dad's Army

The Frank Williams Story

Frank Williams
with Chris Gidney

CANTERBURY
PRESS
Norwich

© Frank Williams and Chris Gidney 2002

First published in 2002 by the Canterbury Press Norwich
(a publishing imprint of Hymns Ancient & Modern Limited,
a registered charity)
St Mary's Works, St Mary's Plain,
Norwich, Norfolk, NR3 3BH

www.scm-canterburypress.co.uk

British Library Cataloguing in Publication data

A catalogue record for this book is available
from the British Library

ISBN 1-85311-494-4

Typeset by Regent Typesetting
Printed and bound in Great Britain by
Biddles Ltd, Guildford and King's Lynn

CONTENTS

PREFACE

On a recent Saturday evening, almost 25 years after the recording of the final episode of *Dad's Army*, memories of one of the happiest periods of my career came flooding back into my mind.

With other surviving members of the cast, I was attending an amateur performance by the Tring Festival Company at the charming Court Theatre in Pendley. The evening was called *A Tribute to Dad's Army*. The company had been doing the show since Tuesday, six performances in all, including a matinee that afternoon. The theatre had been packed at every performance. The talent of the cast combined with the enduring popularity of the programme had given them one of their biggest successes. The show itself consisted of two episodes from the television series – 'The Deadly Attachment' and 'The Godiva Affair' – which were reproduced on stage by permission of Jimmy Perry and David Croft. It was clear from the audience's reaction that their words had lost none of their power to produce gales of laughter.

Some pieces of narration had been specially written to cover any necessary scene or costume changes. Part of this narration described how the series had come into being and gave some description of the two authors. As I sat there in the audience, I thought of the chain of events that had led to the creation of what is probably one of the best loved television comedies of all time. The first event in the chain was the young Jimmy

Perry, aged 16, becoming a member of his local Home Guard and serving there until he joined the army. The next important event was his walking across St James's Park one summer's day in 1967. He heard the bands playing in the distance for the changing of the guard. He thought of the soldiers in their scarlet tunics and remembered how during the war the Home Guard in their drab khaki battledress had taken their turn in doing this duty. That evening, sitting on the train going out to Stratford East (where he was working as an actor with the famous Joan Littlewood theatre company), with memories of his time in the Home Guard still in his mind, the idea for a comedy series suddenly hit him. Then, having written the first script, he put it aside for a few weeks until he found himself working as an actor for David Croft in an episode of *Beggar my Neighbour*. He showed the script to David who liked it. The BBC agreed to do the first series and the rest is history.

Recently, Jimmy and David have both talked about some of the casting discussions which took place and it is fascinating to wonder what might have happened if some of the other names mentioned had been cast in the roles – fascinating, but pretty impossible. The actors who finally appeared on the screen are now so closely identified with the famous characters that one cannot imagine anyone else playing the parts. That first series grew into nine in all. Over 80 episodes of the programme were made. It was adapted for radio, made into a feature film and produced as a successful musical stage show which ran for six months in London, followed by a six-month tour of the provinces. Since the programme finished in 1977, it has been repeated on television many times. It has been sold abroad and videos of the programme continue to be popular. There is an Appreciation Society here in the UK, with a thriving branch in New Zealand. It has been described as a television legend and I am very proud to have been part of it.

So what was the chain of events that led to my involvement with the programme? I suppose that the key to it was getting to know Jimmy Perry. I first met him when he was running the repertory theatre at Watford. I had known the theatre for many years as a member of the audience, so I suppose the first event in the chain that was to lead me to *Dad's Army* was my parents' decision to buy a house in a place where the nearest repertory theatre was the Watford Palace. And it is here that my story begins.

I

SUBURBAN SECURITY

In 1931 Edgware was part of the rapidly growing sprawl of London suburbia. Houses were going up and people were moving in. Parkside Drive was a road like thousands of others springing up all over North London, with detached and semi-detached houses designed for middle-class families. Many of the first occupants were retired couples; there were also families with grown-up children and a smattering of those expecting their first child or, as in my parents' case, having just acquired their first child.

After making my first entrance in a local maternity home, it wasn't long before I was carried over the threshold into number 26. This was to be my home throughout my child-hood and the early years of my adult life. The house consisted of a dining room, drawing room, kitchen and scullery, with bedrooms, a bathroom, lavatory, and so on upstairs. There was also a walk-in airing cupboard, which was to prove a useful if rather obvious hiding place when playing 'Hide and Seek' at birthday parties. A better hiding place was the large cupboard under the stairs where the outdoor clothes were kept. Here I could conceal myself behind the overcoats and mackintoshes, hoping that if the person opening the door did spot a pair of shoes, they would not notice the feet and legs rising from them.

There was a garden at the back with a lawn surrounded by flowerbeds. At the top left-hand corner there was a rockery and at the right-hand corner a large flowering cherry tree.

Next to this was the 'Gnomes Garden'. This was my domain. Having won one at a funfair and having read about them in various fairy stories, I was rather into gnomes – I have a feeling my parents were not. So a compromise was reached and the gnomes were confined to this small area that belonged to me. My father even carved a small notice to place in front of it saying 'Gnomes Garden' so there could be no doubt. Next to it there was a tiny pond in which there were goldfish. The gnome who had a fishing rod stood there patiently for years never catching anything, while his companions sat on their toadstools contemplating life.

On our left lived the Senker family whose son Peter was to become my closest childhood friend. On the right were the Carliers and their daughter Ann. With Audrey Trotman who lived over the way, we were to form the nucleus of the children who played together in our street.

We had a maid. It sounds rather pretentious for an ordinary middle-class family, but it was not unusual in those days. Many of our neighbours had one. They were usually Irish girls who had come over to England seeking employment and perhaps hoping to experience some of the excitements of living in a big city. Ours was Nancy Cavanagh; the Senkers had Lilly Casey. I was very fond of Nancy and would spend hours in the kitchen chatting to her. She was infinitely patient and never seemed to mind that a lot of her time was taken up scuttling around from room to room, probably clearing up after me!

My mother was the secure centre of our family life. She was always there, comforting me when I was upset about something, drying my tears and giving me a hug. She had a strong personality, but she was warm and understanding and she was fun. She was forthright and clear in her thinking and would probably have made a good businesswoman. As it was, like most women of her day, she was perfectly happy to be a 'faithful wife and mother' and care for my father and me.

She was an extremely good cook, and I rather doubt whether Nancy had much of a look-in in that area. Cakes were a speciality and it was a great treat to be allowed to scrape the bowl after the cake had gone into the oven. At Christmas time she made the puddings, the mincemeat and the Christmas cake. My father and I would be summoned to the kitchen to have a stir for good luck.

Sometimes I would go shopping with my mother. If the shop was not crowded, I would sit on one of the chairs provided for the customers; if it was, I would clutch her hand as she went round the various counters. I was fascinated to see the bacon slicer producing the thin rashers that we would have at breakfast. Then it was on to the next counter where the assistant in his white apron would use two wooden butter pats to weigh up the required amount of butter from a huge, square, glistening mound in front of him, patting it into shape and wrapping it before handing it over. The sugar and the dried fruit were all weighed into little blue bags and then we would move on to the biscuit counter. Here there were jars and tins containing various kinds of biscuits. Oval Maries and Digestives and perhaps some Rich Tea would be ordered. At this point, there would be an anxious tug at her sleeve from me. 'Oh yes, and some Teddy Tail biscuits, please.' Teddy Tail was a character in a strip cartoon for children in the *Daily Mail*. They were my favourites. I liked the taste, but the main thing was that Teddy's picture was on the front of them. Eggs were counted into a paper bag. How did we ever get them home without breaking them? Unless my memory deceives me, the only thing that was pre-packaged was tea, and maybe even that was at a later date.

Stanley J. Lee was a drapery emporium. A large shop with counters all around, it was a fascinating place. Mother would make the purchase and, when she handed over the money, the assistant would place it, with the bill, into a wooden container that was clipped on to a wire overhead. A pull on a lever and it would go whizzing away to the cashier in the centre. Seconds later it would come whizzing back with the right change. Did it ever go wrong? Did the change ever go to the wrong place? It never seemed to. It was like magic and I could have watched it for hours.

My father, a very quiet and gentle man, had wanted to be a doctor, but with a large family to educate, the fees involved would have been out of the question. An early photograph shows a handsome man, wearing the tightly fitting, single-breasted jacket of the day with starched white collar and silk tie neatly in place, his strong face half-smiling from beneath a straw boater. He was very good looking and I suspect he was something of a ladies' man in those early years. He was a very caring person and a particularly good listener. It was he who taught me to love books. Reading a lot to me while I was young, it was he who inspired my interest in all manner of writings. When he read *Oliver Twist* to me I remember feeling a particular excitement in learning how Bill Sykes went on the run through Hendon, now a suburb near us. I was fascinated as my father explained that it would then have been a small village outside London and very different from the busy shopping centre I knew.

I became an avid reader, and could often be found sitting in a corner or on my bed with a copy of anything from Enid Blyton to Captain Marryatt. I have never understood the modern denigration of Enid Blyton. Of course she was middle class, but so were many of her readers. She may have had a limited vocabulary, but I believe she did more to stimulate the imagination and inspire a love of reading than almost any other children's writer of the time. She put ordinary children like me into wonderfully adventurous situations. Perhaps without a brother or sister as a playmate in those early years, these books enabled me to live a lot of my life in the world of my own imagination.

Of course I did play with other children. When Peter Senker's younger sister Joan, and Ann Carlier's younger brother Neil were old enough, they were allowed to join with us, but strictly on the understanding that they were junior partners in anything we might be doing. Audrey Trotman and I were around the same age, but it was a male-dominated society so I was the leader in all we did. If we played at being at school, I was the headmaster. If we played at doctors and nurses, I was the doctor. Ann was allowed to be a nurse because she had been given a dressing-up nurse's uniform as a birthday present. The others all had to be patients. If we played at being a family, Audrey and I were the parents and the others our children.

The Senkers always made me feel welcome. They were Jewish, which seemed to mean that while I went to Sunday School on a Sunday, Peter went to Hebrew classes on a Saturday, and rather mysteriously this apparently involved reading backwards! I was quite often there on a Friday when Mrs Senker would light the Sabbath candles and say a prayer. At certain times of the year they used entirely different crockery. On these occasions ordinary bread seemed to disappear from their table, and they had something called matzos, big square pieces of unleavened bread. After the Passover, ordinary bread appeared once more on the Senkers table, while any leftover matzos were given to my mother, who rather liked them. I found all these different religious traditions fascinating.

While playing in each other's back gardens or in the local park, we would invent secret hiding places and imagine ourselves in the kind of situation which years later Enid Blyton was to invent for her *Famous Five* series. On wet days we would sit indoors and play the usual board games: Ludo, Snakes and Ladders, and later Draughts. The frustration of having to drop all the way down a snake just as one had nearly reached the top was infuriating. I daresay it was good for the soul, although it didn't feel like it at the time.

We often went out all together as a family: visits to friends; trips to the zoo; and, joy of joys, the annual visit to see Father Christmas at Selfridges. I told him what I wanted for Christmas but was always slightly surprised that he didn't know already since, with my parents' help, I had written him a letter, listing my requests. These expeditions usually ended with tea at Lyons Corner House where a small band would play popular tunes of the day as I ate my egg on toast followed by some kind of exotic pastry or perhaps a knickerbocker glory.

It was my father who began to show me the world beyond Edgware. We would travel to London on the recently opened underground, and he would take me to see Big Ben and the Houses of Parliament, Westminster Abbey, Trafalgar Square, St Paul's Cathedral, the Monument, and so on. He would tell me all about them and he was very knowledgeable. He had in the past given lantern-slide lectures about London, probably back in his home town of Cowbridge in Wales where many of the people would never have visited the great metropolis. After one of our trips, out would come the long leather box containing the slides and we would revisit the places we had seen during the day. With my mother as the audience I would chatter excitedly on about what I had learned, pointing out something on the picture in the manner of a true lecturer.

The slides were four-inch pieces of square glass that were placed inside a metal lantern that resembled a large rectangular biscuit tin with a cylinder sticking out at the front. This cylinder housed the lens that threw the pictures onto the screen – a piece cut from one of mother's old bedsheets fixed to a piece of wood top and bottom to keep it taut. It was then hung by a cord on the picture rail in the drawing room.

Soon I wanted to share all this with my friends and my magic lantern shows were a big hit with all. They were enthralled as we plunged the room into darkness, and began the show. I worked the slider from left to right and right to left, revealing pictures of all the famous buildings. With all my newly acquired knowledge I would naturally provide the commentary. Sometimes, in my excitement, I would put a slide in upside down, much to the delight of the audience.

Later, history gave way to fun when Father purchased some slides of children's stories. 'Cinderella', all in full colour, followed 'Puss in Boots'. Doing these shows and getting an audience reaction was probably the first time I realized I had a desire to entertain.

Eager to build on my reputation as a local impresario, I was thrilled when my father arrived home with an Episcope. It worked like a magic lantern, but I could cut out a picture from any magazine and throw its image onto the screen. The result was that my imagination now knew no bounds. Whereas before I was tied to the slides that could only be bought, now I could invent any storyline, illustrate it with my own pictures, and amaze my friends even more. I kept the cut-out picture of King George V and Queen Mary for last as the show would always end with the National Anthem played by my father on the piano. Just when I thought we couldn't do any better, I was given a Pathescope. This was the forerunner of the home movie projector, and when enthusiasts demanded their own camera, eventually gave birth to the home movie industry.

There were various kinds of Pathescope, and mine was an 'Ace', with a handle that when wound provided a two-minute sequence of moving pictures. Mickey Mouse and Popeye soon became regular guests at our house. The films were encased in a black metal container which fitted onto the projector and had to be carefully fed through the 'gate' making sure that the sprockets on the side were in the right place. These films were made of nitrate and were extremely flammable, the little red triangle in the corner reminding the owner to keep it away from any type of open flame, or face an event even more serious than those portrayed on their new gangster movies.

Perhaps the picture was a little unsteady and difficult to watch at times, but this new magical wonder took my imagination further than ever before. These moving picture shows were to lead me further into my future love of films.

My father's hobby was woodwork, and he was an extremely able amateur carpenter. When I was quite young, he made me a child's desk. With draws down each side of the knee-hole, it was a beautifully crafted miniature of the conventional pedestal desk. I don't know whether he hoped it would help to stimulate my talent for writing or not, but it certainly did. I was very proud of it and sat at it writing my plays and feeling very grown-up and important. Next, at my request, he made me a toy theatre. While my friends watched, I would move the cardboard cut-out characters around the stage, improvising the plot and dialogue as I went along.

My attempts to get my friends to take part in live drama were less successful. Most of the efforts rarely got beyond the first two or three rehearsals. I was, of course, very ambitious. One project was *The Scarlet Pimpernel* – I had just read the book. I was, naturally, Sir Percy Blakeney. Later, having seen a film about his life, I decided to do a play about Handel, with myself in the title role. I could rehearse this on my own and I agonized movingly over the effort of writing the 'Messiah'. None of these projects ever came to fruition and perhaps it was just as well. One year a Christmas gift of 'Ernest Sewell's Conjuring Outfit' further stimulated my eagerness to entertain, but I think that the success of the effects were due more to the cleverness of the apparatus than to my slight-of-hand skills. Realizing that a box that made a coin disappear could only be performed once to the same audience, I was delighted to discover the existence of card tricks. I spent hours rehearsing these effects on our pet dog and had even more fun presenting them at the concerts. On most occasions they worked well, but I was always prepared for any embarrassing mistakes that might arise.

When handing out the pack at one particular concert, followed by the standard instructions to choose a card and then replace it, I suddenly realized that I didn't actually know what the card was. With the pack now in my hand I waffled for a moment before resolutely showing the spectator his supposed card. When the victim announced that my card was not correct, I firmly responded with 'Don't be silly, this is definitely your card. You must have forgotten it!' He looked at me uncertainly for a moment and then agreed that he might have done. Obviously I had, by now, learned to speak lines with conviction.

Whatever the entertainment we always finished as my father struck up 'God Save the King'. Even if it hadn't been used elsewhere the faithful Episcope with the pictures of their majesties would come into play again at this point. The entire drawing-room audience stood to attention and then Mother came in with the refreshments.

It was my patriotism that caused me to realize that adults do not always behave as a child feels they should, when I eventually arrived at kindergarten school in 1936. I was just one term into my new class when the death of King George V was announced. The whole nation went into mourning and I got a day off school. On my return, I was deeply upset to discover that my teacher had lined her desk drawer with a newspaper portrait of the late King. I was shocked beyond belief, and told my parents that this was just not right!

Abiding memories of this school consist of doing lots of things with raffia and sitting on the floor trying to fasten an elusive strap on my shoe with a button-hook. We learned basic spelling by helping ourselves to little baskets in which there were small cards with words printed on them. I suppose it was an early version of 'look and say'. The baskets were graded according to age and I soon got fed up with my junior one and helped myself to something a bit more senior. The teacher spotted me, took the basket away saying it was much too difficult for me, and handed me the junior one again, so it was back to boring old cat, bat and mat. It was all very frustrating.

My next school met in St Andrew's Church hall while they waited for the building of a new school to be completed. It was a dual-purpose building designed to serve both as a church and a church hall. The holy table, choirstalls, pulpit and lectern could be screened off at one end, and there was a stage at the other end. Was this perhaps an apt expression of what were to become the two most important elements of my life: the world of the Church and the world of entertainment?

It was at this venue that, apart from my drawing-room appearances, I made my public acting debut. Empire Day was always celebrated with gusto, and my primary school made significant efforts to have their children involved. Even at such a young age, my aptitude for performing must have been spotted, and I was picked to appear on stage in a pageant designed to show how the Union Jack was constructed and how it represented England, Scotland, Ireland and Wales. Parents sat row upon row, waiting for their little angels to appear, as the music from the crumbling piano came to a halt. Whispers of expectancy gave way to urgent hushes to be quiet. Each trembling child was to appear on stage representing one of the countries. As my father had come from Wales I was considered to have Welsh connections and would represent that country. My part in the drama was secured, but with one problem: Wales was not actually represented in the Union Jack.

'I am the cross of St George,' said the first wobbly voice, brandishing his shield with its red cross.

'I am the cross of St Patrick,' said the next.

'I am the cross of St Andrew,' said the last.

They all held their shields proudly in front of them. Then it was my turn. No shield for me. I came on carrying a daffodil and said very firmly, 'My flag is not shown in your Union Jack, but my country is part of Great Britain all the same.' I might not have had a shield, and my emblem might not have been part of the Union Jack, but for a small boy with a yellow flower, it was an historic moment. An actor had been born. It was at this early stage in my life that I realized how little I wanted to be a traindriver or policeman when I grew up. Acting was going to be the thing.

I had long realised that my parents were somewhat older than the parents of other children, but it did not really bother me. I also knew that unlike most of my other friends' fathers, my father did not work. He was retired – whatever that meant. When I asked him to explain it to me he did so.

Grandfather had owned a large drapery business in Wales and had a large family of children to match. My father's mother had died when he was just 12, and my grandfather had married again. It was understood that my father was to take over the family business when he was old enough, and so was sent to learn more about the trade at one of the large department stores in London. However, the new and modern ways of millinery and fashion discovered by my father did not sit well with Grandfather who was firmly stuck in traditional ways. Eventually Father decided that he did not want to be part of the family firm, and so pursued other work. When in due course he inherited some money he decided to invest it and take early retirement. With perfect timing, I arrived shortly afterwards.

My father's Christian name was William. This meant that his full name of William Williams was a bit of a tongue twister, and had earned him the nickname 'Twice' when he was at school. I was later intrigued to discover that it was also the name of the great Welsh hymnwriter who wrote 'Guide me, O thou great redeemer'. My mother also had a dual name, but of a different kind. Her real name was Alice but she was called Theresa by my father and his family. The reason for this was something that I never got to understand. To add to this confusion of names I had been baptized Frank John, but throughout my childhood was always known by my middle name. I only started to use 'Frank' when I became an actor. To this day, when sending Christmas cards to some of my more longstanding friends, I have to stop and consider which name to use.

Though Mother had been confirmed in the Church of England, Father, being a good Welsh Nonconformist, had not. We all worshipped at the local Presbyterian church where my parents were actively involved. Father taught a Bible class for boys, and Mother was on the working party for the annual sale of work. For some reason, I did not like the Sunday School there, but agreed to attend the one in St Andrew's Church where my primary school met. There were always a couple of hundred children there for the first part. The parish of Edgware of which St Andrew's was a part was very firmly in the evangelical tradition. I rather enjoyed the jolly choruses and children's hymns – although I was not too sure about the idea that Jesus wanted me for a sunbeam – and I was quite happy to 'build on the rock' and to wave my Bible in the air as we sang 'Draw your sword. Use your sword'. After all being together for this communal singing, we split into various classes of about 10 or 12 children. This was where the real teaching was done. There was a strong emphasis on biblical teaching and the need for a personal relationship with God, which, although I have now moved away from the evangelical tradition, provided me with a firm basis for the future.

Alan Staines was a splendid young Sunday School teacher who encouraged my faith enormously. Somehow he managed to relate to us in a special way. We respected him, and learnt more as a result. He was instrumental in persuading me to join the Campaigners, a uniformed organization much like the Scouts but with an emphasis on definite Christian teaching. The meetings would follow the usual pattern of games and so on, but at the end there was what was known as 'Clan C'. We would sit on the floor in the shape of the letter C, while the leader would give a talk (usually related to a Bible passage), and then we would have prayers. The Campaigner salute was in keeping with its Christian ethos. The left arm was held horizontally across the chest, parallel to the ground (this signified ruling out the self). This was for the Juniors, but when you reached the Inters (I never did) this gesture was combined with the rather more conventional salute done with the right arm pointing to the cap badge which had the words of the Campaigner motto on it: 'Unto Him'. So that was what Campaigners were meant to do: negate the self and look to Christ. It was all very admirable but I was never quite sure why you had to become an Inter before the second part of the equation came into play.

Evangelical organizations of the time were very suspicious of anything to do with drama and acting, so it was surprising that it was in the Campaigners that I found a way of expanding my stage experience even further. In a Campaigner concert I appeared on the platform (we were not allowed to call it a stage) and said 'I do my daily dozen, I bend and touch my toes, I close my mouth when breathing . . .' There was more, but perhaps fortunately I cannot remember the rest. This daft rhyme was to give the impression that I was athletic, which I most certainly was not. I would much rather sit and read a book than do sports. It was my first experience of having to play a role for which I felt I was entirely unsuitable. In later years I often felt frustrated at being typecast. On this occasion, all I could think was how inappropriate it all was.

It was as a Campaigner that I was presented with a New Testament which had John 3.16 printed on the flyleaf. The word 'whosoever' was left out of the text with a dotted line in its place on which I was instructed to write my own name. When I had done this it read 'For God so loved the world that he gave his only begotten Son, that Frank John Williams who believeth in him should not perish, but have everlasting life.'

Again the emphasis on the personal relationship – not the whole truth, but an important one.

From my earliest days my mother and father made sure that I always said grace before meals. For example,

> Thank you for the world so sweet,
> Thank you for the food we eat,
> Thank you for the birds that sing,
> Thank you God for everything.

Yes, I know, it's rather twee but it belonged in that era and, anyway, it is the thought that counts. At night when I was ready for bed, my parents would stay in the room to hear me say my prayers. These too were phrased in a formula of the period: 'Gentle Jesus, meek and mild, look on me a little child. Pity my simplicity, suffer me to come to Thee.' Then a prayer that God would bless my parents, grandparents, uncles, aunts and anyone else I could think of. I'm not sure how far the list went on, but as soon as it was finished and my mother and father had left the room, I would get down to chatting with God in earnest. Now alone, I would lie there for a long time telling Him about all the things that were on my mind.

Perhaps reading some of the books given to my father as Sunday School prizes, which were very concerned with tragic death and orphaned children, had made me fear that I might lose my parents, as most of those poor unfortunate Victorian children had done. I knew above all things that I did not want to be left on my own. I was not afraid of death; I believed in the afterlife. It was separation I feared. So I prayed that God wouldn't let my parents die. Then to make doubly sure I would add, 'But if they do, please let me die as well, so that we can still be together. Amen.' Then it was off to sleep knowing that I had covered every eventuality. God answered the first part of the prayer, so He didn't need to answer the second. They didn't die and I didn't either, so that was all right. In fact, I was to have both parents with me throughout my child-hood and the first part of my adult life.

Fireworks and 5 November went together. One year my heart sank. There were no fireworks left in the shop. To me, the day would be an immense letdown without them. We always had fireworks set off by my father in our own back garden. God was good at sorting things out so I decided to ask Him. 'Please let me have some fireworks. Amen.' Half an hour after arriving home there was a knock at the door and there stood the shopkeeper. 'Mr Williams,' he said, 'I've got this spare box of fireworks that was on order, but no one has come to collect it. I have to shut up shop now, and I was wondering if you would like them instead.' I wasn't surprised. God did things like that. I have no idea why He answered such a selfish prayer. I didn't really think about it at the time. As far as I was concerned He had answered, and that was that. It certainly gave a tremendous boost to my faith!

It was around this time that I had my first introduction to the small screen. 'Would the boy like to see television?' asked Mr Alderton. My father and I had gone into the radio store to buy a new record for my wind-up gramophone. The purchase completed, we had become caught up in the owner's latest acquisition.

Reaching towards a huge mahogany box with a tiny cream-coloured piece of glass at the top, Mr Alderton turned a bake-lite knob. Odd noises were emitted as the screen glowed ready for action. All at once there was the flickering picture of a woman singing. It was like listening to the wireless, but you could see her! It was magic. Here was my Pathescope without a film, but with sound. I thought it was wonderful, but my father was less impressed. He was a devotee of the wireless. 'It'll never catch on,' he said as we walked slowly home together. Even then I knew he was wrong.

It was my father who took me to see my first real movie; we went to the Ritz in Edgware to see *Captain January*. The flickering picture on Mr Alderton's television screen and even my Pathescope paled into insignificance as I watched the clear black and white picture on the enormous screen, and it talked! It starred Shirley Temple, easily the most famous child star of all time. I won't pretend I fell in love with her, but I was captivated – someone of my own age, acting, singing and dancing. This confirmed it. There was no doubt. I knew that this was what I wanted to do.

Not long afterwards, I was standing in a long and winding queue. This time it was outside the Ambassadors cinema in Hendon and I was excited about seeing the long-awaited, first full-length Disney cartoon, *Snow White and the Seven Dwarfs*. It was 1937, I was six, and our local authority was worried that children would be scared by the wicked witch and had refused it a 'U' certificate. I'm glad that my parents took me to see it anyway, and I was far too brave to be scared. I loved swashbuckling adventures such as *The Sea Hawk* and *The Adventures of Robin Hood* with Errol Flynn. He became a great favourite and when he appeared in *The Private Lives of Elizabeth and Essex* with Bette Davis, it made me feel that history could be quite exciting. Having arrived home full of enthusiasm about the story, I was determined to research it further. I asked Father to look up the Earl of Essex in our *Encyclopaedia Britannica*. He did so and I was somewhat disillusioned to find that Hollywood had rather gone over the top in fictionalizing it.

Like many young children, it was pantomime that was my introduction to live entertainment. My first pantos were all at the Golders Green Hippodrome five stops down the Northern Line from Edgware. *Aladdin* starred Freddie Forbes and I sat there entranced as he got the audience to shout out 'Hanky Twanky!' every time he wiped his nose on his sleeve.

The magic of pantomime was important to me. I knew the story and I wanted to stick to it. I was excited to see everything come alive on stage, right in front of me. Unlike film, these were real people and I loved it. I believed in it all. We all went to the West End one year to see *Cinderella* at the Coliseum and in the scene where Buttons tries to cheer her up by making his own coach out of all the pots and pans, my heart sank as I thought that Cinderella would not be going to the ball in a coach after all. Was she really going to meet her prince in this ramshackle affair? Anyway, she was still in rags even if she did have a colander on her head for a tiara. I wanted to see a pumpkin turn into a coach. I wanted to see her rags transformed into a ballgown. Was this really not going to happen? I need not have worried. The Fairy Godmother appeared, and all was well. Cinderella did go to the ball. And in my heart, I went with her. What I did not want to do was to climb up on stage for the traditional song sheet. I was still basically very shy, and crouching down in my seat I would fervently hope that I would not be spotted or picked, and I never was.

The wireless was an important feature of our life at the time. One of my earliest memories of it was not a happy one. My mother and father had gone out and had left me in the charge of our maid Nancy. The Pope had recently died, and – Nancy being a good Catholic – she spent the afternoon listening to the funeral which was being broadcast. I was very scared of all this talk about a dead body. The atmosphere the commentator created was very frightening to a small boy and I couldn't wait until my parents returned to bring an atmosphere of normality again.

Most of the time, however, I loved the wireless. From a toddler I had sat in my little wicker chair beside the set just before teatime, enjoying *Children's Hour* and the stories of Uncle Mac. You could also go *Out with Romany*, and then there was *Toytown* based on stories by the late S.G. Hulme Beaman. I had no idea who this gentleman was and no one ever explained why he was always late, but I loved Larry the Lamb, Ernest the Policeman and Mr Grouser who was always grumbling about something.

I remained an avid reader and the acquisition of a new Arthur Ransome, Dr Doolittle or William book was always a great occasion. William and his gang of outlaws was a particular favourite and the author, Richmal Crompton, continued to produce new ones so that the supply seemed inexhaustible. On many occasions my father would take me into central London, to a store called Bumpus. It was a magical place – row upon row of bookshelves that seemed to stretch forever. I would leave firmly clutching the latest William book with its brightly coloured version of one of Thomas Henry's wonderful illustrations on the dust jacket. I could not wait to get home to start reading the new adventures that Crompton had in store for William and his gang.

A feature of life was the annual family holiday to the seaside. The trunk would go off in advance and when the great day arrived, we would go to the London terminus to catch our train. There would be packets of sandwiches, carefully prepared by Mother and wrapped in greaseproof paper. When I got a bit older, instead of sandwiches, we went down to the restaurant car for lunch and that was even more exciting. I would spend the journey trainspotting, noting down the names of the other engines that we passed. Then we would arrive and have our first sight of the sea. It was a great moment.

Porthcawl was a favourite because to a little boy like me, its funfair was a place of wonderful excitement. You could win china animals at the various stalls and you could ride on the dodgems. You could sit in a car and be hauled to the top of the water shoot and come hurtling down at break-neck speed into the pool of water at the bottom which splashed into a great spray as the car hit it. I would happily have spent the entire day there, but my parents were keen that I experienced just as much fun on the beach building sandcastles and paddling. At Porthcawl there was also a ventriloquist who entertained the children. His doll was called Tommy and I felt the visit was worth it for him alone.

Visits to my grandparents had their own fascination. My maternal grandmother lived in the country town of Ringwood. Life there was very different from suburban London. I went fishing for tadpoles and played marbles with some of the local boys. Milk arrived in churns and was measured into a waiting jug. Hens were kept in the back garden and we would go down and look for the eggs. My grandmother was like an older version of my mother, and I was very fond of her. Many of the family still lived in the area and there was much visiting of aunts and uncles and cousins.

My paternal grandfather was a staunch Nonconformist and Sabbatharian. There were a number of things that we did not do on a Sunday at home. However, when we visited my grandfather the list seemed to extend. I suspect in an ideal world he would have liked me to sit in the corner with an improving book containing pictures of Bible stories. On one occasion my mother took the camera into the garden to take a photograph.

'Not on a Sunday, Theresa!' said my grandfather. I suspect he was too late and the shutter had already clicked. If he was, I've probably still got the sinful photograph somewhere.

It was while we were on a late seaside holiday in Brighton that the real earth-shattering news came. Almost without a word we returned to London. I noticed that my mother had been crying, while my father looked very serious. I was concerned about the fact that my holiday had been cut short. I was aware that something momentous had happened. Arriving home I discovered that my beloved Nancy, who had gone back to Ireland for a holiday, was not expected to return. Little did I know that the impact of World War II was to have a far-reaching effect upon my life well beyond my childhood.

2

HITLER INTERVENES

Once Chamberlain had announced that Britain was at war, clearly things were never going to be the same again. The blackout, seeing sticky tape on the windows to prevent shattering in the event of bomb blast, carrying one's gas mask – all these became part of everyday life. Nothing was ever wasted during the war, and huge piles of waste paper collected from our neighbourhood were stored in our garage. It became the local salvage depot, and the toppling piles were collected and taken off each week to help the war effort. I had no idea how this actually helped the war effort, but I supposed they knew what they were doing.

The wireless, of course, was an important feature of life at the time. My parents listened to the news bulletins and I enjoyed the entertainment programmes. Dominating them all was the immortal *ITMA – It's That Man Again*, but there was also *Happidrome*, *Dick Barton – Special Agent* (whose exploits thrilled us each evening), the occasional Paul Temple mystery series and Valentine Dyall as 'the Man in Black' bringing us an *Appointment with Fear*. The opening and closing lines of *Monday Night at Eight* are still fixed in my mind all these years later:

> It's Monday night at eight o'clock.
> Oh can't you hear the chimes?
> They're telling you to take an easy chair
> And settle by the fireside, take out your *Radio Times*,
> For *Monday Night at Eight* is on the air.

Then at the end:

> Produced by Harry Pepper, and RonnieWaldman, too,
> We hope the programme hasn't caused a frown.
> So goodbye everybody, it's time to say goodnight,
> For *Monday Night at Eight* is closing down.

It was the start of the Battle of Britain and the continuous blitzing of Britain's major cities that really brought the war home to us. Edgware was not a natural target for the bombs but we were sufficiently near London to make it advisable to take shelter whenever the air raid siren sounded. My father was the shelter marshal, helping those who were coming to seek safety from the air raids in the big underground shelter that had been built in the adjoining park. He hated the sense of being cooped up, so having seen all his charges safely installed he would remain above ground watching what was going on in the skies. This underground shelter was a fascinating place for us as children. The dimly lit tunnels deep under the earth were a place of mystery, and if the shelter had been left unlocked we would venture in there with great daring.

The Trotmans' garden backed on to the park and had a gate cut into the fence that gave access to it. As soon as the sirens sounded, a stream of people would move down the side of their house, through the gate and into the shelter. Soon a brick shelter was built attached to our house, so we no longer needed to go across to the park. It would never have survived a direct hit, but in theory it would protect us from blast and falling debris. It seemed strange at first sleeping in there but we soon got used to it. My parents tried to make it as homely as possible. I think there was even a piece of carpet on the floor. There was barely room for their double bed so I had a bunk fixed higher up over their feet. When a plane flew overhead the uncertainty of not knowing whether it of was one of ours or one of theirs could be quite frightening. As an eight-year-old boy this probably didn't worry me too much. Later, of course, there were many opportunities to study pictures of the various types of plane, and identifying them was every schoolboy's ambition. I have to say I was never very good at it.

Looking up into the sky one day I said to my father, 'What are those things falling out of that plane?' I suppose we should have thrown ourselves flat on the ground but we just stood there continuing to look. Although the plane seemed directly overhead the bombs exploded a mile or two away.

We were all having lunch one day when we heard what seemed like an explosion in the skies above. Rushing outside we saw a parachute descending. What was to be done? Two doors away lived Mr Humphries. He was a member of the Home Guard.

'Quick!' said mother. 'There's a German parachutist coming. Go and get Mr Humphries!'

After all, this was the kind of thing the Home Guard was there to deal with. I expect he was alerted but what he did about it, I have no idea. Subsequently we discovered that the German plane had crashed into Broadfields Avenue, a road about a quarter of a mile away. Fortunately it landed in the middle of the road and not on any of the surrounding houses.

I suppose the thing that really brought the tragedy of war home to me was the death of my Sunday School teacher, Alan Stanes. One Sunday, we were told that he had been shot down while serving in the RAF. Someone I knew and admired had died and I shed many private tears that night. It was difficult to believe that he would not be coming home.

While most German planes bypassed Edgware, the odd one did not, and two houses in a nearby road suffered a direct hit. I can remember two little old ladies, sisters I think, collecting as many of their personal belongings as they could and coming to our house. They sat talking about the event as if it was an everyday occurrence, their sense of humour unimpaired.

'We had crushed velvet curtains in the drawing room,' said one.

'And now they really are crushed,' said the other with a laugh.

I thought that was terribly funny. You had to admire such extraordinary stoicism. They were billeted in our house, and I was moved into Nancy's old room. They stayed with us until they were re-housed. Not surprisingly, their experience had left them somewhat nervous. They would jump at any loud noise. Even that was a joke as far as they were concerned. When they left one of them wrote in my autograph book, 'Whenever you hear a bang, think of the two jumpers'.

They were the first of many who came to stay. I enjoyed meeting so many different people. Soldiers and airmen were particularly welcome because they could help me with my collection of cigarette cards. The collection of 'Inns of Old England', 'Uniforms of the British Army' and 'Film Stars' rapidly increased thanks to these visitors. They seemed to take a real interest. 'I've got the whole lot except number 13,' I would say. A few days later one of them would come back home. 'Look what I found in my cigarettes today,' he would say as he presented me with the missing card.

Tea parties for wounded soldiers took place in our back garden. I would hand round the sandwiches and the cakes and the visitors would chat to me, asking how I was getting on at school and so on. It was not uncommon in those days for children to 'entertain' the adults. Some of the visitors would ask politely if I would like to do something for them. I was, however, in many ways painfully shy. I could entertain my friends and perhaps even their parents, but the idea of standing up and doing something on my own in front of strangers terrified me. So I always declined. I felt a bit uneasy about this. I knew I had quite a good voice and I should have been able to sing something at least, but I just couldn't.

I talked about this with my father and he suggested I might

like to join a church choir. He probably felt that singing with other boys would give me the confidence that I lacked. I liked the idea and readily agreed. As St Andrew's did not have boys in the choir, this meant a move to the parent church of the group – St Margaret's, the ancient parish church of Edgware. I liked the idea of dressing up in the surplice and stiff collar with black clip-on bow tie. The collar and tie had to be purchased by my parents and if I remember rightly entailed the sacrifice of a precious clothing coupon.

In accordance with the evangelical tradition, the main services were Morning and Evening Prayer. There was a said communion at eight o'clock, but once a month a communion was tacked onto the end of the morning service. The Ten Commandments were read in full and we led the congregation in singing 'Lord have mercy upon us and incline our hearts to keep this law' after each of them. I would look round the respectable suburban congregation and wonder which of them was in the habit of coveting his neighbour's ox or ass. We were there to lead the singing and not to perform. Anthems and choir pieces were not encouraged. On rare occasions, we did a choir setting of the Magnificat, and on Good Friday we always sang 'God so loved the world' from Stainer's Crucifixion.

During those war years people clearly felt the need of the Church. The National Days of Prayer would see the building crammed to bursting point. Even on an ordinary Sunday, there was a period when the evening service had to be duplicated. We would sing for the first service and then leave halfway through the second sitting, having led the congregation in the opening hymn, the psalm and the canticles. I think we were paid a small sum for our efforts but I don't think we got double time on these occasions. We were certainly paid for weddings. On a Saturday morning, I would often come home proudly and say that the groom had given us all an extra sixpence because we had sung so well! I suspect the motive was more concerned with showing his bride what a jolly and generous chap he was rather than a real appreciation of our voices! I enjoyed the choir and without realizing it probably gained a lot from listening to the sermons. Anyway, my confidence in my singing ability was certainly enhanced.

The war had in no way diminished my interest in acting. In fact if anything, it had intensified it. There were now good war causes for which one could raise money. I had organized a bring-and-buy sale in the garden for Mrs Churchill's 'Aid to Russia Fund' and had been very excited to receive a letter from 10 Downing Street thanking me and seemingly signed by the lady herself. However, bring-and-buy sales were all very well in their way, but I was an impresario and entertainment was the thing.

Being a little older and maybe even a little wiser, I realized that my plans for *The Scarlet Pimpernel* and *The Life of Handel* had perhaps been a bit ambitious. Now I would produce a concert. Armed with my new-found confidence, I would sing and I would audition the rest of my friends and assess their capabilities. As producer, director and designer I had a wonderful time. I organized what I thought was a very splendid bill. Joan Senker, who attended ballet classes, danced 'The Sugar Plum Fairy'. Peter Senker recited, and Ann Carlier played the piano. Of course, we needed programmes. These were done on my Sunday School teacher's printing apparatus. Miss Phillips would cut the stencil on her typewriter and it was then placed in a frame with a sheet of blank paper underneath it. A roller was covered in a black gooey substance and rolled over it leaving the finished print on the blank page. This process had to be repeated for each piece of paper, and I – ever the optimist – overestimated the number of programmes that would be needed. The whole process, therefore, took quite a long time, but she was very patient – as a Sunday School teacher should be!

My material had to match the mood of the nation so, as a

climax, I walked down an improvised set of stairs (I hadn't watched pantomime walkdowns for nothing!) wearing a cloak made of crepe paper, a cardboard crown on my head, a wooden sword in my hand giving a spirited rendition of 'There'll Always be an England' and inviting the audience to join in. Perhaps because the proceeds were going to the Spitfire Fund, the drawing room seemed packed with neighbours and well-wishers. Father had fixed up an old curtain across one end of the room, so it seemed like a proper theatre. He, of course, accompanied the whole thing on the piano and my mother provided the refreshments. It went well, and I felt I had had my first real taste of success. Earlier in the programme, I had sung the wartime song 'Lords of the Air':

> England, our island home
> Land of the Free.
> England unconquered yet
> O'er land and sea.
> Lord of the heavens above
> Answer our prayer,
> God keep Britannia's sons
> Lords of the air.

It was to be 40 years later when I would find myself standing in the wings at the Shaftesbury Theatre in London's West End, listening to this song in one of the most moving moments during the stage show of *Dad's Army*.

The war was obviously having an effect on my schooling and my father was not happy about it. 'All you seem to do is spend your time in the air raid shelter,' he said one day.

Whether we spent more time in the shelter then any other school I don't know, but my father thought we did and he was determined to do something about that. After careful consideration he enrolled me in to Broadfields School, which was about a quarter of a mile from where we lived. This private school took girls through their teenage years, and young boys up to the age of 11. Two large houses knocked into one provided a host of various sized classrooms, and a good homely feel. The headmistress was Mrs Marlow and I discovered recently that a former pupil was the actor Anthony Dawes. Mrs Marlowe's daughter Jean was later also to become a professional actress. Clearly dramatic talent was available but sadly we never performed any plays there. After several happy terms, and as I was growing older, my father began to feel that the strong feminine influence was not appropriate and that I needed to be in a school that more specifically catered for boys. I was to be moved again.

Parkside Preparatory school was the answer. This was, in effect, a reversal of Broadfields. Boys were taken to the age of 12 or 13 and some very young girls were allowed in. It was ruled over by a headmaster, Mr Wilkinson, who for some reason was referred to only as 'Sir'. This word was used not only when addressing him but also when speaking about him: 'Sir did this'; 'Sir did that'. It seemed odd at the time and still does. I soon got used to this change although clearly the atmosphere was very different. Sir would administer the slipper for various misdemeanours, but I was lucky enough to avoid it. Compulsory games of football were something of a nightmare for me, and the weekly sessions when we would go to the church hall of St Margaret's for gym were almost as worrying. I never managed to get more than a few inches up the rope we were supposed to climb, I never managed to land properly when vaulting the horse and trying to do things on the trapeze totally defeated me. I was always thankful when these sessions came to an end and we were back in the changing room discussing the latest film we had seen at the local cinema.

There were, however, compensations. Sir was very keen on drama. We would read simple plays in class, acting them out as we did so. We would also give concerts for the war effort at the local Shakespeare Hall, named, I think, after a local worthy rather than the Bard. This was much more like a proper theatre than our drawing room or even the platform at St Andrew's church. For the first time, I experienced the buzz of a large group of people backstage all taking part in the same show.

In one of these concerts I was cast as the hangman in a Punch and Judy sketch. Dressed all in black, moving on my knees, behind a low table that represented the Punch and Judy booth, I entered with the hangman's noose.

'Now, Mr Punch. You are a very wicked man!' I said to the boy with the big red nose playing Punch. 'You must put your head in there,' I said, pointing at the noose.

'What do you mean? In there?' asked Mr Punch, placing his head nowhere near the noose.

'No, you silly old fool. In there!' I pointed again.

'I don't know how to do it.'

'You don't know how to do it?'

'No, I've never done it before. Show me how to do it.'

'All right. I will show you. You watch me. You put your head in the noose like this and you say, "Boys and Girls, I have been a very bad man and I am going to suff . . ."' At this moment, Punch pulled the rope and I was hanged. Falling down behind the table and crawling off, I was soon hopefully out of sight of the audience.

I was now a regular cinemagoer. My mother would often meet me from school and take me to the cinema. Continuous performances meant that if you were not careful you saw the end of the film before the beginning, with the news and a 'B' feature in between, but it didn't seem to matter. Jeanette MacDonald and Nelson Eddy sang their way into my heart, Errol Flynn continued to swashbuckle, Bette Davis flashed her eyes dangerously and Greer Garson was the most beautiful creature I'd ever seen. I fell madly in love with her. Who can ever forget her luminous smile when she first meets Ronald Colman in *Random Harvest*? This film with its theme of loss of memory fascinated me and was to have a real influence when I started to try to write plays myself.

I sometimes went to the cinema on my own on a Saturday afternoon, but occasionally there was a problem that had to be overcome. In the early 1940s there were three bands of cinema certification: 'U' was 'Universal' and you were allowed in on your own; 'A' was 'Adult' and you had to be accompanied by a grown-up; 'H' was for 'Horror' and you were not allowed in at all. Horror was the thing that the authorities felt should be kept from the younger generation. The 'X' film did not arrive until much later with its censorship against gratuitous violence and explicit sex. If the film that I wanted to see was a 'U' there was no problem, but if it was an 'A' and my parents didn't want to see it, I had to find someone else. The most common way to do this was to approach someone going in at the same time and ask them to take you in. You handed them the money, walked in together and then sat in different places once inside. Of course one always chose a kind, motherly woman, but nonetheless it was an extraordinary routine that could never happen today. At that time it was quite commonplace and no one seemed to worry. Maybe it illustrates the sense of trust that existed in the community at that time.

Around this time, I discovered the world of musical theatre. My mother took me to see Ivor Novello's *The Dancing Years*. Later we saw *Arc de Triomphe* and *Perchance to Dream*. I loved the colour, the music and the sentimental sadness of the story. Variety Bills at the Golders Green Hippodrome were a revelation to me. I saw the famous piano-playing duo Rawicz and Landaeur there. Radio series of the day such as *Happidrome* were featured and gave me the chance to see characters that had only been voices until then. As I watched many of the great music hall names of the time, little did I think that years later I would see them lovingly and accurately impersonated in the *Dad's Army* stage show.

Parkside Preparatory School should have provided me with some security, but we were still at war, and soon after I joined the school was bombed out. Another move down the road to a house in Green Lane was followed after a few months by another evacuation to Edgwarebury Lane. Wartime was certainly not a period for settling down in one place.

When I reached the grand old age of 12, I was on the move again. Many children had been evacuated since the beginning of September 1939, but I had remained at home. Although Edgware had avoided the worst of the bombing, the danger was still there and my parents now felt it would be safer to get me away from London. Ardingly College was a Woodward School, founded in the Anglo-Catholic tradition. 'I am sure your son will get a good education there,' I overheard our evangelical rector saying to my father one day. 'But the religion will be totally, totally wrong.' I had no idea what this meant and anyway it was the least of my worries. I knew or at least I hoped that the days of *Tom Brown's School Days*, where boys were persecuted for saying prayers by their bedside, tossed in a blanket, or even roasted, were well and truly in the past. I suspected that the tales of more modern school storywriters such as Gunby Hadath, with midnight feasts and the discovery that the sadistic housemaster was really a German spy, also only belonged in the realms of fiction. However, I had little idea of what the reality would be.

I didn't notice what sort of weather it was on the day of departure because my heart was really in my boots. My father, mother and I travelled on the underground and I had the same kind of feeling which I now experience on a first night: a knot in my stomach and a stoic acceptance of the inevitable. I was in for it and there was no going back. Arriving at Victoria Station for the school train, my heart sank even further when I noticed 200 or so boys on the platform, all saying goodbye to their parents. Some were nonchalant, some were in tears, and I was frozen to the spot. I didn't know what to say, and I don't think my parents knew either. The good-byes were brief. One hug from Mother and a handshake from Father and they were gone.

The moment was rescued by one of the masters who ushered us all onto the waiting train. Captain Hett was in charge of the new boys.

'Aha! There's the whistle,' he heartily announced. 'We're going now!'

When the train didn't move, the two boys sitting beside me started to giggle. I was in far too tense a state to join them. The wretchedness of my feelings intensified as the train bore me away from everything that made me feel secure. After what seemed an eternity we arrived at Haywards Heath and boarded another train that arrived at Ardingly a few minutes later. I had never been to the area nor seen the school, and was still terribly uncertain what to expect. Clutching my overnight bag, we started walking and I hoped that my trunk that had been sent on well in advance had arrived safely. Suddenly into view came a large red-bricked building which in spite of my forebodings looked reasonably friendly in the evening light. As I followed the rest of my group towards my allocated dormitory, Captain Hett unexpectedly stopped me.

'Oh Williams, aren't you supposed to be in the Junior House?'

'No, Sir,' said another boy. 'He's wearing long trousers.'

'Ah, so you are,' said Captain Hett, as if seeing them for the first time. 'You must be older than you look.'

I was now shown what was to replace my bedroom. Thirty beds, all with red covers and iron bedsteads, stood in two rows down each long wall; it all seemed very clinical. I stood there in the vast dormitory and the knot in my stomach tight-ened. Feeling isolated and lost, I wondered how I would ever come to terms with my new situation. The rest of that day, tea in the big hall and my first night in the dormitory passed in a blur. It all seemed to be happening in an unreal world as though I was in a dream from which I would soon wake up.

Whether it was homesickness or perhaps I was genuinely ill, two days later I was confined to the sanatorium with a high temperature. So I spent the first fortnight of my time at Ardingly under the eagle eye of Sister Fell, a formidable lady who as I was later to discover was adept at detecting malingerers trying to get off games or dodge a class for which they had failed to do their prep. She would administer a noxious liquid and send them back into school with a hearty 'You'll be all right now boy. You're perfectly fit to play games.' It was rumoured that if you chewed toothpaste before going to see her, it would send your temperature up, but I never tested this out. Her assistant, Miss Hoon, was a vague, ethereal lady who was much more of a soft touch.

During my time in the san, I decided to come to terms with my new situation. When I returned to the main life of the school, things started to take on a new shape, and I determined to make the best of my time at Ardingly. I made many friends, and there were many things about the school which I enjoyed. The lessons were interesting and I found to my surprise I even enjoyed the biology where we dissected frogs. English was another favourite subject and my friend Flatman and I would compare notes during the break in prep over the latest short story we had been required to write. One master, R.G.G. Price, wrote for *Punch* and I was very impressed to meet someone who actually had his work printed. I told him I wanted to be a writer and that I thought I would like to write plays. 'Ah yes Williams,' he said. 'If you write a novel you can say "The Duchess made an amusing remark". If you write a play, you have to tell us what the amusing remark is.' He was right, of course, but I have always found that dialogue comes more easily than elaborate descriptions.

Life at Ardingly was spartan. The day room, in which we younger boys lived, moved and had our being, had wooden benches round the edge, with lockers above them and a table tennis table in the middle. There was a distinct lack of home comforts, so I was very grateful when one of the masters invited me to his room where there was a roaring gas fire, easy chairs, and a sofa. He would give me tea and toast. I would sit next to him on the sofa and after the tea and toast his arm would go round my shoulder and his hand would go up my trouser leg. Chatting to the other boys, I discovered that I was not the only one to receive this treatment. Inevitably this eventually came to light and we returned one term to find that he had been quietly removed.

Some prep school headmasters gave their young charges a lecture on the dangers and temptations they would face at their public school. Perhaps because most of the boys at Parkside were destined for local day schools, Sir had not thought it necessary to do so. My father had told me the facts of life and I suspect there was something about the reproductive process in there but the only thing that stuck in my mind was his final injunction, 'Therefore, although it is always important to give up your seat to a lady, it's even more important if the lady is pregnant.' None of this was much help in equipping me for life in an all-male environment. I had read John van Druten's famous play *Young Woodley*, in which a prefect at a public school falls in love with his housemaster's wife, but this seemed an unlikely scenario and so was not much help either.

Those of us in the senior school were strictly forbidden to have anything to do with, or even speak to, those in the junior school. I had no idea of the reason for this. When at the end of one winter term we had a joke Christmas-present-giving ceremony in the dormitory and the prefect was given a large laundry basket out of which jumped one of the younger members of the dormitory, I just didn't know what the joke was. My innocence in these matters was not unusual in my generation. Eventually I realized that there were quite intense friendships between an older and a younger boy but I doubt whether in that era many of them were in any way harmful.

Indeed, I suspect that while they lasted, they were valuable as part of growing up and coming to terms with one's feelings.

It was wartime and everything was rationed so that the food at Ardingly was inevitably rather basic by modern standards. When a favourite such as a pink blancmange was produced, if there was a little left over it was the fervent prayer of each boy that it was their table's turn to go up for seconds, but it didn't often happen. An urn was placed at the end of each table containing what we called 'hoggy'. This was our version of tea – warm and wet certainly, but very weak and milky. My aversion to very milky tea probably dates from this time.

Remembering what our rector had told my father about the religion at Ardingly, I wondered what to expect. It was indeed different from the plain evangelical services back home. The priest wore bright colours which changed according to the seasons. The service was dramatic and I found that it was something to which I could really respond.

Our chaplain was one of those schoolmasters who sit up and ask to be ragged. He was a saintly man who always saw the best in other people, an admirable quality in a priest but something of a disadvantage when trying to control a group of unruly schoolboys. It was always in Divinity that a substance would find its way into the inkwell on the master's desk, causing the ink to effervesce and stream over the top and onto the floor. It was always there that a boy would contrive to tamper with light fittings so that all the lights would fuse the moment they were switched on. This ragging extended to our confirmation classes when we were learning the catechism.

'What is your name?'

'N or M.'

'What?'

'Well, that's what it says, Sir. Look, it's here in the book, Sir.'

'No, you stupid boy, you're supposed to say your own name.'

'Oh am I, Sir? Well, it doesn't say so, Sir. If I'm supposed to say my name, why does it say N or M?'

And so it would go on.

The chaplain would celebrate the Sunday Eucharist for the school but when on occasions the assistant chaplain celebrated we all noted that we were out ten minutes earlier. On a Sunday morning we would wait eagerly to see who was going to be at the altar. Many were the inward groans when, our hopes raised high as the assistant emerged from the vestry, the chaplain got up and announced that he would punctuate the service with a commentary explaining everything, thus restoring the service to its usual length. I was confirmed in the school chapel and wondered if I would feel any different afterwards. I was not surprised, or even disappointed, to find that I did not. Perhaps the Catholic understanding of the sacrament as a gift from God that depended on His grace and not my feelings had subconsciously rubbed off on me. Objectively I knew something significant had happened, and that was enough.

Before making our first communion, we were instructed about making our confession. We were all given a copy of one of those pious devotional books that were so popular at the time. In it, there was a kind of checklist of sins. It was quite coy at times. 'I have been immodest with another' is one that sticks in my mind. This list caused some hilarity as we discussed it. Some of the more mischievous threatened to confess to adultery or getting a woman pregnant out of wedlock. The inclination to rag the chaplain was still irresistible. When it came to it, I doubt if any of them fulfilled their threats and I think we probably all took it quite seriously. With my evangelical background, the whole concept of confession before a priest was a rather strange one. I had always made any confession that I wanted to make privately to God. I soon found the value of the Catholic practice. 'By his authority committed

to me, I absolve thee . . .' gave a focus on what was happening. 'Go in peace, the Lord has put away thy sin . . .' gave a
remarkable reassurance. 'And pray for me a sinner . . .' showed
that the priest was not there to sit in judgement. When I
received the body and blood of Christ for the first time again
it was the objectivity that seemed important. Christ was there
in the sacrament and I received Him. It didn't depend on my
feelings and over the years I have been grateful for that.

Easter was very early one year and we did not break up
until the following week. We were a good Anglo-Catholic
school and very properly the chaplain decided to introduce us
to the liturgy of Holy Week. Somewhat unwisely he decided
to begin with Tenebrae. 'We have readings and psalms and
there are 15 candles,' he explained. 'After each psalm we
extinguish a candle until there is only one candle left. At this
point all the lights in the chapel will be turned out and the one
candle will be hidden behind the altar. At this point there is a
loud noise, and I suggest you bang your hymnbooks on the
chair in front of you. This sound symbolizes Christ bursting
from the tomb. Then the one remaining candle will be
brought out to symbolize the light of the resurrection.'

The service duly started and we suffered the psalms and the
readings, which seemed interminable. The lights were duly
put out and the banging and crashing ensued. When the single
candle was produced, and after a pause the main lights were
switched back on, a scene of utter desolation was revealed.
Chairs were overturned and hymnbooks had been thrown
from one end of the chapel to the other. The headmaster
stormed out in fury leaving a very red-faced chaplain standing
alone and bewildered. This was an unfortunate introduction
to a service that was later to become very important and
meaningful to me.

The rest of the Holy Week services were accomplished in a
much more peaceful manner. I was particularly moved by the
Veneration of the Cross on Good Friday. There was a rather

worrying moment at the lighting of the new fire at the first Mass of Easter. Our chaplain, obviously anxious to ensure that there would be no hitch at this point, had poured a quantity of flammable liquid over it. As he lit it, a sheet of flame shot into the air and he moved hastily backward, just in time to prevent his cope from catching fire.

I was not to experience these services again for many years until I started to worship regularly at All Saints' Margaret Street in London. This journey through the changing moods of Holy Week to the triumph of the Resurrection soon became the centre of the whole Christian year for me.

3

UNWILLINGLY TO SCHOOL

There was a strong belief among the authorities that the cinema was a place where you could easily 'catch something'. There had been an outbreak of chicken pox which had rapidly spread through the school and had necessitated our dormitory, the nearest to the san, being evacuated and used to provide extra beds for those who were ill. We were distributed among the other dormitories which we quite enjoyed as it made a change. Because of this fear of infection, visits to the cinema were strictly forbidden. It was one of those offences which, if you were caught, would guarantee a very painful visit to the headmaster's study.

We were not, however, totally denied the opportunity to see films. Occasionally a film would be hired and shown to the entire school on a Saturday evening. The projector was an ancient one and the soundtrack pretty distorted, but it was something that was different from the ordinary routine of things and we welcomed it. It was under these conditions that I first made the acquaintance of the famous play *The Ghost Train*. The 1941 film version, starring Arthur Askey, was shown and we all enjoyed it. It was not the last time this play would come into my life, and obviously I had no idea that years later I would be working on a regular basis with its author Arnold Ridley.

Ardingly did not go in for drama very much. However, one term we had a festival of one-act plays. Each dormitory produced something to perform before the rest of the school. In spite of my interest in acting, I was not invited to become involved. I cannot even remember what our dormitory did. Perhaps the frustration of not being part of it has blocked it from my memory. C dormitory, one of whose members was Billy Cotton, son of the famous band leader and later to become Head of Comedy at BBC Television, did a kind of revue, based on a day in the life of the BBC. E dormitory did *The Bishop's Candlesticks*, a play based on an episode from Victor Hugo's novel *Les Misérables*. The convict was played by John Gorst, later to become my local MP. He gave a brilliant performance and as he walked down the hall afterwards, for the first time I witnessed someone getting a standing ovation.

Ardingly was dedicated to St Saviour and when C dormitory gave us their glimpse of life behind the scenes at the BBC, it included a parody version of the signature tune for *Much-Binding-in-the-Marsh*:

> At St Saviour's on the Ouse
> The weather it is perfectly appalling;
> At St Saviour's on the Ouse,
> The jolly old barometer keeps falling . . .

And it did. It fell and fell and fell. It was one of the worst winters for many years. Everything froze up. Captain Hett arrived at the school one day having travelled on skis from his home in the village. So many of us had chilblains that we were allowed back into the dormitory during the daytime (usually forbidden), so that we could plunge our hands into a basin full of hot water and then into the adjacent basin full of cold water. It was supposed to help and I think it did. The lavatories all froze and we younger boys were kept busy carrying buckets of water from a standpipe in order to flush them. We had to do this not only for ourselves but also for the prefects. Everyone was very relieved when at last the thaw set in.

Bath nights were always something of a challenge. For a dormitory of 30 boys, there were 3 baths. The prefects operated a rota system. When it was your turn, you were allocated ten minutes in the wartime regulation five inches of water. Plugs were the problem. Even if there was one for each bath at the beginning of term, a week or so later they would all have disappeared. Some boys stuffed the plughole with the carbolic soap that we used. This was not tremendously effective as it tended to dissolve, and anyway it was a waste of soap in wartime – and would incur the wrath of the prefect if he noticed. I became quite adept at filling the hole with my heel while twisting and turning to wash in the meagre amount of water available to me.

Sometimes we were required to remake the prefect's bed at night. I rather enjoyed this as he had a radio on his bedside locker. I soon realized that if I timed the folding and placing of the sheets and blankets as slowly as possible I could listen to *The Man in Black*. 'This is your storyteller,' it would begin, as I straightened the undersheet. 'The Man in Black, bringing you an *Appointment with Fear*!' If I could extend the bedmaking to the length of the programme I was fine. Quite often the prefect would arrive and say, 'Right, that's fine, Williams', just before the climax of the piece and I would return to my bed and lie awake after lights out, wondering how it had ended.

We were in many ways an enclosed and self-sufficient community. Nothing could have brought this home to me more clearly than the bizarre incident concerning daylight saving. During the war, there was a government decision that the hours of daylight in the summer should be maximized. To achieve this they instituted 'double daylight saving'. I think it meant that the clocks went forward or backward two hours instead of one as in peace time. Whatever it was, Ardingly decided not to go along with it. The result was that our time was one hour different from the rest of the country. It really didn't seem to matter. Our contact with the outside world was so rare that certainly for the boys it made no difference. It was probably more difficult for the masters, having to remember what time the pubs opened and closed. It made letters home rather complicated especially when I was trying to arrange to meet my parents when they came down to take me out for the day. 'So I will meet you outside the chapel, at ten o'clock our time, which is, of course, eleven o'clock your time.' Looking back, it all seems rather unreal, a defiant gesture of independence perhaps. I suppose there was a point to it somewhere.

Twice a term, our parents were allowed to come down on Sunday to take us out for the day. It was something to which I looked forward for weeks ahead. It really seemed wonderful to get away from the place, to see my parents and have lunch somewhere other than the school dining hall. Often on these occasions I would take a friend whose parents for one reason or another had not been able to get there. You had to have an exeat signed by your housemaster on these occasions.

'Kipps' Herring saw boys in his study before tea each evening. You would join the queue and wonder which boys were there for a happy reason like you, and which were there for something less happy. You soon found out. Some boys would go in fairly quickly and emerge again with a smile on their face. Others were there longer and you would hear the swish and crack of the cane as it landed on their tautened grey flannels. The boy would emerge wincing and rubbing his backside. Usually it was three or four strokes. Sometimes a quite senior boy would go in, someone in the First Eleven and probably only a term away from being made prefect. Surely he was there to get a pass signed or something like that. But no, we would hear the swish and crack. It seemed louder this time and it would be six. The young man would come out trying to look nonchalant and unconcerned. Conscious of his dignity, he would keep any rubbing of the backside until he was out of sight.

Discipline was maintained without too much trouble. The

regime was not oppressive and usually seemed fair. Outside the classroom it was almost wholly in the hands of the prefect. They were allowed to beat but ironically ordinary masters were not. Six from a hefty athletic member of the First Eleven was considered to be much more painful then something similar from a housemaster or even the head. Occasionally extra work would be given or special fagging duties, but these were rare and the usual punishment was the cane. The only variant was the number of strokes: three, four or six. It was rarely less than three and for some reason never five. Misdemeanours in the classroom, failure to have done one's prep, or bad work would result in a note from the master in charge which had to be presented to one's housemaster that evening. He would read it, tell the boy to bend over and the strokes would be delivered.

There was a clever, but to our minds, fiendish device to make sure we kept up with our schoolwork. Every fortnight form lists would be posted showing each boy's place in the form. If you dropped five or more places you were put on report for the following fortnight. You were given a form made out like a timetable with a square for each period of each day. At the end of a class the master had to fill in the appropriate square. If he put 'S' you were all right. 'VS', however, did not mean that you were more than all right but stood for 'Vix Satis', which meant you might be in trouble. 'NS' meant you were definitely in trouble. The form had to be presented to your housemaster each evening. A 'VS', particularly if it was the first one on the form, might be dealt with quite leniently – an hour's extra work or something like that. 'NS' always meant a beating – four strokes for the first one and six for any subsequent ones. Getting an 'NS' during the first period of the day and knowing what awaited you that evening was not a pleasant experience.

On one occasion a group of boys from the Lower Fifth were sent to their respective housemasters because of rowdy behaviour in the swimming pool. There was much discussion that evening over the fact that the School House boys had each received four cuts from Kipps Herring, while 'Dusty' Miller had offered the boys in his house a choice: either being banned from the swimming pool for the following fortnight or taking six strokes. Despite the fact that Dusty was known to be a formidable wielder of the cane and six from him would be no joke, the lure of the swimming pool on a hot day was strong and each boy went into the study, opted for the beating and received his six cuts. The last boy actually disliked swimming so had decided to opt for the fortnight's ban, but Dusty was wise to him. 'No point in banning you from swimming, is there?' he said. 'That would suit you all too well, wouldn't it? So no choice for you, I'm afraid. Get over that table.'

Smoking was, of course, a capital offence and very few boys indulged in it. This probably had as much to do with wartime shortages as an unwillingness to take the risk. However, there was a sub-prefect in our house who enjoyed an occasional pipe. One day while indulging in this pastime in a secluded spot, he saw to his horror that the housemaster was approaching. Knowing that his status would not save him, and that detection would result in instant demotion with six of the very best that Kipps could dish out, he hastily shoved the evidence into his pocket. Managing a cheery, 'Good afternoon, Sir', he waited until the danger had passed and then dashed to the nearest water supply to dowse the now smouldering jacket which was threatening to burst into flames.

Remembering my lack of prowess at Parkside, the one thing I dreaded was the thought of compulsory games. They had been a big feature in every school story that I had ever read. Unbelievably, there was a way out. It was wartime and we could opt for working in the school's Land Army instead of playing games. I seized the opportunity with both hands and spent many happy hours 'Digging for Victory'. Under the eagle eye of Dusty Miller, we sawed and chopped wood, dug potatoes, collected turnips and generally helped the war effort. It was quite hard work but it was also fun and to me infinitely preferable to playing football. I happily cheered my dormitory on in the swimming gala, but sport was definitely not for me.

Nothing, however, could get you out of being in the corps. Once a week I would don the ill-fitting khaki uniform and parade under the command of the redoubtable Captain Hett. I stood to attention and I stood at ease. I marched wheeling right and I marched wheeling left. I sloped arms, I ordered arms and I even learned to present arms. I went on route marches, and I took part in field days, thunder flashes exploding all around. But I was never very good at it, which is I suppose ironic as much of my future television career was going to be concerned with the army in one way or another.

Ardingly was a pretty peaceful place during most of the war, although one of the early flying bombs came down and exploded not far away. It had obviously been aimed at the main railway line between London and the south coast but it had missed its target and done no damage. Because it had been so peaceful until then, we had no idea what had caused the loud bang that awakened us in the middle of the night. I think we decided that a rather fat boy had fallen out of bed in the dormitory next door. It was only later next morning that we learned the truth.

When eventually victory in Europe came about, we celebrated VE Day with a great bonfire on the terrace with its view of the viaduct and railway line in the distance. Perhaps some of us remembered that doodlebug that had awakened us from our slumbers. The bonfire was augmented by improvised fireworks in the shape of thunder flashes purloined from the corps armoury. Captain Hett was far from pleased about this misuse of army stores. At any other time the culprits would have been sought out and a number of senior boys would have found themselves bending over for six of the best. But this was not a time for retribution; it was a time for rejoicing. The war against Japan continued, but the conflict in Europe was over and England could begin the long haul back to peace.

My father was getting older and felt he would like to have me around. I had always made it clear that I would prefer to be at home. So with the threat of bombs now a thing of the past it was decided that I would leave Ardingly. Perversely, when it came to it, part of me regretted that I was leaving. I had been a fag, a junior and got through all the difficult bits. But I would never be a prefect. Although in some ways I felt robbed, I knew that the independence that I had learned there was a valuable lesson.

I still wanted to be an actor and tried to persuade my parents to send me to a stage school. The famous Aida Foster School was in Golders Green, not too far away. It had produced a number of stars, such as Jean Simmons, and I felt it would be just the right place for me. Apart from Shirley Temple, I had seen a number of other child stars and some of them were boys. I had seen Freddie Bartholomew, Mickey Rooney and Roddy McDowall playing leading roles. If they could do it, so could I.

Wisely, my parents did not accede to my suggestion. They knew little about the lives of actors, but probably realized that for every highly successful star there were probably dozens who were struggling to make a living. Clearly they also felt that I was too young to make a decision about my future career. My father did, however, make me a promise. 'Go to an ordinary school, finish your education there, and if you still want to become an actor, we will give you our backing,' he said. I determined to enjoy the rest of my school days, although deep down I knew the wish to be an actor was not going to fade.

My final place of education was to be Hendon County School. A grammar school that had a high reputation in the area, it was a short journey by tube or bus from where we lived. It was a great contrast to Ardingly. To start with, it was mixed, so suddenly there were girls around. The greatest contrast, however, was that it was a day school and I was allowed home every evening. Also Saturdays were entirely free. This meant I could resume my visits to the cinema. The Ritz at Edgware, the various Odeons and Gaumonts became regular haunts. This was the great age of British cinema, and stars like James Mason and Margaret Lockwood in films such as *The Wicked Lady* and *The Man in Grey* were attracting audiences to rival anything coming out of Hollywood. Newspaper accounts endowed these British stars with an aura of mystery and glamour, and I believed it all. My fantasy was abruptly shattered one day when I went to stay with my maternal grandmother who lived in Ringwood. I knew that Margaret Lockwood lived nearby, and one day I was walking down the high street when joy of joys, up drove a big open-topped white car and out stepped the lady herself. As I watched, I noticed that she looked every inch the film star. I stood in awe. Then she ruined it all for me by going into Woolworth's!

Britain was also making films of a more serious nature. I saw for the first time the incomparable Celia Johnson with Trevor Howard in *Brief Encounter*. I have seen the film many times since, and it never fails to move me. Then there was *Odd Man Out* which, although James Mason was the star, also featured some wonderful character players from the Abbey Theatre in Dublin. It was a marvellous era and they don't make them like that any more.

Weekly visits to the repertory theatre at Watford became a regular feature of my life. The box office staff soon came to recognize the tall, bespectacled youth asking for his single ticket for the first performance on Saturday. I was fascinated to see the actors playing a different part each week, and after a time I felt I knew the resident company as well as my own

family. I was always excited to see any of them in the street
and out of character. If I was waiting for the bus and saw
Harold Wilkinson rushing for the train, it made my day. If the
stage manager who occasionally played small parts got on the
same bus as me, that was even better although I never had the
courage to speak to her. If one of the company had landed a
part in the West End, my excitement knew no bounds.
'Arnold Bell is in the play at the Criterion!' I would excitedly
announce to my parents. At the first opportunity, I would go
up to the London theatre to see him.

Whenever I could afford it, I went to see plays in the West
End. It was a wonderful time, Laurence Olivier and Vivien
Leigh would be appearing at one theatre, Ralph Richardson
or John Gielgud would be at another. There was Flora
Robson, Edith Evans, Sybil Thorndike and Lewis Casson. I
saw them all and I collected their autographs. I was com-
pletely stage-struck, which is only another way of saying that
I was totally in love with the theatre.

In the midst of all these distractions, I had to give some
attention to my schoolwork. I was fairly well up academically
in most subjects but the fact that I had not done Latin at
Ardingly meant that I was placed in the practical stream.
Given my ineptitude at all things practical, this was, to put it
mildly, something of a mistake. Woodwork classes were a
disaster and anything I made was guaranteed to fall to pieces
if anyone so much as looked at it. For the rest, however, things
went reasonably well. I took my School Certificate and
embarked on the Sixth Form course. At this point there was a
snag. I had in no way given up my determination to become
an actor, but I was anxious to hedge my bets. I might want to
go to university. When I shared this thought with my parents,
they seized on it with alacrity. Was there a possibility that
their son might go in for a 'proper job' after all? The problem
was that in order to read English, I would have to have done
Latin to matriculation standard, especially if Oxford or

Cambridge were to be considered. The answer was a term of private tuition in the evenings, cramming Latin into my head. I had done some basic Latin at Parkside: Mensa, a table; Mensa, O table. I did not understand the vocative, and was delighted to learn in later life that no less a person than Winston Churchill had also queried the idea of addressing a table. Naturally matriculation requirements went well beyond this. My patient tutor strained to get some of it into my head. Passages from Caesar began to make some sort of sense and when at the end of all this cramming I took the exam no one was more surprised than I to learn that I had actually passed. I had achieved the necessary result and I promptly forgot the whole thing.

Thoughts of a career in the theatre were still there, however, and Hendon County was prepared to take these seriously. In English, we read plays aloud although it was Shakespeare and Shaw rather than the simple things we read at Parkside. There were school productions. The staff put on *Blithe Spirit* and I was allowed to help with the stage management. Eunice Holden, who had played Madame Arcati, produced *Make Believe*, a play by A.A Milne. Some of the junior forms took part and this time I was in charge of the stage management. Although heavily involved in the rehearsals, the stage manager is basically responsible for the day-to-day running of the show once the director has left. Props, scenery, calling artistes to the stage, cueing and prompting are all part of his responsibility. When I later came to do a bit of this in the professional theatre, it seemed quite easy in comparison with trying to deal with a number of noisy first formers. One small boy was playing a missionary and I had made him a clerical collar out of folded paper fixed with a paper fastener at the back.

'I've made a spare in case you lose the first one,' I said.

Miss Holden overheard this. 'Clearly, you know what actors are like,' she said. It seemed like an accolade.

During one summer holiday, she married and became Mrs Black. We all heard about this when her picture on the front page of the *Daily Mail* appeared under the headline 'Bottom of Honeymoon Boat Falls Out'. I have no idea what the story was all about, but we all thought it was hilarious at the time. Not surprisingly, she later became a professional actress and I was very excited when I saw her appear in a revue on television.

When it was announced that we were going to do *HMS Pinafore*, I auditioned for the role of Sir Joseph Porter. Apart from anything else, I thought it would be rather fun to have all those sisters, cousins and aunts around. But it was a production that also involved the staff and the part went to Mr Driver, the master who taught French. It was agreed that I would be his understudy. I was sorely tempted to pray that he would lose his voice or something. I like to think that I resisted the temptation, but even if I didn't, it did me no good. He was on every night giving a splendid performance.

A chance to do some real acting came during one of the summer holidays. I joined a group called Dramatours. Father forked out the fee, and I rehearsed the play in a rehearsal room in the West End. We were only amateurs but it seemed very professional. Rehearsals over, I joined the coach that would take the eager company to the various locations in which we were to do our one-night performance. On arrival, we would unload the scenery, put up the set and do an evening performance in the village hall for local workers – from the hop-pickers of Kent to the dairymaids of Sussex. The cast were a wonderful group of people and it was my first experience of being on tour with a company. I was nicknamed 'Tizer'. There were only two under-age members of the group, and we would happily down this sticky, bright orange, fizzy concoction while the others drank their beer. The play was called *Dear Evelyn* and I played the juvenile lead, which was probably a mistake. But it didn't seem to matter. I enjoyed performing it and I enjoyed the social life. I was very sad when it finished and if I needed any assurance that the career I was planning was the right one, that tour gave it to me.

Back at school, the Higher School Certificate loomed. When it eventually came, I did the papers – English, French and History – and sat back to wait for the results. With the exams over, the staff had to decide what to do with us for the remainder of the term. To my delight, it was decided that we should rehearse and perform a play for the rest of the school. It was at this point that *The Ghost Train* reappeared in my life. This was the chosen play and I was cast in the leading role. The play is a comedy thriller. The idea had come to Arnold Ridley after a long and unwelcome wait at a deserted railway station. It is a play that works well even to this day, and it was wonderful to play the part and hear the huge roars of laughter from the audience. I had had no opportunity to perform in school productions at Ardingly or Hendon, but this made up for it all.

4

GATEWAY TO THE FUTURE

My schooldays over and with my Higher School Certificate achieved, I reminded my father of his promise to support me if I wanted to pursue an acting career. Needless to say he was as good as his word. In those days many aspiring actors did not go to drama school. The many repertory companies would take on young people as trainee Assistant Stage Managers (ASM), and I felt this was the way forward for me. So I scoured *The Stage* for possible openings. After replying to several advertisements without success I came across one that looked more hopeful. Their reply showed that it was for a small theatre within travelling distance of home.

The Gateway Theatre, 103 Westbourne Grove, was one of a clutch of small club theatres in that part of London. Some were very daring and avant-garde, specializing in plays banned by the censor. The Gateway was in comparison fairly conventional, showing a number of new plays, interspersed with classics and the occasional ordinary commercial success. The last of these were avoided as much as possible since they involved paying royalties to the author. My father agreed to pay a premium of £30 for my training as a student ASM. This money would be repaid to me over the next 15 weeks, making the princely sum of £2 per week.

The theatre had a certain primitive charm and from the point of view of the audience was quite well appointed. There was a raked auditorium with proper seating looking down on to a stage which although narrow was quite deep. Back stage conditions, however, were less comfortable. Does anything ever change? There were two dressing rooms, one for men and one for women. There was a single wash basin with, if I remember correctly, only cold water. There was no lavatory back stage but there was a thing called an Elsan. Later, this was replaced by another receptacle with a notice saying, 'Someone has broken the Elsan. Please use the bucket which replaces it very carefully.' One wonders what a present-day health and hygiene inspector would have made of it all.

I soon learnt that being the student ASM meant that I was the general dog's body for the company. I made the tea at rehearsals, swept the stage, helped put up the set each week, went out with a shopping list of props to collect, rattled the thunder sheet in the wings, and worked the two turntables that played 78 r.p.m. records at the side of the stage. Although I was, I think, a good ASM, this piece of equipment sometimes defeated me. We played gramophone records on it while the audience were entering the theatre. At 78 r.p.m. these only lasted three or four minutes. If I was playing a part, I had to keep dashing from the dressing room where I was making up, to change the record over. At the beginning of the performance, we always played the National Anthem. On one occasion, perhaps in more of a panic than usual, I rushed to the corner, seized the recording called *National Anthems of the Nations*, placed it on the turntable and out came the Marseillaise. I decided to leave it and doubtless the audience spent the first few minutes of the play looking round for the French ambassador.

We had an author who was rather keen on historical plays. In one of these, a character was required to say, 'Hark, I hear a distant trumpet'. This posed a problem and I consulted with our resident stage director. 'There's a record of trumpet fanfares,' I said, 'but there does not seem to be anything that has a single trumpet.'

'Ah yes,' he said. We've had that before. We use the recording of the Leonora overture. That has a single trumpet call in the middle of it.' He produced the record and it had a yellow crayon line on it. 'You put the needle exactly on that line and you get the single trumpet.'

To my amazement, it worked. Night after night, the actress said the immortal line and I produced the trumpet call. Until, that is, the evening when the inevitable disaster struck. I was probably in a panic once again. 'Hark,' she proclaimed, 'I hear a distant trumpet.' Whereupon I brought in the entire Halle orchestra!

The part of the job that consisted of seeking out suitable furniture for the production was easy enough when the setting was a bedsitter in Notting Hill. We went to an antique shop a few doors away. Over the door it said proudly, 'John P. Dennis and by the grace of God his eight children'. I don't think I ever met any of the eight children but Mr Dennis himself was happy to supply the furniture we needed for a mention in the programme. When it came to furnishing a Baronial hall, things were not so easy. John P. Dennis and by the grace of God his eight children did not have that kind of furniture, and if they had, they probably would not have trusted it to us. So I would return with a moth-eaten armchair and a sofa with its springs coming out. Fortunately, we had a brilliant scenic artist who draped these items with old curtains and other pieces of material and somehow the final effect was always pretty good. I often think of him when I hear of the vast sums paid for the stage settings in some of our subsidized theatres.

The writer of historical plays sometimes demanded suits of armour. I think he must have paid for their hire because the theatre certainly could not have afforded it. I was always dispatched to collect it and instructed to find a taxi to transport it back to the theatre. It was embarrassing enough persuading an unwilling taxi driver to fill his cab with mountains of armour. Arriving back at the Gateway, and asking him to wait while the stage manager raided the three penny bits from the previous night's programme sales in order to pay him took embarrassment to the limits.

Part of the bargain was that I would eventually get to play some small roles. In most theatres this would have meant detective sergeants and the occasional butler. We, however, were not an ordinary theatre. Such roles might come later, but for the moment, my lot was a series of costume parts. Actually, I looked quite good in tights.

The very first play in which I was involved was *The Insect Play*. A fascinating piece by the brothers Capek, it was a parable of human life portrayed in the insect world. The first act, the butterflies, portrays the life of careless social ease. The second act, creepy crawlies, shows ordinary people trying to make a living in their various ways. The third act, the ants, portrays the totalitarian state. I doubt if many actors can claim to have made their first professional appearance as an ant or a snail. I can, for it was in these roles that I was cast. As the second lieutenant of the ants, my main function was to bark out orders and slogans, with my counterpart the first lieutenant. The rest of the cast were ordinary worker ants and trudged from one side of the stage to the other and then ran round the back to join the end of the line and cross the stage again. After that, a quick change to a snail. The shell was constructed of wire netting covered in sacking. We crawled on to the stage, hoping we were still in our shells – they were inclined to get stuck in the wings – and if one of us arrived without it, the audience tended to wonder why there were two people doing snail acting, but only one of them had a shell. Having got there, we had the final lines of what is still a very moving play. This was my professional debut. Later, in television, army captains, vicars and even bishops were to follow, but I still look back at that ant and that snail with enormous affection.

My fellow snail was Liz Smith, later to become well known for her portrayal of eccentric old women. During the season, Liz left to have a baby, only to return for a run of Shakespeare's *Henry VIII* in which her offspring joined her on stage for one performance as the infant Queen Elizabeth. Held in Henry's arms the tot was absolutely fascinated by the king's jewellery, and played with it all the way through the scene. My role as a very minor duke in this production became quite a major part as I acquired all the lines which Shakespeare had given to characters cut from the cast list to save money. This led to a certain inconsistency in the character. Sometimes I seemed to be for Buckingham, and sometimes I seemed to be against him, but no one seemed to mind.

When my 15 weeks at the Gateway came to an end, for some reason they decided to keep me on. They would even continue to pay me the £2 per week, coming from their money rather than my father. I suppose this was cheap labour. Later, this went up to £3. Later still, we went on a profit share basis, which usually consisted of an envelope at the end of the week with a note to say that there were no profits and that I owed the bar 1/6. This extension to my contract eventually enabled me to get my Equity card. This was extremely hard to come by as one had to have worked for 40 weeks to get it, but a further 25 weeks at the Gateway meant that I now qualified to work anywhere. During this time I did my stage management duties and enjoyed a multitude of smaller roles. Detective sergeants, butlers and footmen were now the order of the day, although the chance to get into tights still occasionally came my way.

During lunch one day at home, the telephone rang and I picked up the receiver.

'Hello Frank,' announced the familiar voice. 'There won't be a performance tonight as the King has died.'

I put the phone down and turned to tell my parents the news. My father immediately switched on our wireless. Solemn music was playing, and all the other programmes had been cancelled. The whole country was in mourning. Many women dressed in black and most men wore a black tie. My mother and I went up to town for the lying in state. Westminster Hall had a queue that seemed miles long, but we fell in at the back and wound our way slowly towards the huge doors at the entrance. Two hours later and we were filing past the catafalque. It was tremendously impressive. Despite the continual flow of people, there was a silence that could almost be felt.

We came up to London again three days later to witness the funeral procession. Thousands upon thousands of people lined the route. In the distance we heard the sound of a military band playing the Dead March in Saul. The crowd stood motionless, the silence broken only by the sound of the horses' hooves and the solemn music. It was Chopin's Funeral March now. The closed carriages with the veiled figures of the King's widow, her daughter our new Queen and the Princess Margaret went past. Many wept as the gun carriage carrying the late King went by. King George VI had stayed with his countrymen all through the war and he was much loved. It was the passing of an age.

Throughout this time I had continued my interest in writing and it was at the Gateway that my first play was performed. Entitled *No Traveller*, it was a moderate success. The plot concerned a man who had lost his memory – shades of Ronald Colman in *Random Harvest* – and was probably rather melodramatic. The leading roles were played by Margaret Fry, who had recently appeared in the West End, and Richard Gatehouse, an actor I remembered from my days attending Watford rep. I think it was probably quite well constructed and was written in the style of the commercial plays I had seen over the years. It had light relief in the form of a comic charwoman who played the trombone in a Salvation Army band. It was reasonably well received and I think stood comparison with many of the other new plays that were performed there. With all its faults, it was a great thrill to see what I had written being brought to life on the stage. I didn't make any money out of it, indeed, in common with other new authors at the Gateway I suspect I had to bear some of the cost of staging it. I am not surprised that no West End management rushed to take it up, but at least I felt my career as a playwright had begun.

A number of very big film epics were being made at that time and there were insufficient people belonging to the Film Artistes' Association (the crowd artistes union) to provide all the extras required. Film companies such as MGM opened the doors to members of Equity, and I used this as my opportunity to find out what it was like inside a film studio.

Ivanhoe was produced by MGM and filmed in Technicolor; its list of star names was endless, including Elizabeth Taylor, Robert Taylor and Joan Fontaine. It was filmed at the gigantic MGM studios in Elstree, only a short bus journey from Edgware where I lived. We were called to the studios at seven in the morning to get into costume and to go to make up. With two or three hundred people to deal with this was a time-consuming process. When we were ready, we were directed to the lot, an enormous open air space at the back of the studios. Here an imposing castle had been constructed. Although it was made from only plaster, it looked pretty real from the front. It was visible from the main road and stood there for many years, long after *Ivanhoe* was finished and so probably featured in a number of other films later.

We were filming a sequence in which this vast army of extras were attacking the castle. This required shooting arrows at it, and we were arranged in ranks with the stuntmen who were skilled in the art of archery nearest to the camera. Those of us who were less skilled, or as in my case totally unskilled, were placed as far away from the camera as possible. We would be an indistinct blur in the background. This was just as well as when we were commanded to fire our arrows, I found that mine rarely travelled farther than the rank immediately in front of me. I took some comfort from the fact that most of those around me seemed to be equally inept.

Mid-morning we had a break. Tea or coffee and sandwiches were set out on long trestle tables and were very welcome after all our exertions. Then we were back to the attack again. At the lunch break, we were provided with packed lunches. The studio canteen would have been unable to cope with the large numbers involved, and getting us all there and then back would have been too time-consuming.

In the afternoon we returned to the attack once more. About halfway through, there was the statutory tea break, cakes and biscuits this time. At the end of the day, having washed off our make-up and changed into our ordinary clothes, we queued to be 'signed off'. Then we joined another queue, presented the paper that the assistant had just signed and received our day's pay in cash.

This pattern was repeated for several days. The attack was filmed from every angle. Sometimes there would be one of the leading players in the foreground, while we continued to shoot our arrows. At other times we would see a stuntman do a spectacular fall from the very top of the ramparts. After a week or so of this, we were given a change of uniform. This time we were to defend the castle. Standing on the ramparts, we awaited the onslaught. The skilled archers were now behind the camera shooting their arrows towards us, but there were also machines that launched a great flurry of arrows in our direction at the same time. I was advised by the man standing next to me to fall down dead as soon as any of the arrows came towards us. 'That way,' he explained, 'you're out of it and you can lie around in the sun as a corpse for the rest of the day.' This seemed good advice and I did as he had suggested. Apparently everyone else had the same idea and after the first shower of arrows, there was hardly anyone left to defend the castle.

'That's no good,' said the director through his megaphone. 'Some of you have got to stay alive. I only want a few to fall down.'

The arrow machines were loaded, the archers took their position and we did the shot again with the same result. Realizing it was no use asking for volunteers to keep on their feet, the assistant director went round selecting those who were appointed to die and those who were to remain alive.

The defence of the castle also went on for about a week and then we had a change. We were to be the onlookers in the tournament scene. Our uniforms abandoned, we were now dressed as civilians. I was disappointed to be given a fairly dreary peasant costume of brown sacking and rather envied those of my fellows who were dressed as lords and ladies in flowing velvet robes. I soon realized I had actually done rather well as the heat of the sun made those heavy costumes pretty unbearable, whereas my sacking outfit was reasonably comfortable. As no particular skill was required here, I found myself placed in the foreground of the spectators; and not only the foreground, but close to the royal box. This meant I was able to see at close quarters the glamorous Elizabeth Taylor. She was even more beautiful than she was on the screen. The filming of the tournament took even longer than the sequences with the castle. I marvelled at the skill of the stuntmen, some of them doubling for the leading players, as they galloped at great speed towards each other with their lances. They would fall from their horses at exactly the right moment. Take after take after take, they would repeat the fall in exactly the same way. They were brilliant and I realized what an important part they played in the success of films such as this.

My career as a film extra continued and, for a time I became a member of the Film Artistes Association, as well as Equity. My theatre work, still at the Gateway or other fringe venues like it, paid little or no money. It was a great bonus to be paid in cash at the end of a day's filming. It was also more interesting and more fun than working in a shop or washing up in a restaurant. I think for a while that I also held on to the fantasy that I might be 'discovered' while working in the background. After all, I had read that many of my cinema heroes had worked as extras at one time. Even the great David Niven had started in this way.

Lying on a stretcher for *The Lady with a Lamp* I watched as Anna Neagle glided past. Would Herbert Wilcox, the director, suggest that she stopped by me to minister to my wounds? Even though I had no lines to speak, I would at least have the opportunity to show emotion. But it was not to be. Ironically a still was taken as she passed me and it appeared in the magazine *Picturegoer*. I was clearly recognizable, but still only an extra.

It was at Shepperton studios that I was finally upgraded while working on the film *The Story of Gilbert and Sullivan*. In this film I was part of the massed choirs in the Albert Hall singing in the first performance of *The Golden Legend*. I was also featured as one of four angry men, seen walking out on the great master because he was wasting his time on nonsense like *HMS Pinafore* instead of oratorio. Curiously, it was being featured and therefore recognizable that finally convinced me that working as a crowd artiste was probably harming rather than enhancing my career. There was a clear distinction in the eyes of directors and casting directors between those who were crowd artistes and those who were actors.

It was with some regret that I decided I would have to stop working in this area. The regret was partially financial – I would certainly miss the money that I was earning – but I would also miss working with a remarkable set of people. Those who made up the crowd on any film were an extraordinary cross-section of British life. There were retired actors, and variety artistes supplementing the money they earned elsewhere; there were old Etonians and borstal boys. I had spent many happy hours chatting with them on a variety of subjects during the long waits between takes. It had been fun, I had enjoyed their company and I would miss them.

With the occasional small parts continuing at the Gateway, I had often found myself juggling my diary between theatre and studio. There had been days when I had stood around for hours on set as an extra, praying that I would be released on time to catch the bus back to Westbourne Grove for the evening performance. While the Gateway served to offer experience in theatre, and the extra work in films paid the bills, neither was moving me forward in any sort of constructive way, and at the speed which I desired. Even though I had written and directed my first play, *No Traveller*, at the Gateway, still no one had spotted me live or on film and it seemed that the time was right to make a decisive move forward.

Though television transmissions had started in the 1930s, they had been discontinued during the war years. Once they began again I found myself visiting family friends, the Freedmans, on a regular basis. The screen was about the size of a small sheet of paper. In spite of its size, it had a quality that was much better than the one I had seen in the shop six years earlier. It took many years for the price of televisions to come down sufficiently for most people to afford one. The 1953 Coronation of Queen Elizabeth II was probably the occasion that sold television to the mass audience. We still did not possess one and so on the day of the Coronation, my parents and I all gathered round the Freedmans' set to watch the young Queen being crowned. We all raised a glass to her as she left the Abbey to drive back to the palace through the cheering crowds.

It was my constant nagging that eventually caused my parents to agree that we should have a set ourselves, and it was a great day when it finally arrived in the corner of our drawing room. This little box was to become an increasingly influential element in the life of the nation. It was a great source of entertainment. For me it was a new challenge. I did not just want to sit in an armchair watching it, I wanted to be there on that tiny screen.

As television was an up and coming medium I decided that this was where my career should now move. In the absence of an agent I began to write to directors whose names I had culled from the *Radio Times*. I soon realized that this was getting me nowhere: 'Dear Mr Williams, Thank you for your letter enquiring about the possibility of appearing in our new drama series. It would be very difficult to see every actor who writes in and I therefore suggest that you attend one of our group auditions in London.'

Realizing that thousands of young hopefuls were all trying to get a place in this new area of the profession, I wondered whether it was worth even trying. However, I decided to do so. What had I got to lose? I applied and learnt that I would need to do three pieces. I knew I would need some help.

Christabel Currie had wanted to become an actress, but her parents had decreed that this was not a suitable career for a young girl in her day. She had kept her interest in the art alive by teaching drama and elocution. As voice production was her speciality, she soon had me contorting my mouth and tongue, doing exercises which on occasion I still do to this day. These lessons over, we concentrated on the pieces that I was due to perform. I rehearsed them so many times I felt as if I could have done them backwards. As well as the customary audition excerpt from one of Shakespeare's plays, I performed as the elder brother in *The Winslow Boy*. It was a speech that required my being on the telephone. In the scene, the brother picks up the phone to answer a reporter enquiring about his younger brother who is embroiled in a court case. 'Oh I don't know,' he says. 'He's just like any other kid. Doesn't wash and so on. Oh I say, don't take that too seriously, he does wash sometimes of course.'

I felt it was a part that suited me rather well and I would have liked to play it. I never did, although ironically I was to do the play many years later in Vienna, but playing the part of the father. As I stood in the wings listening to the young actor doing the telephone call, my mind often went back to that early audition at the BBC which had started it all.

The third piece, from a contemporary play *The Hidden Years*, concerned a young schoolboy talking about his feelings for another boy. I think Miss Currie found this a bit sentimental but it enabled me to show emotion and I wanted to make it clear that I could play a wide range of parts. Even in those days I had great ambitions to be taken seriously.

I was soon invited to present my pieces, at the BBC in Lime Grove. They didn't seem to react and I felt pretty sure that this audition process was merely a way of dealing with the growing number of people wanting entrance to the new medium. I left feeling neither one thing nor another. Even if it hadn't done any good, I reasoned with myself as I sat on the bus, at least I could say I had done the BBC audition. This would mean that they couldn't fob me off with it any more when I wrote in for other parts.

I continued to write to various directors and producers whenever I heard that there was a new programme idea being developed. Mentioning the fact that I had already done the television audition seemed to pay off, because after several months I began to receive some signs of interest. Caryl Doncaster received one of my letters enquiring about her need of teenagers for a series of dramatized documentaries entitled *The Rising Twenties*. 'The Call Up' was one in the series that featured six young men doing their first six weeks of National Service training. I must have been what she had in mind, and I found it hard to believe that after a short interview I was cast as a country yokel recruit who couldn't do anything right, which was just as well because I couldn't do anything right anyway.

The basement hall of the Church of the Annunciation in Marble Arch was to be our rehearsal base for the next three weeks. The thought of going through my paces with an army drill sergeant from Aldershot terrified me. Memories of the corps at Ardingly came flooding back. Fortunately, as he watched in amazement my ineptitude at drill movements, I was able to explain that 'It's OK, I'm not supposed to get it right anyway.' The sound of six teenagers marching up and down and the bellowed commands of the drill sergeant must have sent certain shock waves through the building, because at one stage a young curate arrived looking harassed and said 'Sorry, but could you be a bit quieter as we are trying to have our service upstairs!'

Not having to perfect my drill was a relief when it came to performance, for in those days, television was always live. The church hall was exchanged for the BBC studios at Lime Grove. We were introduced to the lights and the cameras and for the first time saw the sets which up until now had only been represented by taped marks on the floor. Standing in exactly the right position is important in television if the cameras are going to be able to get the correct shot. We went through this many times in several technical rehearsals. Then came the moment of truth. With all thoughts of the many millions of people who would be watching firmly removed from our minds, we went through this live documentary and by some miracle it went as it had done at rehearsals. When it was all over and the red light was turned off in the studio, great relief was the overwhelming feeling of the moment. We had done it. It was performed as the viewer saw it, but unlike my appearances on film, I was never able to see or judge the performance for myself. My parents had gone next door to the Senkers' house to see me act on the box, and when I returned home they were very complimentary; I felt that my television career had got off the ground.

However, I still had a lot to learn. During a tea break on

'The Call Up' I discovered that every one of my peers had an agent. It was not only the fact that it was easier to gain work if you had an agent, I realised, but also the fact that they were all being paid more than I was. My fee was 18 guineas for the entire job – three weeks' rehearsal and the transmission. They were all getting 21 guineas. I was three guineas short and determined to find an agent as soon as possible. Over the years, I was to end up having more agents than most people have had hot dinners!

When Caryl Doncaster recalled me for another of her documentaries I was well prepared with my new agent negotiating on my behalf. *Those Who Dare* was transmitted live, but gave me my first taste of location filming. The documentary related how in the 1930s a group of borstal boys and two of their warders marched up the country from Feltham to Nottingham where they physically built the first open borstal at Lowdham Grange. As they marched up the country, they were put up for the night in various church halls and hostels, and cooked for by ladies of the parish. All these interior scenes were to be transmitted live from the studio, but the outside scenes were pre-filmed at Feltham and Lowdham Grange. Initially, we found this experience quite frightening as Feltham contained some very high security inmates and we were often locked inside with some quite tough juvenile delinquents. Lowdhan Grange was quite different. As we emerged from the coach in our 1930s borstal boys' uniform, we were approached by one of the older warders. He sighed as he spoke. 'Ahh. You're the sort of lad we used to get in borstal. We just get a load of old riffraff these days!'

In the more relaxed surroundings of Lowdham Grange, some of the real borstal boys were used as extras. For their own sake it had been decreed that the young criminal faces should not be seen, which led to some amusing moments of upstaging as many of the boys were quite eager to become overnight film stars. Several of the boys used the excuse of our filming round a campfire one night to abscond. They were all recaptured pretty quickly, but it gave me a great insight into a world that I had never seen, and an appreciation of the wider world of television.

The next three years saw me playing all manner of parts from children's series to serious drama. I was asked to play a small part in *Clive of India*; again, it was to be transmitted live. This was to be a big production. The director, Rudolph Cartier, had constructed a jungle set in the studio. The camera-man was called upon to track two of the characters as they walked through the jungle together. For television at that time, it was tremendously ambitious. I watched one of the studio monitors and was lost in admiration when I saw how good it looked on screen. Doing that type of epic production within the confines of a television studio was really ahead of its time.

Of all the actresses that I had worked with up until then, it was Thora Hird who stood above the rest. *The Queen Came By* produced in 1955 told the story of the staff in a Victorian drapery store preparing for Queen Victoria's Jubilee procession to pass their window. Thora was the ultimate professional. She seemed totally natural in the part of the senior seamstress and mother figure of the family business. She had played it with great success in the West End and to begin with I was somewhat in awe of her. However, she was so friendly that I soon began to feel at ease. The director started by saying, 'Now Thora, the camera will be over here for this shot.'

'Oh don't worry about all that,' Thora replied. 'I'll just do it, and you shoot me as you see fit.'

She was right. The more camera conscious an actor is, the less convincing it all becomes. In rehearsal I watched the rest of the cast. Peter Bull and Maureen Pryor were in the production. 'I'm really not as good as all these,' I said to myself. 'They'll notice how bad I am and want to re-cast my part.'

All actors are insecure, but, among such a starry cast, I

was more insecure than most. It was my first big chance of a decent part and I didn't believe it was really going to happen. Surely at the last moment they would get rid of me? Of course, my fears were groundless. We completed the three weeks' rehearsal, and at the end of it the play was transmitted live on a Sunday evening. It went well and I even survived a scene in which I had to play the banjo, carefully shot so that I had my back to the camera while someone else played behind the set. Friends who had seen it said it looked quite convincing. They also seemed to think that my performance was all right. This was just as well as I had to do it again. Repeats in those days before recording meant that the entire cast had to reassemble and perform it live once more. For some reason, we had a different camera crew, so all the technical rehearsal had to be repeated for their benefit and again it went without a hitch. I had now completed my first real play on television.

It was this production that first introduced me to the dread actor's disease known as corpsing. Corpsing usually occurs when something unexpected happens and an actor starts to laugh uncontrollably and is unable to stop. The more he tries to control it, the worse it gets. It is probably all to do with nervousness and tension, but if you suffer from it, there is little you can do about it. Sometimes it occurs when a situation or a line in a play, not necessarily a funny line, strikes the actor as particularly amusing. Every time this line or situation comes up, however much he tries not to, he will corpse. If you are given to corpsing, it is absolutely fatal to play scenes with someone who also suffers from the disease. During rehearsals for *The Queen Came By*, I found that Maureen Pryor was such a person and in rehearsal after rehearsal, we disgraced ourselves at the same point. Fortunately, it was a scene in which only the two of us were involved, so the other members of the cast did not have to put up with this appalling behaviour and the director was remarkably patient.

In the play Maureen played a shopgirl who was rather keen

on me. Trying to persuade me to take her to the celebration fireworks display in Hyde Park, she had the line, 'and Mr Wallasey, there's a set piece of the Queen fifty feet high'. I know it's not particularly funny, but for some reason we thought it was. The moment she said it, one or other of us would start to giggle, the other would join in and the rehearsal came to a halt until we had managed to pull ourselves together. We were both worried that we might do it on transmission, but the terror of doing a live performance saved us on both occasions. Some years later I did another play with Maureen. On the first day of rehearsal we talked sternly to each other and agreed that we would behave ourselves this time. There was one danger line, but we managed to cope with it, until the day when all the heads of ATV came to see the final run through in the rehearsal room. The sight of all these important people must have overcome us. That was the moment when we lost it once again.

One of my worst corpsing incidents occurred with the wonderful Pat Coombs. I was playing her rather soppy boyfriend and she wanted to get me alone in the garden. 'Come and see my bird bath,' she invented wildly. We exited and moments later I returned. 'Someone has stolen her bird bath,' I announced. 'She hasn't got a bird bath,' said the redoubtable Peggy Mount. 'Not now she hasn't,' I replied.

That was it. We both thought it was hysterical. The moment I uttered the line, we both dissolved. This went on for several days and we could see that Peggy was not pleased with us.

'We must pull ourselves together,' said Pat to me one day. 'If we don't, Peggy's going to get so cross.'

She was right. The day came when Peggy had had enough. 'You two are going to do that on the recording, if you're not careful,' she boomed. It should have pulled us up short, but somehow it only made it worse. We took even longer to recover on that occasion. Despite the fact that the programme was recorded and the terror of live television was no longer there, we did manage to get through without disgracing ourselves, but only just.

5

THE BIG SCREEN BECKONS

I had worked on stage, and now on television, but the big screen still eluded me. When my chance came to appear in a cinema film, it combined both my religious beliefs and my career as an actor.

J. Arthur Rank was a British millionaire who made his money in flour. A deeply committed Methodist, Arthur Rank entered film production because he thought it was an excellent medium to preach the gospel through religious films. At a time when the Church still tended to condemn the entertainment business in particular, Rank put his money into black and white short films, which were shown in local chapels and village halls.

The success of Rank's films were to be taken far beyond what he had ever imagined and by the mid 1940s, his business acumen had led him to become the biggest film producer in Britain. The Religious Film Society, formed in 1933 to promote the use of film for Christian purposes, led to the formation of the British National Film Company a year later. As chairman of the new Rank Organization he invested heavily in the British film industry, acquired several film studios, including Pinewood, and controlled the Gaumont and Odeon cinema chains. It was in Rank's religious film department that I got my first break in the movie business.

Shield of Faith was based on the true story of a football team that was killed in an air crash. Mervyn Johns played a padre who was ministering to the bereaved. I made my film debut in a flashback sequence set in World War I playing the part of a dying soldier. As the padre hovered over me while I lay dying among the chaos of the trenches, I recited my first lines on film: part of the twenty-third Psalm. The script suggested that this sequence strengthened the padre's faith, so that later he was able to cope with the desolation of the air crash and its bereaved.

As it was 1955 and the film was in black and white, my wounds did not look too horrific, and the fake blood was kept to a minimum. My look of agony was probably enhanced by the fact that I had dreadful toothache at the time; so all the groaning was quite real. As soon as the filming was completed, I went to see my dentist, Dr Rhys Herbert. He was a rotund, jolly Welshman, and was assisted by Miss Rhys Herbert, his sister. When I had visited him as a boy, accompanied by my father, he would often ignore me while he reminisced about the great Welsh rugby players. On learning that I had become an actor, he said, 'I think I could have made an actor myself.'

'Fatty Arbuckle. That's what you'd have been,' retorted his sister.

Now sitting in his chair I told him that I had just done my first film part. 'I've just been dying in the trenches,' I proudly announced.

'Well, you'd better not tell your mother about that,' was the only reply he could manage.

Remembering my time as a crowd artiste, it was a strange coincidence that my first part in a commercial film should be in *The Extra Day*. It was made at Shepperton and was partially set in a film studio. The plot centered around a can of film that had been lost on the way to the lab. The final day's shooting has to be redone and the story revolves around the effect this has on the lives of the extras who have been recalled. Arriving at the studios, I was somewhat overawed to discover that I was sharing a dressing room with the great film actor, Bryan Forbes. I was highly nervous but he was extremely laid back and even climbed out of our dressing-room window onto a flat roof that gave him the chance for a touch of sunbathing while waiting to be called. Having got into my costume and make up by 8 am I sat in the dressing room, going over my one or two lines, and awaited my call to the set. This wait seemed so interminable that at one point I wondered if we had been forgotten entirely. Bryan was still enjoying the sunshine outside the window, so I presumed all was well.

Eventually our call came, and we were escorted into the waiting throng of actors and crew. My role in *The Extra Day* was as an assistant cameraman and I spent the next few days sitting on the little seat beside a camera on a crane which went up and down alarmingly. Knowing that the job of an assistant cameraman meant fiddling about with focus and other technical things, I tried to look as if I knew what I was doing. It was only a small part, but at least I felt that my film career had begun. On the last day of filming, Bryan Forbes gave me a lift back to Richmond Station, and talked in a general way about marriage, and I, as a bachelor, responded as best I could. I had no idea why this had been the subject of our conversation until the next day when I read in the newspapers that he had announced his engagement to Nanette Newman.

I was still doing quite a lot of work on television and was always eager to pick up any tips from actors who had more experience than I. 'I've always thought it was a good idea not to shave on the morning of the transmission,' said one. 'It gives a clearer definition to the outline of the face on camera.' I tried it, but as I had a very pale beard it probably didn't make much difference one way or the other.

I soon learned the importance of being as natural as possible when playing a straight role on television. Successive directors had to tell me that I was doing 'too much' in a close up. My early days in the theatre had taught me to project and be slightly 'larger than life' so that the performance would register even in the back row. Now I had to learn to tone it down. When not in a scene I would watch the monitor and realize that those who had really learnt the television technique did very little, particularly in close-up. As the camera came in, it seemed as if it could see right into their souls. Wherever possible I heeded Thora Hird's earlier advice to pretend that the camera wasn't there, but sometimes it just wasn't possible. In the days of live television you sometimes had to cheat to get the right camera angle. 'Frank, can you lean right back in your chair when you say that line, otherwise I can't get the shot,' would come booming from the director's box over the studio loudspeaker system. On the transmission, I had to remember these little bits of extra direction.

My time in television was never a substitute for the theatre. Visits to see plays at the Watford Palace remained a regular part of my life whenever I had some free time, and I even worked there on one or two occasions. The Watford Palace had for many years been run by the Melville family. I learned recently that John Le Mesurier's first wife was June Melville, who had directed a number of the plays that I had seen. When the Melville family retired from running the theatre it was taken over by Jimmy and Gilda Perry. Having played a doctor and a barrister in *Witness for the Prosecution* for the Melvilles, when the Perrys took over they invited me back to appear in *Honeymoon Beds*. This was to be my first professional engagement with the man who was later to become famous with David Croft for many television classics, including, of course, *Dad's Army*.

I found Jimmy to be a most approachable and likeable man, and one who was always positive even in the direst of circumstances. Disaster could be striking all around him and he would still smile and say, 'Its all going very well, isn't it?' Jimmy was always ready to listen to new ideas and when I showed him the script of a play I had written, he agreed to do it. *The TV Murders* is about a group of people watching television when one of their number is mysteriously murdered. It was probably not a great play but the audience seemed to find it reasonably entertaining. It was subsequently performed by a number of other reps and I had the opportunity to play the lead when it was at the Intimate Theatre, Palmers Green, in north London. One of the things I find very interesting about this business is that something that seems relatively unimportant may lead to something that has a profound effect on your career later. How was I to know that meeting and working with Jimmy and being chairman of his Patrons' Club would make him think of me nearly 20 years later?

ITV had begun broadcasting in 1955, and was rapidly catching up with the BBC in its output. For actors this was a golden opportunity for more work, and over the next few years I frequently switched between the two channels. It was Granada Television that was to provide my first taste of instant recognition. When I was first starting in the theatre, I often wondered what it would be like to be recognized in the street. The first time this happened, I was walking down Coventry Street in the West End of London when a man stopped me.

'Didn't I see you on television last night?' he asked.

This was it. Fame at last. I smiled modestly. 'Yes, you could have done.'

'Thought so,' he replied. 'You were awful!'

When the telephone call from my agent came, he explained that they had a small part for me in a comedy series and it would be rehearsed in London but transmitted from Manchester. 'That'll be a week's work then,' I thought, and noted the dates in my diary. However, *The Army Game* was to become ITV's first big comedy success. My agent explained the plot. 'They've got this tall guy called Bernard Bresslaw who plays one of the soldiers and his catchphrase is "I only asked". William Hartnell plays a sergeant major who is starting to behave very oddly and the army has decided to call in a psychiatrist, and that's where you come in. By mistake the psychiatrist gets Bernard Bresslaw instead of William Hartnell!'

They were a friendly crowd and I got on very well with Bernard. Playing the scenes with him was a joy. During rehearsals William had let slip an extremely mild swear word, and then turned round to see a young actress within earshot. 'I'm terribly sorry my dear,' he apologised. 'I really didn't see you standing there.' One just didn't swear in front of a woman. How times have changed!

After a week's rehearsal, most of the cast flew up to Manchester, but William Hartnell and I said we would prefer to go by train. William could be a little overbearing at times. When we had lunch together on the train he seemed to complain about everything. Every time he was asked whether he had a sufficient portion he said, 'No, I'd like some more.' I could see the waiter getting more and more irritated, and I think the size of my own portions suffered as a result. Over lunch he gave me a long lecture about the fact that I only had a half page in *Spotlight*, the profession's casting directory. 'An actor of your standing should have a full page,' he said.

It was all very well for him, he had been a film star for many years, and he could afford a full page. I could not. He went on like this for most of the journey and I wondered if this was one of the reasons why the others had chosen to go by plane. I had seen many of his films and I greatly admired his work. It was William Hartnell's appearances in *The Army Game* that caused him to be chosen by the TV producer Verity Lambert for the role as the BBC's first Dr Who.

Upon our arrival at the Granada Television Studios we rehearsed the show with the cameras before doing the final performance as a live transmission. The size of the sets and the lack of space for the studio audience meant that they were seated in the canteen next door watching the episode on monitors. Their laughter was to be fed back to us through loudspeakers in the studio. As the opening titles began and the first scene went into action all seemed to be going well. The studio audience was obviously enjoying the show as there was much laughter coming from next door. My first entrance went down well and all seemed to be going smoothly. Suddenly the laughs stopped. For a moment our hearts stopped as well as we wondered if we had hit a part of the script that was hideously unfunny. We carried on in silence for a time until one of the technicians whispered that the sound system had broken down between the canteen and the studio. It was a relief to know that the audience was still laughing even though we couldn't hear them.

Once the transmission was over, we all knew it had gone forever as programmes were never recorded in those days. However, many years later I met someone who said he had seen a repeat of the episode in question on the Granada Plus channel. I told him this could not possibly be so because only two episodes of *The Army Game* had ever been recorded. These had been done on film and kept for use in an emergency if for any reason the live show could not be transmitted. He was still insistent that it was the one with me as the psychiatrist. He sent me the videotape of the episode and indeed it was the one in which we worked with the silent laughter. I was interested to note that the laughter, although inaudible to us, had been heard by the watching millions.

In those days producers did not seem too worried if an actor appeared in the same series playing a different character. Over the next few months I played quite an assortment. In one episode I played the part of a doctor. It opened with my listening to a soldier's heart through a stethoscope. The actor was Percy Herbert, a big muscular man who always played very tough roles. He lay on the examination bed and I hovered over him waiting for the floor manager to give the signal for action. It came and I placed the stethoscope on his chest. The noise of his heart pounding in my ears nearly drowned out the dialogue. The terrifying thump, thump, thump, brought home to me how much of a strain live television was in those days.

For a time I hovered between life and death for *Emergency*

Ward 10, the late 1950s version of today's *Casualty*. My contribution began as I pushed my way through joints of hanging meat in a butcher's shop, opened the door and collapsed straight into Charles Tingwell's arms. Thereafter I was in bed with a brain tumour over the next six weeks. Filmed in the middle of winter, we were not happy that the dressing rooms were across the yard in another block. We had to brave the elements and walk backwards and forwards along a snow-covered pathway, and I was only wearing pyjamas. I made up for it in the episode following my operation in which I spent the whole time tucked up warmly in bed without having to say a word, surrounded by lovely nurses and anxious doctors. 'What a splendid way to earn a living,' I thought.

Unlike the medical series of today, in which every cut of the scalpel is shown in brilliantly coloured close-up, nothing like that was ever seen on the screen. When an operation was performed, all the viewers saw were surgeons and nurses looking worriedly at the patient. My operation was nevertheless extremely convincing, but I was not there. The viewers saw the doctors looking down as they discussed the operation, but did not see me at all. It was live television, but I was sitting comfortably at home being rather moved at their obvious concern about my condition. It was particularly poignant when one nurse was so upset she went out to have a little weep in the corridor! However, all was well and I pulled through.

The next day I was on a tube train going back to the studio when I heard the woman opposite me say, 'See that man over there, Mabel? Isn't he like that Malcolm Thingamabob in *Emergency Ward 10*? The one who's just had that awful operation?'

'Don't be silly,' replied her friend. 'He'd be far too ill to be travelling on a train!' Such is the magic of television. My time on *Emergency Ward 10* came to an end with my character having happily recovered. In fact all the patients seemed to recover on that programme. Once I had had my operation and my head was heavily bandaged, they got interested in someone else.

At home things were not easy. My father had become increasingly ill and he was now housebound. He needed constant nursing and the strain was beginning to tell on my mother. 'You need a break from all this,' our GP told her. 'I can arrange for Mr Williams to go into a nursing home so that you can have a fortnight's holiday. I think it's essential for your own health.' My father backed him up and my mother reluctantly agreed. He went into a local nursing home, and she went down to Hampshire to stay with her sister.

When I went to visit Father, he had become so disorientated that he didn't appear to recognize me. 'Who are you?' he said, staring at me in bewilderment. He then proceeded to talk to me, about me. 'My son comes to see me, you know,' he said.

I was shattered and didn't know how to respond. As I was leaving I met Mrs Senker who had come to visit my father. 'I've been to see him but he doesn't know who I am,' I said feeling very distressed.

'I'm sure it's only temporary, and he'll be all right when be gets back home,' she reassured me.

She was right. Two weeks later my mother returned and once my father was back home in familiar surroundings all was well.

One night my mother came into my room and woke me up. As she stood by my bed in the darkened room, I knew that something was wrong. 'I think we had better call the doctor,' she said.

It took only a few moments for our family GP to certify that Father had died. Mother and I spent the rest of the night downstairs, comforting ourselves by talking about the old times. There is so much to do after a death that in a strange way the reality of what has happened does not quite sink in. The contacting of the relatives and the funeral arrangements has to be done in such a short time that there is no opportunity to stop and think about yourself. It's later that the real grieving begins. Although I grieved deeply over his death, he had been ill for some time and his death was not totally unexpected. I was happy that, at 76, he had enjoyed a good life. My greatest sadness was that he didn't see me develop my television career.

As a 26-year-old, who had lived with his parents, I was none the less reasonably independent and, unlike an uncle of mine, certainly knew how to boil an egg. My sense of independence was to increase when my mother decided that she would like to move back to Hampshire in order to be with her immediate family. I would have to find somewhere to live and started scouring the adverts in the local paper for flats to let. After a number of unsuccessful sorties I came to the conclusion that if at all possible I should try to buy something, and I discussed this with my mother and our family solicitor. It was agreed that my mother would lend me the money to buy something and I would pay her interest on the loan.

Once again, I set out on my search. It was a good time to buy and houses for sale seemed more readily available than flats to let. Eventually I found something that seemed ideal: a turn-of-the-century terraced house in a road down which I had often walked with my father as a boy when he was going to the bank. It was near to the shops and the underground station, and the cinema in which I had spent so many happy hours was on the corner. The survey showed that there were some problems but the price meant that I would be able to afford to have them put right. Contracts were exchanged and I was now a house-owner in my own right.

Hoping that my meagre and unreliable actor's income would support such a financial move, I was happy that the lower part of the house was let, and my sitting tenants would provide a small but secure supplement to my earnings. As

soon as it became mine, I inspected the property. There was
dry rot and every room of my flat needed redecorating. Blast
damage from a bomb which had fallen nearby during the war
had shattered the damp course, and downstairs was pretty
wet by any standards. The work involved pulling up all the
downstairs floorboards. Arriving home one day I decided to
pop in and see how my tenants were coping with the disrup-
tion. The scene that met me was almost surreal. The family
were crowded around the boiler in the kitchen on the only bit
of floor that had not been removed. With their chairs packed
on the small wooden island it looked as though they had
encamped on the edge of an abyss. I made some inane remark,
smiled feebly and retreated hastily up the stairs.

Now it was back to the agent to see if there was any more
work on the horizon. I was delighted when a few days later
Granada Television phoned my agent to say that the current
commanding officer was leaving *The Army Game* and that
they wanted me to do six episodes as the new character of
Captain Pocket. Six episodes became seventy-five over the
next three years.

The opportunity to become a regular character was
immensely satisfying. Hut 29 was part of an army barracks at
Surplus Ordnance Depot, Nether Wallop, Warwickshire, and
here lived a group of squaddies doing their National Service.
As they grumble and plan ways of skiving from their duties,
the silly ass officer, played by myself, would try to bring some
order to the proceedings. Some of the original cast had now
left and Bill Fraser had taken over from William Hartnell as
the sergeant major. The viewing audience had not been sure
if they liked this change at first, but after a few episodes
Sergeant Major Snudge was accepted as one of the great
comedy characters of British television. His co-star Alfie Bass
('Excused Boots' Bisley) had played many film, and television
roles. Among others in the cast were Norman Rossington
(Private 'Cupcake' Cook), and Charles Hawtrey (Private

'Professor' Hatchett). Corporal 'Flogger' Hoskins was played by the inimitable Harry Fowler. The show was now being rehearsed and transmitted from London, and the old Chelsea Palace Theatre had become its resident home. The stage area and stalls had been adapted as a studio. The audience sat in the Dress Circle and it was an interesting combination of live theatre and live television all at the same time. I became aware that quite often a rather jolly friend of Bill Fraser would join us for drinks after the show. Pamela Cundell eventually married him and she was later to become Mrs Fox in *Dad's Army*.

We did one episode each week, starting rehearsals on the Monday in a local church hall and going into the studio on the Friday. Having done the show we would get the next script so that we could read it ready for rehearsals for the following week. Apart from this, Saturday and Sunday were free and I would often take the opportunity to visit my mother in Ringwood. It was unfortunate that on one visit I developed bronchitis. Running a high temperature, I was forced to telephone the producer to say I would be unable to do the show. They wrote in a temporary part for another actor to cover me. I watched the two episodes and he was very good. Arriving back after my two weeks of sick leave I was slightly concerned that my replacement might have been so good that they would want to get rid of me and have him instead. Fortunately they did not.

Back in the studio I had a slight feeling of nervousness when faced with quite a tricky piece of dialogue to remember. I had in the past copied numbers and words onto my fingernails and nonchalantly looked at my hands while reading and delivering the line. I had always felt that it was a dangerous thing for an actor to write a line down and hide it on the set in case he comes to rely on it too much. In this instance I was about to break my own rule. I decided to place a line reminder on a piece of paper on the desk I was using on set, and all went well until the performance. Before my line was said, one of the other actors marched in and placed a file of papers on top of my desk, right on top of my reminder. I was slightly thrown by this, but managed to remember the line. It was a salutary lesson and stopped me resorting to this in the future.

To give a bit of a change from the normal life of the camp, the writers wrote an episode in which 'Excused Boots' Bisley dreamed about the history of the regiment. The dream sequence occupied most of the programme. I appeared as Queen Boadicea with a long green dress and horns coming out of my head. To show that we were in a dream, a smoke machine was used. It was being operated by a new member of the crew who had obviously not had a lot of practice with the equipment. When the sequence started the young fellow set the smoke machine off but somehow failed to turn it off again. Before long the whole studio looked like the London smog. Still going out live, it got totally out of hand and became so thick that we couldn't see each other or even the set. Disembodied voices continued to emerge from the gloom, as we battled on regardless. We certainly couldn't see the cameras and it seemed likely that they couldn't see us. Goodness only knows what it looked like to everyone viewing at home.

Another episode involved my playing two parts: myself and my twin brother. As Captain Pocket I rushed out of one door, put a mac on over the costume, and rushed back in another, as my twin. I had a minder who grabbed me, pulled the mac on or off as appropriate and pushed me back in the right direction. It was quite easy really. All I had to remember was that with no mac I was Captain Pocket, and with it, I was not. Simple!

One script required Geoffrey Sumner, now playing another officer, and myself to be completely soaked through. The only way to do this quickly was to run off the set, straight to the nearest dressing room and jump fully clothed into a bath of cold water. I got out and Geoffrey took my place. No squeamishness about sharing the bathwater. After all this was the army! We returned to the studio dripping water everywhere. Why did I ever think acting was going to be glamorous?

The news that I was going to have to fly in the following week's episode seemed somewhat puzzling. I never knew what was actually going to happen until I was given the script, but rumours abounded. Was 'Excused Boots' Bisley going to have another dream in which I was transformed into Peter Pan? When I read the script, all was made clear. The plot concerned a rocket which was supposed to be sent to Perthshire and I had sent it to Persia by mistake. While trying to sort this out, the rocket was inadvertently launched while I was still holding onto it. The Kirby Flying Company was called in to ensure that I could fly upwards in safety. I was strapped into the harness with a wire attached and after a number of practice runs I felt reasonably confident that all would be well. My ascent with the rocket was the climax of the episode and when the moment came I shot into the air and duly disappeared from sight. The studio audience applauded as the credits began to roll and, suspended about 20 feet above the studio floor, I breathed a sigh of relief.

I waited politely for the technicians to return me to ground level but nothing seemed to be happening. I looked down and the studio audience were beginning to leave. 'Excuse me,' I said. No one took any notice.

'Excuse me,' I said, louder this time. Still nothing.

'I'm still here.' It was a bellow by now, but everyone continued to ignore me. What was the matter with them all? I continued to shout for what felt like hours, but they all seemed to be totally oblivious. Just as I was beginning to feel that I was in some kind of nightmare, I saw Harry Fowler look up and point at me with mock surprise. I should have known. Harry, always the practical joker, had persuaded them to leave me hanging for a time. When I eventually reached terra firma everyone seemed to think it had been a wonderful joke.

I saw the funny side and laughed too, but made sure Harry bought me a large drink in the pub afterwards.

Towards the end of 1959 *The Army Game* was invited to appear in a sketch before Her Majesty the Queen Mother for that year's Royal Variety Performance back in Manchester. As it was not possible for us all to be presented to her we drew lots on who would represent us. The lot fell to Alfie Bass. This was somewhat ironic as in conversations with Alfie I had gathered that he did not really approve of the Royal Family as an institution.

The continual contracts for *The Army Game* brought a sense of security, and certainly improved my bank balance. It is a fallacy that all actors are millionaires but for the first time in my life I was reasonably secure. Money had never been the most important aspect of my work, I wanted to enjoy what I was doing and play parts that I felt were worthwhile.

Each year having done 39 episodes of *The Army Game* we had a summer break. In one of these I did a film. *Inn for Trouble* was a film version of a popular ATV series *The Larkins*, which starred David Kossoff and Peggy Mount, the wonderful screen battle-axe. In the first episode of the television series, the cockney family were awaiting the return of their son who was coming back from the army. They employed an artist, played by me, to paint their son's portrait as a welcome home gift. I had done the episode and thought no more about it. When it was decided to transfer the story to the big screen the producers watched a number of episodes to get the flavour of it. Seeing my performance they decided to give me a role in the film. This is another example of the way in which something that seems unimportant at the time can lead to something else.

The film made clever use of several famous names playing small cameo roles, including Irene Handl. When she arrived to do her day on the film, I sat in the studio restaurant with Miss Handl and she was accompanied by her snappy little dog.

Someone came over to speak to her and the dog promptly bit him. 'Oh yes,' she said. 'He does that from time to time.' It was such a wonderfully bizarre throwaway line that I couldn't help but smile, though I don't think the victim found it so amusing.

I came in and out of the film quite a lot, and had to ride a moped. Not being one of the most practical actors around and hating anything mechanical, my problems began the moment I tried to start the wretched thing. I was supposed to start the moped and ride off at great speed. Somehow, whatever I did with the pedal it just chugged and rattled and then died. When a member of the technical crew came over to assist I was embarrassed when he just touched the pedal and the machine burst into life. The director was amazingly patient and in the end decided that the only way round the problem was for a member of the crew to start the bike, dive out of sight behind the hedge to avoid being seen and then I would mount and ride off. Even this required several attempts; he would start the engine, dive behind the hedge, I would mount the bike, but I would somehow manage to stall the engine. Eventually I got it right and set off down the road at a reasonable speed. As I approached the pub that I was aiming for I slowed down but my anxiety got the better of me and I stopped long before the mark outside the tavern door and the moped spluttered to a halt. 'We'll have to go again!' said the director. 'You must get to the mark, Frank.'

Down the lane once more, I jumped on, the moped's engine growled, the crewman fell into the hedge, and I blasted off into the distance. This time I was so determined not to stop too soon that I drove the moped towards the inn, went past the white stop mark, and straight through the door of the pub! Those inside stared at me in amazement. I apologized profusely and wheeled the miserable piece of metal back outside. Thereafter it was decided that a double was to be employed whenever I was required to handle anything remotely technical, for which I was profoundly grateful.

However, in a later scene no doubling was possible. I had to ride a horse as part of the hunt. Dressed in hunting pink, it soon became clear that I was no horseman and I was relieved when they gave me a very quiet animal. In fact it was so quiet I couldn't get it to move at all. I had visions of the hunt moving off and being left behind. I need not have worried; A.E. Matthews at the age of 90 was the master of the hunt. He had a much more spirited horse, and was clearly a good rider. At the given cue, he moved off without any effort and my horse, after a quick look round, decided it might as well follow.

Once the location scenes were completed, we went into the studio to film the interior of the pub. The place was full of dogs yelping and yapping and we had to rise above the racket in order to deliver our dialogue. 'Get those dogs out of here!' shouted Peggy Mount in her role as the landlady.

Many of us were being paid on a daily rate. We were getting short of time, and the director was anxious to get the last scene in the can as soon as possible. Having been word perfect all day long, A.E. Matthews suddenly appeared unable to deliver one of his lines. Every time the camera ran, he stalled mid-sentence and apologized.

'Does anyone mind if we call 15 minutes overtime to get this shot finished?' asked the director. We all agreed, but when the scene was repeated, Mr Matthews dried once more.

'I think we'll call it a day, and come back tomorrow,' said the director with an air of resignation.

As we all started to leave, A.E. Matthews turned to me and whispered 'There ya go boy. Got us both an extra day's work there!' He gave me a huge wink and disappeared back to his dressing room.

My first appearance in the film was in a bath singing 'Colonel Bogey', but once in the can they found there was a copyright problem with that tune, so I was called back into the studio to dub 'Annie Laurie' over the top.

When the film eventually arrived at my local cinema the

1. Where did you get that hat?

2. Who said I couldn't drive?

WHY NOT HAVE IT ENLARGED ?

4. With my parents and Jo the dog in our back garden

3. A pre-war photo-weighing machine in Brighton

5. Juvenile lead?

6. As the dying soldier with Mervyn Johns in *Shield of Faith*, Rank Films 1955

9. As Barrabas in *The Substitute* with Gilda Perry as Mary Magdalene, 1960

10. My play, *The TV Murders*, at Watford with (L to R) *back row*: John Clegg; Judy Parfitt; Michael Bevis. *Front row*: Mavis Pugh; Judy Knowlson; Nick Haig, 1960

11. Captain Pocket from the *The Army Game* making a personal appearance at a 'minors matinee', 1960

12. Now available for detective roles!

13. *Murder by Appointment* goes on tour

manager, wishing to capitalize on the fact that one of the actors was a local resident had a large photograph of me displayed outside the cinema. He chose a 'still' from my opening scene. I had just got out of the bath to answer the telephone and appeared semi-naked with a towel round my waist. This confirmed the worst fears of the more staid members of the church congregation. 'I think that photograph outside the cinema is quite disgusting!' said the disapproving voice next Sunday. 'If that's really what you want to do with your life, Williams, then it's up to you.'

It *was* what I wanted to do with my life; there was no contradiction between my faith and my work as far as I was concerned. They were good people at the church, but the fact that they seemed so blinkered was beginning to cause a tension within me. Fortunately, younger members of the congregation and our young curates believed that drama, dance and music were indeed gifts from God which could be used positively.

During this period church life was always a way of remaining anchored. Our curate, Donald Smith, and his wife, Violet, would invite some of the young people down to their home and provide a wonderful supper of bacon and eggs. They were a lovely couple and became close personal friends.

I have never married, so friendships have been very important throughout my life. Some of those formed at St Margaret's Edgware are with me still. Donald and Violet, together with their successors Ted and Audrey Roberts, have remained close friends throughout my life. Because Donald and Ted were nearer to our own age they were able to understand and empathize with the problems which can worry young people. In spite of his evangelical background, I can remember Donald agreeing to hear my confession and pronounce absolution when something was particularly troubling my conscience.

It was at one of the evenings at the Smiths' house that I first met Betty Camkin. A hospital secretary, Betty was one of those people who was always able to listen and contribute to our group discussions. It was the beginning of another life-long friendship. We both belonged to what we referred to as the 'odd' Bible study group. It acquired this name when our rector, announcing some parish activity or other, added, 'I realize some of the people will not be there as they attend some odd Bible study or other.'

It was at one of the meetings of the 'odd' Bible study that we discussed fasting. While everyone in the group seemed to feel that this was no longer required I decided to be different and suggested that it was still a useful discipline. Was I hankering for the more Catholic understanding that I remembered from Ardingly? The discussion was over and I was clearly in a minority of one. Refreshments were passed around, but for some strange reason I didn't get any! Nobody seemed to notice and I was too embarrassed to say anything. When I told Betty afterwards what had happened she burst out laughing and I joined in. For many years afterwards it was a standing joke between us.

Our church congregation included the President of the Protestant Truth Society and the General Secretary of the Lord's Day Observance Society. In many ways the church was very rigid, with visits to the dance hall, cinema and theatre being regarded as sinful and totally unsuitable for a Christian. As my mother was leaving church one day, she was confront-ed by a member of the congregation who said, 'Mrs Williams, I don't understand how you can allow your son to be an actor. Do you realize that the word "actor" in Greek comes from the same word as "hypocrite"?'

I've no idea what my mother replied. She was never rude but she would have made it clear that this was a view she did not share before she went on her way. This view was not untypical among the church membership. I once heard someone state with great confidence that the Bible made it clear that the cinema was evil. 'Paul tells us to eschew the unprofitable works of darkness,' he said. 'When you go to the cinema you are in darkness so clearly the cinema was one of the things he had in mind.' Who could argue with such brilliant logic? It taught me that you could take any text out of its context and make it prove anything you wanted.

I decided to try to bring the two important elements in my life together by writing a Passion play. *The Substitute* presented the Crucifixion in modern dress, and would tell the story of the Passion from the point of view of Barabbas. Our Lord would never appear, but the other characters in the narrative would talk about the things they had seen and experienced. Once I started, I found it very interesting trying to combine the different accounts from the four Gospels. I spent many hours looking at what St Matthew said and then comparing it with St John. In the end I hope I produced something that was reasonably coherent.

I went to see our rector and asked him if he would allow me to produce it in the church hall. Knowing the views of some of the older members of the congregation, he was obviously a little worried. Eventually he agreed to the idea, a courageous decision on his part. He also suggested that we should involve some of the other churches in the production. We ended up with a truly ecumenical cast. Slightly to my surprise, a large number of younger members of our congregation were happy to be part of it. I was to play the part of Barabbas myself and the play was directed by another member of the congregation who was a journalist. We presented it for three performances and it was well received, although our poor rector got an anonymous note from someone who wrote, 'You have let Jezebel into our church in the form of a Passion play'.

During one of the breaks in recording *The Army Game* I had the idea that I would like to produce a professional production of *The Substitute*. In doing it in Edgware I had taken the theatre into the church, I now wanted to take the church into the theatre. As I knew that this would not appeal

to Jimmy Perry as a commercial production, I approached him
to ask if I could hire the theatre and the company and put it on
myself. Jimmy was careful to listen but warned of the perils of
putting on one's own play, particularly when I told him what
this one was all about. Undeterred by Jimmy's reluctance, I
explained that I had already produced the play in my own
church, where it had been quite a success. It had gone so well
there, that it seemed only reasonable to hope for a similar
success in a professional theatre, I argued. In spite of my
enthusiasm for *The Substitute,* I could see from Jimmy's face
that not only did he think it would not work, but that he
wanted to spare me the embarrassment of a large financial
loss.

'How much will it cost?' I enquired.

Jimmy was keen to encourage while being realistic, but he
also had to consider the business side of the theatre. He suggested £300 for the week. He agreed to pay the actors their
usual salary and I would play Barabbas for nothing. The
theatre would keep the bar takings and programme sales.
Sensing that I had been let off quite lightly for a new producer, I offered to pay him a percentage of the box office takings.
Jimmy, convinced that I would lose more than my shirt over
the production, refused the offer so long as all the expenses
were met. Determined to prove Jimmy wrong, I worked hard
on the publicity and advertising and I wrote to various church
leaders, to every incumbent Catholic priest and Free Church
minister for miles around, and it worked. We played to near
full houses every night. As well as the regular theatre-going
audience, church parties came from miles around and I hoped
that it helped bring the Passion story closer to those who saw
it. Betty had organized a party from St Margaret's Edgware to
see the production and among them was our new rector. An
ascetic man who was certainly no theatre-goer, I was moved
when Betty told me that at the weekly prayer meeting he had
said that he felt God's work was being done at the Watford

Palace that week. At the end of the run, I had a substantial sum of money to give to the charity, and working on this play with Jimmy and Gilda did much to cement a friendship that remains to this day.

6

CATS, GUINNESS AND ALLSORTS

My first introduction to the world of commercials came from Guinness. 'They want you to do an advert to be shown in the cinema,' my agent explained. 'It's one of a series about people who have invented weird and wonderful things. When these amazing contraptions don't work, they down a pint of Guinness and immediately, all is well.'

It was certainly something different, and it sounded as though it might be fun. When I got the script I saw that my invention was to be a suit that enabled the wearer to walk through walls. When the suit refused to work, I was to drink the famous black liquid and the wall would disintegrate as I touched it. The commercial was in English for England, but Guinness had a lot of money tied up in France, so it was to be made in a studio in Paris. This was very unexpected, but it would be good to be able to see Paris at someone else's expense. The director of the commercial was French and did not speak much English. I arrived on set dressed in my super-suit, and we tried the first shot. The director gave me very long and involved instructions, all in French. He spoke so fast that I only understood one word in ten.

'What does he want me to do?' I asked the interpreter. The instructions had certainly sounded extremely complicated.

'Oh, just camp it up a bit!' he said.

I ran towards the wall, and slammed into it. I did not want the interpreter to tell me that the director wanted to do the shot again, but he did just that. It was too late to ask for some padding, so I launched myself at the solid wall once more. After several more attempts the director seemed satisfied. At last the scene showing that the super-suit did not work, was safely in the can. I sat down to recover from all my exertions while they prepared the next shot.

Drinking the Guinness was going to be the worst bit. I had never been good at drinking vast quantities of anything, and Guinness was not my favourite beverage. Furthermore the director wanted me to down the pint in one go, and no trick glass had been provided. I was given a very full glass and wondered how many takes this would involve. When the director shouted 'Action!' I took a deep breath and downed it with what I hoped was a look of enjoyment. This was real acting. There was a moment of suspense while I wondered whether the director would ask me to do it again, but to my relief he seemed pleased with my attempt.

Now we came to walking through the wall. The special effects department showed me how it would fall to pieces as soon as I made contact with it. It looked easy enough, and confident that this would happen, I ran at the wall at full speed. The wall seemed even more solid than it had been in the first shot, and only one brick fell feebly out of it, about halfway down. Because I was expecting it to disintegrate I was not prepared for its sturdiness – it felt as if I had dislocated my shoulder blade. There was much excited shouting in French, and I gathered that profuse apologies were being offered to me, alongside assurances that it would definitely work next time. I cannot remember how many times we did the scene. Sometimes a small section of the wall at the bottom would fall away, sometimes a few bricks at the top. Eventually, I was getting desperate, but with one final effort I managed to hit the wall with sufficient force to make it all collapse, and I was through. There was a round of applause from everyone in the studio. I thought it was for me, but discovered it was aimed at the technicians who had apparently got it right at last. The day's work over, I was glad to get back to the hotel and enjoy a hearty dinner. I chose a good bottle of claret to accompany the meal and I was thankful that there was not a drop of Guinness in sight.

A few weeks later the cinema manager in Edgware telephoned me. 'Frank, I have just seen you in one of the advertisements. If you want to come and see it, you'll be here all week.' I went to have a look, and it seemed to work quite well. It was quite funny and by the miracles of technology the French background actors were heard muttering in perfect English. I think the feature film that had been chosen to accompany my few moments was quite good too!

The Guinness advert was the only one I did for the cinema, but as ITV came into being, television commercials became a useful new source of income for many actors. Bassett's Liquorice Allsorts had a commercial set in a jewellery shop. A set of diamonds was arranged on one red velvet tray, and individual Bassett's Allsorts arranged on the identical tray beside it. I was the jeweller. I was astounded to learn that rather than use prop jewels, they had hired real ones. The gems sparkled in the studio lights, and I was not surprised at the strong presence of security guards looking on. Despite the fact that diamonds are known to be a girl's best friend, I think the customer was supposed to find the Allsorts even more attractive than the jewels. I never cease to marvel at some of the extraordinary ideas that some advertising copywriters produce.

'Tunes' are those wonderfully strong, cherry flavoured, square-shaped sweets designed especially for a blocked-up nose. The producers decided that I was the ideal person to advertise them. They liked the way in which I said the word 'Tunes' in a slow and rather nasal voice. I had to say the word as if I had a severe cold, and then repeat it as if my illness had miraculously disappeared. I did this several times, until the director was happy. It took only a couple of hours to film but became an extremely successful commercial that ran for a long time. With the repeat fees, I probably earned more in that short time than I would have done working in the theatre for many months. I also got used to strangers suddenly coming up to me in the street and saying 'Tunes' in my face. There's really no answer to that!

I did one commercial for a frozen food company, but I cannot remember which one it was. It was to advertise a complete roast dinner, direct from the freezer. The food had to look so perfect when it was seen in close up that someone was actually allocated the task of polishing the sprouts in case any of the gravy had spilled on them. In the plot I am watching a cricket match when a very large lady sits on my packed lunch. When I get home, my mother, hearing that I have been deprived of my lunch, instantly produces the wonderful roast dinner and all is well. It was a commercial that was shown a lot and made quite a mark, albeit in the wrong direction. Whenever people came up and said, 'We love the advert where the fat lady sits on your sandwiches, it does make us laugh,' I would ask, 'Do you remember which frozen food company it's advertising?' and they never did.

On another occasion, the coalboard wanted me to play the devil in hell. In the make-up room they covered me in black hair, stuck on with spirit gum, which I knew would be very difficult to remove. Only then did they inform me that due to a break down in the boilers, the studio had no hot water. I wondered idly how I was going to get on at the end of the day, but at that moment this was the least of my worries.

'Who's that?' I asked, noticing a man in a boiler suit standing behind the camera.

'Oh, he's there in case the fire gets out of hand,' came the helpful reply.

'Fire?' I asked.

'Yes. He's got a fire extinguisher, in case you catch alight.'

I was given my position and told that it was essential that I did not move as the camera angle was critical. Then they lit the fire. The flames shot up and seemed dangerously near. I was suddenly very thankful for the little man in the boiler suit armed with his fire extinguisher. It's amazing what they got away with in the early days! I sat there for hours while they shot the scene from every angle. I got very hot but miraculously no damage was done and I was very relieved when the director finally called it a day. Now came the problem of removing the hair. Even after the make-up department had removed the worst of it, I still looked a mess and the cold water was no use at all. I had visions of everyone retreating in panic as I tried to board the tube looking like some wild creature that had escaped from the zoo. Fortunately, the director took pity on me, and bundled me into his car. He took me to his flat where I was able to take a long hot bath and wash off all the remaining hair. He even gave me a large whiskey afterwards and I think I deserved it.

'Delikatt' was the food that no self-respecting cat could resist. This was the message that the makers were eager to get across to their audience of cat-lovers. The script was simple. The moggy was sleeping on his plush chair, was awakened by his alarm clock, and then I, as his loving owner, handed him a silver tray with a portion of his favourite food for his breakfast. It was, of course, Delikatt. The problem was getting the cat to go to sleep. It sat on its chair grooming itself and determined to stay wide awake. Every now and then it would pause and look at us. I could swear that there was a grin on its face as it held court. Every time it looked as if it was dropping off, any slight sound in the studio made it look up, decide it was not a good time for a nap after all, and we were back to square one. The crew played cards to pass the time, and we all whispered and walked around on tiptoe. It was the first time I had ever been told to keep quiet so that a cat could get its sleep, but I was not too worried as I was aware that my pocket was filling up with overtime payments. I think it took most of the day to get that scene in the can.

This was not a short commercial. There were several scenes for me to do with my new-found friend. Next day we were on location for the opening shot. Riding down the road on a bike with my co-star in the basket on the front, I was terrified that it would jump out as I cycled and that I would run it over. 'Oh, that's OK, Frank,' said her owner. 'It's well trained.' She was right. It did not budge, and the outside shot was done in one take. Fortunately the powers that be decided that it didn't look good from a safety point of view. It might encourage people to do the same with their untrained cats, and if there was an accident Delikatt would be blamed, so this sequence ended up on the cutting-room floor.

Now it was time for more inside shots. My cat gave a tea party at which I served Delikatt to the assembled guests. I went round the table taking their orders offering the different flavours. Getting my cat to look at me as I approached and asked for its order was easy enough, as it knew me by now and we were quite good friends. The others were not so co-operative. Walking round the table and trying to get the attention of each cat in turn was a nightmare. First one would ignore me, and then after an almost successful round taking orders, the final cat would decide to jump off the chair altogether and have nothing more to do with it. After 20 or 30 takes we managed to get something that looked reasonable.

The final sequence was in a restaurant. The storyline ran that my co-star and I had become such good friends that I took her out for a meal. I would have pheasant, but my friend would prefer Delikatt. She was to sit on my lap, and when my mouth-watering pheasant was brought in, she would ignore it, preferring the Delikatt which another waiter had brought for her. We knew she liked Delikatt, as she had eaten it with

every sign of enjoyment in many previous takes. It now
became clear that she also liked pheasant, because as soon as
the platter arrived, she made a beeline for the dish thinking
that all her Christmases and birthdays had come at once. She
leapt off my lap, grabbed the bird and desperately tried to
drag it away, determined to tuck in as quickly as possible.

'Can you just try harder to keep her on your lap?' asked the
director.

'I'll do my best,' I replied.

We started again and I held the cat very firmly as the
pheasant was placed before us once more. Again, as soon as
she saw it, she struggled to get free while I struggled to hold
on. She got very cross and decided the only thing to do was to
scratch me, which she did. First Aid came to the rescue
with antiseptic and a plaster. Now my grazed hand had to be
kept out of sight to maintain continuity. I sat there with her on
my lap trying to restrain her with only one free hand. I need
not have worried. This time when the pheasant arrived, apart
from a sideways glance, she completely ignored it, and I
wondered why. As I released my grip, she moved sedately
towards the dish of Delikatt and began to eat happily.
Apparently, this time they had sprayed the pheasant with
something which was clearly a complete turn-off as far as the
cat was concerned, and we were able to complete the scene.
After all this, I knew what people meant when they said never
work with animals!

I was still worshipping at St Margaret's, when one Christmas
a friend invited me to go with him to the neighbouring parish
of John Keble for Midnight Mass. The church was located
on the boundary between Edgware and the adjacent suburb
of Mill Hill. It had been built in the late 1930s as one of a
number of new churches designed to serve the new communi-
ties that were springing up all around the outskirts of London.
Architecturally it was unusual and unconventional for its
day. A square building, it had a wide sanctuary and a High

Altar that was visible from every seat in the church. Founder members were fond of telling you that the start of the Consecration Service had been delayed because the then Bishop of London was late, having been involved with the abdication crisis.

I went to the Midnight Mass not knowing what to expect, but as soon as the service started I felt at home. I was taken back to my days at Ardingly. The clergy wore vestments, the music was splendid and it had a feeling of drama. The liturgy expressed the joy of the Incarnation in a way that I had not experienced for years. Every part of me responded to it. I think I knew from that moment that this was where I really belonged. After that first visit, I began to attend more regularly. The attitude was very different from St Margaret's. It was life affirming. All the things that had been so suspect there, such as the cinema and the theatre, were seen as gifts that should be enjoyed, and because of this my chosen career also seemed affirmed.

The main service was Parish Communion at 9.30. It was not extreme and would, I suppose, have been described as middle-of-the-road or prayerbook Catholic. The congregation were welcoming and friendly and made me feel at home. The service was followed by the parish breakfast of coffee or tea with bread and butter and marmalade. I learned that in the early years, before the war, there had been ham and eggs!

For a time I continued to attend St Margaret's as well as my new-found church, but I soon realized that I would have to make a decision. The rector who had been at Edgware through most of my adolescent years and early adult life had moved on and his successor was a godly man, but I found that his asceticism created something of a barrier and made it difficult to get to know him. He was a preacher in a style that was already becoming old-fashioned. Sermons lasted well over 30 minutes and consisted of meticulous examination of biblical texts. He believed strongly in having a series of sermons on a particular subject. The sermons would have a different title each week and one younger member of the congregation when we had suffered a particular series for months on end was heard to remark, 'It doesn't matter what he calls it, it's still flipping Philippians'.

I felt it would be wrong just to disappear without a word from the church in which I had worshipped all my life, so I made an appointment to see the rector. He was very courteous but obviously disapproved. He said that at least I was not going to a totally different religion, although his tone implied that he was not quite sure that this was true. He warned me that I would not get the biblical teaching that was the staple diet of his ministry at Edgware. 'The most you can hope for,' he said, 'is perhaps ten minutes on the Gospel of the day.' As I had recently sat through several months of 40-minute doses of 'Abraham the Friend of God' the prospect of ten minutes on the Gospel of the day seemed rather enticing.

John Keble Church became my main spiritual home from that time. I did not miss my friends at St Margaret's as I continued to meet them socially, and at John Keble I made some of those new and lasting friendships which have always been so important in my life. Richard Buck came to the church as a young curate to serve his title. He, probably more than anyone else, opened up to me the riches of the Catholic understanding of the faith. The things that I had half understood and half appreciated at Ardingly became central to my way of thinking. I still believed that a personal relationship with Christ was important, but I also realized that it was important to be part of something bigger. The presence of Christ in the Blessed Sacrament, not dependent on my feelings but just there, became central to my worship. I began to understand the role of the Saints and the place of the Blessed Virgin Mary. Above all, I came to know that my relationship with God was not dependent on the strength of my faith, but on His Grace. It gave a wonderful sense of freedom and release. It was Richard who introduced a number of us to the church of All Saints' Margaret Street. I had visited this church once many years before, in the days when the congregation was still segregated, men on one side and women on the other. The two sexes were allowed to sit together at the back in what was known as 'mixed bathing'. By the time Richard took us there, the church had moved on and men and women were allowed to sit together.

Being middle of the road, John Keble had a somewhat simplified version of the Holy Week liturgy. It was to the High Mass of the Paschal Vigil at All Saints' that Richard took us and it was a revelation. My memories of it from that one time at Ardingly were now quite dim. In any case, Margaret Street was on a bigger scale altogether. The waiting in the darkened church, the sounds only partially heard of something mysterious going on outside, the reflected glow of the new fire flickering over the church door and the entrance of the Paschal candle into the church proclaiming the light of Christ, was wonderful drama and yet so much more. The light being passed from one candle to another until the whole church was a sea of lights, and the Exultet with that marvellous insight that the light, although it is divided is never diminished, moved me in a way that I could barely grasp. The service proceeded with the readings telling the story of God's plan of redemption, the prayers, the Litany of the Saints and the renewal of baptismal vows. Then came something that I had never experienced before. I do not think it had happened at Ardingly, or if it had it had been done in such a small way that it had made no impact on me. The celebrant intoned 'Gloria in Excelcis Deo' and suddenly the darkened church sprang into light, bells rang out and the organ thundered. It was extraordinary and a frisson ran up and down my spine. This was proclaiming the joy of the Resurrection in a way that was totally new to me. 'Christ is risen,' it said. It left no room for doubt. When the Mass was finished, I came out full of joy and excitement. I felt

I had not only heard about and listened to the story of the Resurrection, but also that I had actually experienced it.

For me, that service and the extraordinary week that precedes it is the centre of the Christian year. The liturgy of Holy Week enables you to travel with Christ from the cheering crowds of Palm Sunday to the quiet of the upper room and the last supper with the washing of the disciples' feet and the new command to love one another. It takes you to the garden of Gethsemane to watch, and then takes you through the desolation of Good Friday as you stand at the foot of the Cross. Finally it brings you to the moment of victory on Easter Day as you exchange the greeting, 'Christ is risen, alleluia.' 'He is risen indeed, alleluia.' If for any reason I have to miss any of this, I feel a real sense of deprivation.

When Richard Buck left John Keble he was succeeded by Edward Holland, later to become Assistant Bishop in Europe and then Bishop of Colchester. He carried on the good work which Richard had begun. I have good cause to be grateful to both of them and they remain friends to this day.

John Keble Church had a drama group which had been formed in the days before the church building itself had been completed, when the congregation were worshipping in what was later to become the church hall. They called themselves 'The Good Companions' – J.B. Priestley's famous novel was popular at the time. When I first knew them they already enjoyed a reputation for productions of very high quality. It was through this group that I made another of those lifelong friendships that have always been so important to me. Barrie Wyse was a young student when I first met him. He was an active member of the group and played a number of young leading roles. He left Mill Hill to take up his first teaching post in Beverley in Yorkshire. He has lived there ever since and he and his wife Vera always make me feel very welcome. Whenever I have performed pantomime in the north of England, they have gone to great trouble to enable me to spend Christmas Day with them. Whenever I stay there I am always made to feel like one of the family, rather than a visitor. I am godfather to their son Pascal.

It would obviously not have been appropriate for me to be involved with 'The Good Companions' as an actor, but I was happy to share in what they were doing in other ways. One event involved a sponsored reading of the entire works of Shakespeare – or at least all the plays. Groups sat in each corner of the church hall with an allotted mixture of comedies, tragedies and histories. I was working at the time and was only able to join my group after a day in the studio. We were reading *A Midsummer Night's Dream* when I lost concentration for a moment and there was a pause. My neighbour nudged me and I read the next line, 'When my cue comes, call me.' Yes, I know it sounds contrived, but it really did happen! Obviously, the timing could not be exact and as each group finished their allotted task, they went over to see how the others were getting on. When only one group was left still reading, there was a good crowd around them and a great cheer went up as the final line of their play was pronounced.

Although I could not be involved as an actor, it was with 'The Good Companions' that I first tried my hand at directing. It was here that once again *The Ghost Train* came into my life. I enjoyed directing it enormously and it was fascinating to see it from another angle. I rather regretted that the elaborate instructions for producing the sound effect of the train going through the station, which were so meticulously described in the acting edition and involved, if I remember rightly, garden rollers and sheets of corrugated iron, were no longer necessary now that we were in the era of tape-recorded sound effects. It was, however, interesting to work with the stage management to achieve the visual effect of the train arriving and leaving, and working out how Julia could break the windowpane without the danger of broken glass all over the stage.

'The Good Companions' also gave me the chance to develop

my writing skills in a different way. I wrote a couple of
pantomimes, and even appeared in one, substituting for an
Ugly Sister who had been taken ill. Fortunately, I had written
the character as someone who repeated everything her sister
said, so learning the lines at the last minute was not too much
of a challenge! I also wrote one play about the friendship
between a young actor and an eccentric old lady who lives in
the flat below him. I called it *Two Children on a See-Saw* and
it was the group's entry at the local drama festival that year. It
won the prize as the best new play, although to be honest
I have to say that it did not have very much in the way of
competition. I subsequently added two more acts to make it
into a full-length play and I live in hope that one day someone
will want to do it!

The week after my two and half years for Granada on *The
Army Game* had finished, I was asked to go and see the great
director Rudolph Cartier. He was the leading television director of that period and I had worked for him on several occasions in the past.

'My secretary tells me you have been in some programme
on the other channel which I have not seen, called . . .' – there
was a pause here while he looked at the paper in front of him.
'Ah yes. *The Army Game*. I have no idea what this is, but
never mind.'

I waited for what was coming next.

'Now. I am doing *Anna Karenina* with Sean Connery and
Claire Bloom, and there is a part for you. *Anna Karenina* is a
long and a rather heavy piece, so I want you to come and
bring light into it.'

By television standards this was an epic, and obviously this
was why Rudolph Cartier had been chosen to direct it. The
costumes were quite beautiful and the colours brilliant. It was
sad that this production was made just before colour television had really begun. Even in black and white it looked
magnificent. My role was as a jolly young man who loved to

dance with the ladies and one scene involved dancing with the beautiful Claire Bloom. 'Like a dream you float, dear lady!' was my line delivered as we swung across the ballroom together.

'When you say the line you must be right under the chandelier because that is where we have hidden the microphone,' said Mr Cartier.

This shows just how primitive live television still was in those days, but we were used to this sort of thing and I managed to time our dance perfectly so that my line was spoken exactly below the shining crystal.

It was during the shooting of *Anna Karenina* that I became quite friendly with a young actress, June Thorburn. She had made a number of films and over the three weeks of rehearsal I enjoyed chatting with her and comparing experiences. She was a lovely vivacious actress and brought even more light to the production than I did. One Sunday a few years later I was listening to the news when I heard that June had been killed in an air crash. I was very shocked and when I went to church that evening it was uppermost in my mind. Although I had not seen her for some while, I remembered her with great affection. It seemed such a tragic waste of a young life. The anthem that night was 'The Souls of the Righteous are in the Hand of God'. It was very poignant and extraordinarily appropriate.

I hoped that appearing in something else immediately after the end of *The Army Game* was an indication that I had avoided being typecast. Rudolph Cartier might not have seen the programme but it seemed that everyone else had. Once *Anna Karenina* was completed, I began a very lean time. I was not best pleased at one interview when a very experienced casting director took one look at me and said, 'Sorry, but we don't have any soldiers in this film.' It seemed that I was destined to play silly ass officers and that was that. How would I ever be able to break out?

7

THE TEMPERATURE RISES

Eventually, Captain Pocket and *The Army Game* faded from people's minds and a new generation of directors arrived who were prepared to take a risk with someone who had been identified with a particular role in the past.

Diary of a Young Man was a series directed by Peter Duguid and Ken Loach. It followed the fortunes of a young man through various experiences in his life. In each episode, I played a different part, but always an authority figure. It was an interesting concept and one that I thoroughly enjoyed. When the young man got married I played the registrar who performed the ceremony and then later in the same episode the lawyer who dealt with his divorce. Trying to make all the characters different was something of a challenge but I hope it worked. One sequence involved night filming at Box Hill in the Surrey countryside. We stood in the darkness ready for the first scene. Suddenly our arc lamps lit up the whole area, and out of the bushes leapt several young couples with very red and surprised faces. It was a magic moment.

The series was undoubtedly ahead of its day and I wonder if it still exists in the archives. The leading actor was a young man called Victor Henry, one of the great young talents of the period and after appearing together we became very close friends. He was something of a drinker, and into wild parties, and we should have been like chalk and cheese, yet something within us clicked. One day he suddenly asked me whether I would be a witness at his wedding the following day! I was happy to agree, but sadly the marriage didn't last very long. It was typical of Victor to do things on the spur of the moment. Six years later when Victor was standing at a bus stop, a bus went out of control, hit a lamp standard, and this crashed down on top of him. He was in a coma for several years. His mother would play the tapes of all his programmes in the hope that it would bring some response from him, but none of this worked, and he subsequently died. I had been to visit him in hospital and he just looked as if he was sleeping peacefully. It was difficult to believe that he had never come out of the coma. Just before the accident he had recorded *Diary of a Madman* in which he gave a masterly performance of a man slowly going mad. I had recorded it on video and I found it quite agonizing to watch knowing what had happened to him.

When I watched it with Betty, she said, 'You can't ever wipe that off the tape.'

'No, but neither will I be able to bear to watch it,' I said.

My mother was enjoying living in Ringwood and being near her family. She had joined the Women's Institute and had become actively involved with the church and made a lot of new friends. I would go down to stay with her for a few days between jobs and for the occasional weekend. From time to time, she would come up to stay with me, taking the opportunity to catch up with her Edgware friends. When she was with me, it always gave me great pleasure to take her to the theatre as she had taken me when I was a boy.

When she became ill, the doctor did not seem too concerned and while I went down to visit as often as possible, I knew that with all her family around, there were plenty of people who would take care of her even when I wasn't there. However, when she was taken into hospital in Salisbury, I realized that things were more serious. When I went down I stayed at a pub next to the hospital in order to be as near as possible. Of course, when I said my prayers each day I prayed that she would get better. I did not consciously add 'Thy will be done', but I have never believed that prayer is about changing God's mind, rather it is something which he can use to do his perfect will.

Betty and her parents were very supportive and I spent a lot of time at their house. One day when I was going up to have a meal with them and thinking about my mother, I sent up a silent prayer for her healing. Immediately an inner voice spoke so clearly that I stopped in my tracks and stood still for a moment. For the Christian death is never a disaster. It is in fact the final and greatest healing of all as the person leaves their illness and all the other trials and tribulations of this life behind and enters into the fuller life in Christ.

The next time I was down in Salisbury, I visited mother in the afternoon. Hospitals still had quite strict visiting hours in those days, so I went out for a long walk to fill in the time before my evening visit. When I got back to the pub where I was staying, a message was waiting for me asking me to go to the hospital as soon as possible.

With my heart thumping, I arrived to find my mother in an oxygen tent. Her condition had deteriorated suddenly and she was now unconscious. I sat with her and held her hand until I realized she had stopped breathing. I called a nurse and she confirmed what I already knew. I was numb. Leaving the hospital I went and sat in a nearby church. I tried to pray, but somehow my mind would not function.

Returning to the pub I told the landlord and his wife what had happened. They were extraordinarily kind and immediately offered me the use of their own sitting room so that I could be alone.

I telephoned Betty with the news, and she was, as always, sympathetic and supportive. I knew my mother wanted to be buried with my father so the funeral would take place in Edgware. The present rector had not really known my mother so I telephoned Donald Smith and asked him if he would take the service. He had a church in Suffolk at this time but readily agreed to come down. I went over to Ringwood to break the news to Mother's family. Back in Edgware, I set about putting a notice in the *Times* and the *Daily Telegraph*, getting service sheets printed and so on. The need to do things kept the major part of my grief at bay.

Although the rector of Edgware was not conducting the funeral, it was taking place in his church and I had made all the arrangements for this over the telephone when I was down in Salisbury. I now needed to call and confirm one or two things. I was not particularly looking forward to the interview as I had always found him a rather austere man who, at least as far as I was concerned, lacked any real warmth. I think he felt that the resurrection promise meant that mourning and grieving were something of an indulgence. Whether it was divine intervention or not, when I called at the rectory he was out. I had a long and helpful talk with his wife. She seemed to understand how I felt and I was extremely grateful for that.

My mother had died at the end of July and the Bank Holiday weekend intervened before the funeral. I spent most of it with Betty and her family. They had friends staying with them and the group included a small child. Somehow the normality of it all helped. When the day of the funeral arrived, the church was full with family and friends. I was moved to know that so many people had come and was particularly touched by seeing people that I had not expected to be there. I realized how well liked she had been. As I knew he would, Donald took the service with great sensitivity, recognizing the need to mourn and grieve but pointing to the joyful hope of the Resurrection. I retained my composure at the funeral, but wept many tears in private. I was left with the most tremendous and overwhelming feeling of being alone. The family ties that had kept me had now gone, and it was difficult to come to terms with this new situation.

The bond between a child – perhaps particularly a son –

and his mother is a very strong one. My mother and I had not lived together for a number of years, but still the sense of loss seemed overwhelming. Perhaps those who marry and enter into a relationship, which we are told is stronger than the tie to parents, can face the loss of a parent in a different way. As a single man it was not so, and I felt utterly alone. The psalmist knew something of this, 'I went heavily as one that mourneth for his mother.' I mourned and I grieved. Sometimes I managed to push it into the background but it was always there. A small incident such as coming across my mother's work basket with its needles and threads and spare buttons could bring it all back with a stab that was almost physical. Gradually the intensity of grief faded, but not for a very long time. Work, of course, helped and the next ten years of my life were to provide a constant flow of varied commitments. Perhaps this is just what I needed to ease me out of the many years of *The Army Game* and its typecasting, or producers' assumptions that I was now either too expensive or unavailable.

A welcome break came when I was asked to go to Paris for an episode of *Maigret*. The location filming was great fun but I didn't really understand the plot while we were doing it or even when I subsequently saw it on the screen. The most important thing about this production was that it was the beginning of another of my lifelong friendships. It was here that I first met Anna Turner. She had been an up and coming star in the 1940s and had played a lot of West End roles. As a number of us who were on location sat in a restaurant near the Opera House, a whisper went round that the President was attending the opera that night. As soon as she heard the news, Anna got very excited and jumped up to look out of the window to see if she could see De Gaulle pass by. As she was quite short, she was unable to see anything, so she stood on her seat to get a better view. She found it difficult to understand why the waiters and the other customers were not similarly enthusiastic, but presumably they could see the

President at any time. Anna's zest for life is something I have come to know well over the years, and it's always wonderfully refreshing.

Alongside episodes of *Z Cars* and *No Hiding Place*, two popular police series of the 1960s, I did *Hugh and I*. This series featured Terry Scott and Hugh Lloyd. It was directed by David Croft, and this was to be my first meeting with the man who was later to co-write and direct *Dad's Army*.

In another series called *The Gnomes of Dulwich*, Hugh and Terry played garden gnomes. I was in an episode in which the gnomes had been purchased at a Labour Party Bazaar by Mary Wilson, wife of the Prime Minister. They stood at ground level contemplating the legs of the various guests at a garden party. Clad in Carnaby Street trousers (it was quite difficult to find anything that fitted me in that haunt of trendy young people) I wandered around as a society photographer. As the audience only heard my voice and saw my disembodied legs they were never quite sure who I was, but I decided that this was my one chance to play royalty and that I was Lord Snowdon.

It was around this time that I contracted mumps. The child downstairs had caught it and had decided to pass it on. I was to find out that all the stories that I had heard about adult males catching this nasty disease were quite true.

When the doctor arrived I ventured to air my fears. 'Is it true, that this can make one impotent?' I asked.

'Not necessarily,' he replied with a laugh. He seemed to find the whole idea amusing, but I certainly did not!

Betty came round each day to minister to me. 'Let's take a look at my temperature,' I said.

'Listen,' she replied. 'We know perfectly well that you're ill, what does it matter what your temperature is?'

I still insisted that it needed to be checked. She reluctantly agreed, but as she shook the thermometer in preparation it flew across the room and under the bed. I got quite cross. She got frustrated. But we started again. 'There you are. It's over 100!' I declared triumphantly.

'That's because it broke when I threw it across the room,' she said. Eventually it all became too much and we both collapsed into laughter.

I was not the best patient, and could not wait to be able to get back to work. When I was still convalescing but no longer infectious I was offered a *Comedy Playhouse*: a one-off, half-hour comedy. Deciding that if I had a car to and from the studios I could cope with it, I accepted. The part was an angel in a programme called *Friends in High Places*. Feeling as I did it was hard to look angelic, but I think I managed, and earnt some money into the bargain.

Punctuality at rehearsals is always important, but sometimes there are legitimate reasons for being late. Cars do break down, and trains do get stuck in tunnels, but the best excuse for being late at rehearsals I have ever heard was on an episode of *The Tales of Saki*. We were all sitting round the table reading through the script and awaiting the arrival of the leading lady. This was the last episode in a long series on ITV, and we chatted and laughed together while we waited for her arrival. Eventually it was decided that we should start without her, and while several other actors tut-tutted about her absence, someone read in for her. Suddenly the door flew open and she made a wonderfully dramatic entrance.

'Oh my darlings,' she declared. 'Last night I went to bed and dreamed that the series was over. When I woke up this morning, I had a terrible shock. There was a script pristine and untouched and I thought my goodness, there is still another episode! So I rushed here as quickly as I could, and that's why I am late. I really am so sorry my darlings.'

What could anyone say in the face of such a wonderful story?

When I agreed to appear for the Children's Film Foundation in *Countdown to Danger* I was taken off to Alderney where it was being shot, and was booked for five days. The word about my inability with mechanical things had obviously not been passed on, for in this film I was required to drive a car. They had paid for me to have some driving lessons before I went out there. Even though I was to drive on an island with one policeman, no traffic lights and very few roads, the driving instructor insisted on taking me out onto the busy Edgware Road. I thought it was quite unnecessary for us both to suffer in this way, and wondered which of us would have the nervous breakdown first. Alongside my constant confusion about which pedal did what, I was always convinced that the car would never fit between whatever was approaching. Despite all this, I think I was seen as a bit of a challenge and he said to me at the end of our few days together, 'You know, if you were to persist with these lessons, you'd probably be a very good driver.'

At that moment I had already decided that driving was not for me. 'No thanks,' I replied. 'I'd rather take the train.' This was to be my philosophy for the rest of my life.

Once on Alderney I did my best to convince the director that he should get someone else to drive the car, but he wouldn't listen. I had already done a scene in a boat where I had rowed out from the shore as they filmed, only to find that I couldn't get back. As the boat drifted out to sea, I shouted for help, and the Assistant Director had to strip off and swim out to rescue me. You would have thought they would have got the message by then, but they hadn't. Still insisting that I should drive, they took as many precautions as possible, and even closed down all the roads in the vicinity. I was left staring in trepidation at the old vintage banger. I soon proved myself incompetent once again when I climbed in and could not even start the miserable thing. When they got it started, they found I couldn't stop it. When they wanted me to go forwards I went backwards and nearly ran over the cameraman. I really couldn't do anything with it, and after much wasted time, a double was eventually used to get me out of trouble.

'Now Frank,' the director said. 'There is one shot where we can't use your double. We really have to see you driving the car, stopping, and then getting out, all in one go.'

'Well, I'll give it a try,' I said nervously.

'The only problem is,' the director took in a long breath, and looked in the opposite direction, 'you have to drive it towards the edge of that cliff.'

My heart stopped for a moment as the significance of these words took hold. 'Well, I'll give it a try,' I repeated feebly and climbed inside the driving seat. I didn't need to start the engine because the shot began at the top of a steep hill, and all I had to do was to freewheel down to the fatal point.

'Action!' shouted the director.

I took a deep breath and released the brake. The car began to move, slowly at first, but soon gathering speed as it rolled down the steep gradient. My foot was poised over the brake pedal all the way down. All I had to do was press it firmly at the right point. Cliff edge approached and then I was there. Down went my foot and to my intense relief the car stopped. I was so overcome with my achievement that I almost forgot the next essential bit – getting out of the car having put on the handbrake – but I remembered just in time which meant that the scene was shot in just one take. This was just as well as I could not have gone through it all again. Looking back, I realise I must have been mad to agree to it, but when you're young you don't always act sensibly, and anyway, I'm still here to tell the tale.

The one thing that is not predictable at any time of the year is the weather. We shot in brilliant sunshine for the first four days, but just before they completed my part, the weather turned miserable, and it meant that I remained on the island having a wonderful holiday on Alderney while they waited for the clouds to clear. The rest of the cast could do other shots that didn't involve me, so while they were all slaving away I wandered off to explore. Sadly, about a week later the sun returned, they got my shot, and I was sent home, but for me, *Countdown to Danger* had certainly lived up to its title!

'Frank, I've just been talking to a record producer who wants to do a recording of *Henry V* and they want you to play Gower,' said my agent one day.

'Are you sure?' I asked, wondering why they had thought of me. I was not a radio actor so knew nothing of the technique of working in sound alone. I had done no Shakespeare since the days of the Gateway, and no one was likely to have seen me there anyway. My agent also seemed somewhat surprised at the offer. 'Well, they've got an all-star cast with Richard Burton and a whole lot of other people, but I do wonder if they are mixing you up with Frank Finlay who we also represent!' he mused. This was just what I needed to boost my confidence! However, they had asked for me so they could have me, and off I went to the first day's recording. It was certainly an experience to remember, and as I watched Richard Burton at work I was awestruck at the natural way he performed in front of the microphone.

As this was my first time at acting with just my voice, I was tremendously nervous, and the whole experience of reading with a script in my hand seemed very strange. At one point the instinct to do moves got the better of me and Kenneth Griffith came over to me and said, 'Frank, this isn't a television studio. You must stand still in front of the microphone otherwise it doesn't work.'

I think the record was eventually given away with packets of Cornflakes but it was an interesting experience, and making my first excursion into audio acting in such illustrious company gave me some confidence when later I did a lot more radio.

Back in the television studio, the part of an elderly professor in Aldous Huxley's *After Many a Summer* awaited me, but there was a strike by the cameramen. It wasn't that they wouldn't work at all, but that their union had decided that they should only 'work to rule'. This added the strange complication that they would pan during a shot but not track. In the script, the director had already marked where and how each shot was to be done, and now had the task of revising it as best he could. It is amazing how difficulties can be overcome and he proved this triumphantly. In spite of the problems the programme was a great success and I doubt if the viewing audience had any idea that there was anything amiss.

Jimmy and Gilda Perry had left the theatre at Watford, and it was now being run as a civic theatre by Giles Havergal, later to become artistic director of the famous Glasgow Citizens Theatre. He invited me to be in a rather daring new play by Norman Bogner. *The Waiters* was about a husband and wife, played by Patricia Burke and myself, but the audience did not know that we were husband and wife until the end. The couple are in separate rooms in the same hotel each having a fling with their own waiter. The theatre still had the Lord Chamberlain as a censor in the 1960s and anything to do with homosexuality was definitely taboo. I can only think that somehow he had not noticed that there were scenes between two men. Perhaps he felt it was all right as there was nothing explicit on stage. One night, we had arrived at the scene in which my waiter, played by Peter Cleall, was trying to get some money out of me.

'We'll talk about that after we've had a kip,' my character said.

Agreeing, he came over to the bed on which I was lying. I pulled him towards me, expecting the lights to fade as we had rehearsed. Unlike previous performances, however, we got to within a few inches of each other and the lights were still full on. Staring at each other with a mixture of surprise and panic, Peter suddenly muttered in his deepest voice, 'Oh no! My wife's out-front tonight, and she only likes me in butch parts!'

That did it. The dreaded corpsing disease came over me and I started to giggle helplessly. In the past when we had got to that part, we could hear the banging of theatre seats as some people left in disgust, but on this occasion a stunned silence hung in the air until the lighting operator woke up and plunged us into darkness.

'Oh we did suffer for you darling,' said Patricia as we came off stage.

'Well, he was no help,' said Peter pointing at me. 'All he did was giggle!'

I apologized to Peter, and in the interval, the lighting man came to apologize to both of us, but by this time even Peter had seen the funny side and we were both laughing about it.

The second half was no better. In the final scene the husband and wife are packing to go back home. During rehearsals Patricia and I had done our best to cope with the fact that the characters were supposed to smoke. Eventually Giles, who was directing, could stand it no longer.

'You look ridiculous,' he said. 'It's not going to work because it's obvious neither of you have ever smoked. Why don't you eat After Eight mints instead?'

We were more than happy with the idea. Unfortunately, on this particular night, the stage management had forgotten to keep the chocolates in a cool place, and they had been on a plate in the wings throughout the performance. When I reached for the After Eights in the last scene, all I managed to grab got was a sticky, gooey, brown mess. I offered them to Patricia, but she wisely declined. Somehow we both managed to avoid corpsing. It was just one of those nights.

N.F. Simpson was probably the leading British writer in the movement known as the Theatre of the Absurd. His *One Way Pendulum*, with its chorus of weighing machines singing the Hallelujah Chorus, and *A Resounding Tinkle*, had both enjoyed an enormous success in the West End, so I was delighted to be offered a leading part in his new play *The*

Cresta Run which was to be presented at the Royal Court. I was even more excited when I learned from a newspaper gossip column that my 'wife' was to be played by my heroine from *Brief Encounter*, the wonderful Celia Johnson. The new season at the Royal Court was to open with three plays in repertoire. As well as *The Cresta Run*, there would be *Shelley* by Ann Jellicoe and Edward Bond's *Saved*. Most members of the company were in more than one play, but as Celia was only doing *The Cresta Run*, the management decided that I would not be involved in the other productions so that I would be free to rehearse my scenes with her.

I arrived for the first rehearsal with some sense of trepidation. The Royal Court had a reputation for being somewhat avant-garde. The thought of playing opposite an actress who had been one of my idols for years was also a little daunting. However, on that first day I felt my fears were groundless. The company all seemed pretty normal and Celia Johnson was very friendly and welcoming. Once we started rehearsals, however, my fears began to reawaken. The director was very different from others with whom I had worked. He had a distinctly modern approach and obviously felt that he should allow the actors to explore the script for themselves. I did not find this at all easy, and Celia seemed somewhat disconcerted by it as well. We were both used to being told what to do, certainly when it came to working out the moves.

'Where would you like me to go?' Celia asked.

'Where you feel you would like to go,' came the reply.

'I'd like to go where you tell me to go,' said Celia. However, she decided to try to work his way. 'Frank, you move down there and I'll come to you,' she said.

Celia looked to see if the director thought this was a good idea but by now he was lying flat on the floor, eating an apple and staring at the ceiling. He would give an occasional glance in our direction but for most of the time he seemed happy to leave us to our own devices.

Suddenly he spoke. 'As this is a play by N.F. Simpson,' he announced, 'we should have a lot of pauses.' We waited for more. 'As with Pinter,' he added helpfully.

After a few days of this, Celia decided she could take no more. I received a phone call at home. 'I'm afraid I've got some bad news for you, Frank,' said the voice of the stage manager. 'Celia Johnson has asked to be released from her contract and we are going to have to recast.' I was disappointed not be working with my heroine but I was not entirely surprised. Avril Edgar who was in one of the other plays took over and rehearsals re-commenced.

During rehearsals I had another bad attack of the corpsing disease. I was playing an ordinary suburban man who gets embroiled in the world of espionage. In order to infiltrate Russia, I disguised myself as a bear (well, it was Theatre of the Absurd!). I came on stage in my bear costume, and Avril took one look at it and unzipped it saying scornfully, 'What circles you expect a thing like that to give you the entreé into, I can't imagine.' Every time I looked at her outraged face I started to go. Knowing I could not risk disgracing myself in an important new play at the Royal Court, I took myself off to see a hypnotherapist. He got me into a light trance and told me I would not wish to laugh at this point and I have to say it actually worked.

Avril was wonderful in the part but somehow the play never quite came together. The notices were not very good, and most of the critics found the play disappointing. The management had decided that our play, being a comedy, would be the most commercial. We had more scheduled performances than either of the other plays. In the event, we were the least popular and played to quite poor houses. Edward Bond's *Saved* was the big success of the season, with its notorious scene of a gang of youths stoning a baby in a pram. N.F. Simpson was deeply apologetic and said he felt he had let us down, but I still think *The Cresta Run* is a marvellous play and with a different production might have been a great success.

I was asked to stay on with the company and do some other plays, but I had lost heart, and I had heard rumours that some of the other directors went in for the kind of rehearsal where most of the time was spent doing exercises or pretending to be some inanimate object. On a television programme a drama student had explained that the most difficult thing he had ever tried to be was a bent hat pin, in pain. I certainly did not want to get involved in anything like that, and anyway there was other work on offer so I decided that my stay at the Royal Court would come to an end.

N.F. Simpson wrote some quite successful half-hour television plays and I appeared in two of them. The title of one sticks in my mind, and was firmly in the true absurd tradition: *'The Best I Can Do by Way of a Gate Leg Table is 100 cwt of Coal.'* The script was quite funny as well.

I am very grateful that I had the opportunity to work with some of the great comics of the time. These performers are always one-offs, and once they have left us they are utterly irreplaceable. Even if their type of humour didn't always make me laugh, I admired their artistry and skill. Who can forget the opening sequence of each episode of *Here's Harry* as Harry Worth walked down the street and surreptitiously looked around before diving into the doorway of a shop? Standing against the corner of the shop, with the window acting as a mirror, he looked as though he was doing the splits in mid-air. Despite being a very big television star, Harry was a very approachable man and very friendly. He treated everyone around him as an equal and we all enjoyed working with him.

I had heard that Charlie Drake was difficult, and I can understand some of the reasons why this may have been. The pressure of carrying the whole show on your shoulders can be very great. If the show doesn't work or the script is unfunny, it's the star that the public tend to blame. In my experience most comics are perfectionists, and demand much of themselves and others. When I arrived for my first day's rehearsal on *The Worker*, I found that it was Charlie Drake's practice to have one room in which he worked, and another where the rest of the cast waited. He did not like the idea of rehearsing in front of other people. After sitting around for some time chatting with my fellow actors, I was summoned to do my scene as a supermarket manager with Charlie Drake, and then banished back to the room next door. One rather grand, elderly actress came out of his rehearsal room and announced in her best Lady Bracknell voice, 'Well, it was never like this with John Gielgud!'

We were supposed to call him Mr Drake, and eventually some, including myself, were allowed to call him Charles, but never Charlie. There were times when he seemed to pick on a particular member of the company, and make them feel they could do nothing right. Occasionally, a young and inexperienced actor could even be reduced to tears. Nevertheless Charlie Drake was popular with millions, was a great performer, and I worked with him a number of times. I have to say that whatever he may have been like to other people he was always very nice to me.

In 1968 I had my first encounter with Tommy Cooper. Sitting in the studio canteen one day at Teddington I saw a producer look across and say something to his companion. He came over to me and said, 'Hello Frank, what are you doing next week?'

'Nothing,' I said.

'OK, how would you like to do an episode of *Life with Cooper*?'

It is amazing what being in the right place at the right time can do. Rehearsing with Tommy was hilarious. Never letting a gag go to waste, he entertained us as much in the coffee break as when we were actually rehearsing. When the first morning's rehearsal was over, we split into groups and went to different pubs for lunch. I had gone with some of the new faces on the series, while the others went with Tommy. I soon found out why. When our small party returned an hour later, we found the rehearsal room deserted. After waiting another hour, we went to the other pub to see what had happened to everyone else, and there they were with Tommy still entertaining. Thereafter we went to the same pub with Tommy at lunchtime, which meant we didn't need to move until he did. This elongated break, often until three o'clock, was due to the fact that Tommy, like many stand-up comics, clearly didn't like rehearsing very much.

I did several more episodes of *Life with Cooper* and they were all as much fun as the first. With Tommy, we soon got used to preparing for the unexpected, and while this could have been difficult the atmosphere was so relaxed and such fun that we all found we could cope with it.

The Square Peg was a film that starred Norman Wisdom. I was disappointed that the scene in which we were to appear together was filmed separately. I was playing a character who was chatting to him via a field-telephone, and, as I filmed my scene, someone else was reading Norman's lines in for him. It was extraordinary to do a scene with someone so well known without ever meeting them. It wasn't to be long before I worked on a number of other films with Norman and met him face to face. *A Stitch in Time* saw me playing an incompetent St John's Ambulance man, struggling with my stretcher as if it were some impossible deckchair. In *The Bulldog Breed* Norman was accidentally sent into space in place of me, and I spent several weeks as an astronaut wandering around with a huge glass globe on my head. Norman was a wonderful person to work with because he had so much energy and enthusiasm. He is definitely one of the great comic talents of our age.

The 1960s had been a busy and varied time and I had

become quite adept at moving between film, television and theatre. I had established a niche for myself as one of those supporting actors who could pop up anywhere. The question was, where would it be next?

8

THE MOVE TO
WALMINGTON-ON-SEA

Little did I know that when the phone rang that spring day in 1969 that it would become a life-changing moment. It was my agent who was at the other end.

'You've worked with David Croft before, haven't you Frank?'

'Oh, yes,' I said. 'I did a couple of episodes of *Hugh and I* for him.'

'And you know Jimmy Perry?'

'Yes, for a long time, since the days at Watford.'

Where was all this leading?

'Well, they want you for an episode of *Dad's Army*.'

Although the programme had been popular for well over six months, I was unfamiliar with it. I had never seen it, and to be honest I didn't know a great deal about it. 'They want you to play a vicar,' my agent said.

'Well . . . yes . . . I can do vicars,' I replied.

'They've done two series already, and they want you for the first episode of series three,' she said.

'Fine.'

'It's called "The Armoured Might of Jack Jones".'

'Righto.' I replaced the receiver, quickly made a note of the first rehearsal day in my diary, and awaited the contract.

On 19 May 1969 I set out for the London Transport Training Centre, an unlikely venue for a BBC rehearsal room. At the time, I had no idea that this was the beginning of one of the longest and happiest chapters in my career.

'The Armoured Might of Lance Corporal Jones', as it was later re-titled, was my introduction to a remarkable cast of actors. Edward Sinclair, who played the verger, was the kindest of men and he and I became great friends. He was a man who had actually been born in a theatrical trunk because his parents were a music hall act and he would often accompany them on tour. As a boy when travelling on the train between dates, his parents would hide him under the seat to avoid paying the fare when the ticket inspector arrived. Although a great lover of the theatre, Edward felt that his responsibilities as a husband and father to two sons had to come first. He decided that the theatre life was too precarious for someone in his position. However, the theatre was in his blood, and he involved himself as a keen amateur writer, director and actor. Once he felt his family were old enough not to rely on him financially he decided to embark on a professional career. One of his first roles was with *Dad's Army* and what a wonderful job he made of the verger. Edward said that he based the character, with cap and duster, on a real verger he had known in his youth.

Bill Pertwee, the irascible air raid warden, was the scapegoat and seemed to spend most of his time shouting and falling into water. Bill tends to play himself down, suggesting that 'I'm not really an actor at all, just a "turn"'. He had spent a lot of time in the theatre as a comic, but by the time *Dad's Army* had finished he was going on tour to play Candida's father in the play by George Bernard Shaw.

'How are you going to play that, Bill?' I enquired.

'Oh, it'll be just like the air raid warden, but without the tin hat,' he said.

Bill was to become a good friend and over the years, he,

Edward and I became a kind of unholy alliance both on and off the screen.

The platoon themselves were a marvellous bunch of characters. There was Ian Lavender, the 'stupid boy', who regularly did the *Times* crossword. David Croft's wife, Ann, who had seen him at drama school, realized that he was not only a good actor but also the one around whom all the girls were flocking after the performance. He was clearly something of a heart-throb. Ann suggested him for the part of Pike. David and Jimmy readily agreed. A lot of the characters were an extension of the actor who was playing them. The exception to this was Ian, as he is very far from being the stupid, petulant boy we see on screen. He is a highly intelligent man and would often compete with John Laurie to see who could finish the *Times* crossword first. When we did pantomime together a few years later, the *Times* and its crossword puzzle became a regular feature of our dressing room. I have never been able to do crosswords and Ian tried in vain to teach me. He would tell me the clue just as I was going on stage, but when I came off, I had no more idea of the answer than when I had gone on. Even when he told me what the answer was and explained how he had arrived at it, I still did not really understand.

James Beck, who played the much-loved Private Walker, was about the same age as me. He was an extremely good and talented actor. A cheerful and good-natured man, he would, I believe, have become one of our most popular character actors had he not died so tragically young.

Arnold Ridley, who played Private Godfrey, was a product of a bygone era and was perfect as the gentle character of the piece. He was about the same age as John Laurie who had played all the great classical roles in film and theatre between the wars and was a master of the facial expression. The part was originally written as a fisherman, and it wasn't until later that he was turned into an undertaker. Most of the cast pretended to have a sort of love–hate relationship with the show. With tongue in cheek one day, John reminded Jimmy Perry of all that he had done in his career, ''Tis a strange thing, Jimmy. I played all the great classic roles at Stratford between the wars, and now I've become a household name doing this rubbish of yours.'

Clive Dunn was, of course, much younger than the character he portrayed. It was fascinating to see a comparatively young man create so convincingly the character of Corporal Jones. Clive had already played this dithery type of character in *Bootsie and Snudge*, which incidentally was a spin-off from *The Army Game*. It's a small world. It was quite something to rehearse with Clive without costume and make-up and then see that transformation take place for the cameras later in the week. For me, some of the most joyous moments of the series come when he embarks on one of his endless reminiscences while Captain Mainwaring listens with ever-increasing frustration.

Arthur Lowe himself was often perceived as being rather like the character he played, but this was an unfair assessment. He wasn't pompous, but he certainly didn't suffer fools gladly and always knew his own mind. He was something of a perfectionist but he also had an ability to laugh at himself. He had a reputation for not learning his lines very well, and the seemingly inspired pause you often see is probably him grappling with a lapse in memory. At one point David Croft became quite exasperated with him.

'Right Arthur,' he said. 'Here are four scripts. One you can leave in the rehearsal room. One is for you to take with you as you travel. There's a spare one. And another one for you to keep at home.'

'Home?' said Arthur. 'Oh no, no, no. I won't have rubbish like that in my house!'

For me, some of Arthur's funniest moments were achieved in the simplest way. For example, whenever Captain

Mainwaring fell over he always resurfaced with his spectacles and hat awry. This comic moment was repeated in episode after episode. It didn't matter how many times you saw it, it always got an enormous laugh. To see Arthur do a drunken scene was a revelation. He never over-did it, but the slightly unsteady walk, the glazed eyes and the attempt to keep his dignity worked perfectly. It was brilliant stuff.

I had already met John Le Mesurier when I did a dramatized documentary on television called *Children in Trust*. Unusually, Hattie Jacques was playing a straight role as a downtrodden housewife who had seen her children taken into care because she was incapable of looking after them herself. John and Hattie were married at the time and during a break in the rehearsal room, this vague man suddenly appeared and said, 'Oh Hattie darling, I can't find the marmalade.' His image on and off stage was built around being helpless and he used it to great advantage as I was to find out later. It seemed that almost any British film from the early 1940s onwards had John appearing in it. He won an award for playing the lead in a television production called *Traitor*. Turning to my friend Betty one day he said, 'I've got this award you see, but I really don't know what to do with it. It says on the bottom "John Le Mesurier – Traitor"! If I put it on my mantelpiece, how am I going to explain that to people?'

Jimmy and David often used the actors' idiosyncrasies as part of their character. John Le Mesurier was a case in point. His diffidence and 'Do you think that's really wise, Sir?' was as much part of him as it was of Sergeant Wilson.

'The Armoured Might of Lance Corporal Jones' was significant for a number of reasons. It was not only my first appearance but also marked the debut of Mrs Fox played by Pamela Cundell. It has a young Nigel Hawthorne in a cameo role and was the first time Jones's van had been seen as the platoon's new mode of transport. David Croft had seen Pamela Cundell do a marvellous wink in a television show. On the strength of this he cast her as Mrs Fox, and in this episode Pamela gives the same mischievous wink at Corporal Jones. In the episode, the platoon are using Jonesey's van as an ambulance on an exercise to see how they would cope in the event of an invasion. I had one short scene in which, as the gullible vicar, I allowed Frazer and Jones to take gas from the vicarage fire to fill the gasbag used to fuel the van. We rehearsed for a week and then performed it in front of a live audience with the location filming slotted in at the appropriate moment on overhead monitors for the studio audience to watch and follow the storyline. Having recorded that first episode, as far as I knew that was the end of it; but, of course, it wasn't. The vicar was recalled for further episodes during 1969 and over the years for many more. For me, it was the beginning of a magnificent time working with wonderful people in a programme that 30 years later is as popular as ever. Is it any wonder that I view that first episode with such affection?

I soon found that the rhythm of rehearsing and recording *Dad's Army* was not unlike *The Army Game*, but without the stress of a live transmission. The whole programme was recorded within half an hour, but any necessary retakes were done at the end. At first, rehearsals took place in various church halls, or the dreaded boys clubs that seemed to retain the odour of stale sweat left behind by those who had used it the night before. We eventually moved to the high-rise block soon known in the business as the Acton Hilton. This was a building that had two or three rehearsal rooms on each floor. Soon, most of the BBC shows rehearsed there, and it was not unusual to bump into Morecambe and Wise or the Two Ronnies in the lift on the way up or down.

Drying – or forgetting one's lines – is every actor's nightmare. Usually this was not a problem to me, but in one episode, it certainly was. My scene was with Harold Bennett who played Mr Bluett. He was most famous for his portrayal as Young Mr Grace in *Are You Being Served?* In the rehearsal room he had been having trouble with his lines. When it came to the recording *he* was perfectly all right – I was the one in trouble. In the scene, I was sitting in my study and Mr Bluett called me to the window to complain about what the platoon were up to in my garden. I moved to the window and my mind went blank. There was a terrible pause and then I said, 'I'm terribly sorry, but I've no idea what I'm supposed to say.'

The audience laughed sympathetically and the studio manager brought the script over to me and showed me the line. I returned to my desk and we started the scene again. I moved to the window and again nothing. By now panic was beginning to set in. On the third try I think I managed it. At the end of the transmission I apologized to everyone in sight. Arnold Ridley's wife Althea who had been in the audience said, 'Don't worry, Frank. It can happen to anyone.'

John Le Mesurier, who was a kind man, said, 'We were all worried about Harold. Perhaps that's what threw you?' I knew it wasn't true, I wasn't worried about Harold at all. I was just worried about me.

The art of comedy depends on good timing, and Arthur Lowe and John Le Mesurier were masters at this, especially in the scenes they shared together. There was a scene in which Mainwaring gets carried away and institutes a court martial for a very minor offence among his men. He informs Sgt Wilson of this and after the inevitable 'Is that wise, Sir?' Wilson walks around Mainwaring's desk saying, 'Oh dear, oh dear, oh dear.' It sounds very boring on paper, but I was lost in admiration as I watched it every day in the rehearsal room.

On the screen it was David Croft's sense of timing that enabled him to cut away to a close-up of Mainwaring's reactions at just the right minute. David's brilliant cutting and editing was as important to the show as any of the actors' performances. Any camera shot that had been missed would be re-shot at the end of the performance. John Laurie would be asked to do a surprised expression. The camera would focus on his face, the cue was given, and to the delight of the studio audience he would go through a series of contortions leaving David with a multitude of possibilities to choose from.

As rehearsals and recording progressed I got to know my character very well. The vicar was petulant, not always very nice, and I don't think he was a terribly good advert for the Church. Usually harmless, he could certainly be devious on occasions. I have sometimes been asked whether it worries me to play a character whose actions might be seen as poking fun at the Church. I usually reply that the fun is not at the expense of the Church but of the vicar. I really do not think that clergymen can be treated as an endangered species who can only be shown in a good light. Bank managers do not feel they are being unfairly treated because Mainwaring is pompous and greengrocers don't suggest that Warden Hodges gives them all a bad name.

Dad's Army was now regularly topping the television ratings. Over the years, as the series continued I was contracted to do more and more episodes, until the last season when the vicar was in every one. Nobody could ever have foreseen the immense success the series would enjoy in the future. Apart from Ian Lavender, I was the youngest member of the whole cast, which makes you think. The extraordinary thing was that in spite of their age, most of them seemed to have far more energy than I did. It was only when the programme was almost coming to an end that Arnold Ridley said plaintively one day, 'In the early episodes, I used to run around a lot, but I don't seem able to do quite so much of it now.' One day I was reading the autobiography of William Douglas Home and discovered that someone he had known was described as being 'rather like the vicar in *Dad's Army*'. So there was a Timothy Farthing look-alike out there somewhere!

My agent rang me one day to tell me she had a strange request for a photograph. It had not come from a fan but from the police. 'They are looking for a particular criminal, and the only description they have is that he looks like the vicar in *Dad's Army*! They want your photograph to issue to all their officers as they go around asking if anyone has seen this man!'

Whether they caught the criminal or not, I never found out, but I wondered for many weeks afterwards whether I would be suddenly jumped on and arrested.

Jimmy knew I was a practising churchgoer and this meant that I became a sort of advisor on most things ecclesiastical. I would say things like, 'This stole is the wrong colour for this particular time of year'.

'Oh, but it's a lovely colour!' the wardrobe-mistress would say.

'Yes, but it's wrong.'

The costume and set designers paid great attention to detail on the series, and made sure that everything was perfectly in period. The pair of spectacles I wore had authentic wartime frames. With plain glass I couldn't really see through them, but eventually they were sent away and the lenses were made up to my prescription.

When on location, one room at the hotel was given up to the wardrobe department. Here, all the costumes and personal props were stored. One day we came down to breakfast, only to hear that this room had been broken into during the night. One of the things stolen was my Homburg hat, and I wondered why someone would want to steal it in the first place.

I found the time spent on location with *Dad's Army* was idyllic. Thetford, in Norfolk, was where we would film all the exterior shots for a whole series during the spring or autumn. It is a beautiful part of the country and quite flat, and so very popular with the crew as they struggled with heavy sound equipment, cameras, and old wartime vehicles. The flatness was also a great relief to the elderly cast! Many would bring their wives with them, who would potter around making sure their husbands were being looked after with plenty of tea and scones from the refreshment wagon. Sometimes the scene at lunchtime looked more like a Derby and Joan picnic than a group of people making a television production.

The television caterers were actually very good, and cooked lunches were served on long trestle tables in the sunshine. Various comments on this were passed during the day. 'Well yes, yes,' said Arthur in true Mainwaring style. 'The steak pie was very good today, you know.'

The lovely surroundings were always enhanced by what became known as 'Croft's Weather'. David was always extra-ordinarily lucky with the weather. It was an ongoing joke that if anyone was considering going away for a holiday in the UK, they should go when David was planning his location work, because he always had absolutely perfect weather. In all the years, I can only remember two or three days when we had to stop filming for rain, and even then it wasn't for terribly long.

The Bell Hotel, Thetford, had become our annual home-from-home for the two weeks' filming work we did at the start of each season. It was a good idea to have everybody more or less together in the same place. Those who could not be accommodated at The Bell stayed at the nearby Anchor Hotel. I would sometimes drive up from London with Teddy Sinclair, but others caught the coach from BBC Television centre. It often seemed as if we had all arrived at once, creating havoc in the hotel foyer like a reunion of long-lost friends who hadn't seen each other for years. Bits of The Bell were quite old, but there was a modern extension that had been added. It had the atmosphere of an old pub hotel, but with all the modern facilities. It was also very conveniently placed for all the various locations dotted around the area. The reaction of the other hotel clients was sometimes a joy to observe. There they were, having a quiet country holiday, when suddenly the entire cast and crew of a famous BBC series descended upon them without warning. It was true to say that we took up so much room at the hotel that there were not many vacant rooms. However, the few members of the public that had managed to book in were open-mouthed at breakfast as one by one each member of the platoon arrived for the first meal of the day, usually in *Dad's Army* costume in readiness for filming. I always made a point of not wearing my clerical collar and tied a scarf round the top of my shirt. I didn't want to add further to the confusion by introducing what might seem to be a real vicar in the midst of it all. Teddy only donned the cap, cassock and the famous duster once breakfast was over.

Fans on location could sometimes be a problem. In the busy town of Thetford the residents were used to us and quite happily allowed us to get on with our work. However, if we were working anywhere near one of the local villages, as soon as word got round that we had arrived, we were often inundated with a live audience watching our every move. It can be difficult if lots of people suddenly want autographs while the director is trying to get everyone organized for the next shot. Obviously we did not ignore them but we were all aware that time on location is extremely precious, and a lot has to be done in the short time available. If one of the bystanders ever coughed or sneezed loudly enough to be picked up by our microphones, it was back to square one. One day, a whole load of fans suddenly appeared from nowhere. We all signed their books and bits of paper. Arthur was not prepared to be so obliging. 'Oh no, no, no. I don't do that when I'm working.'

Later that same day, another army of fans arrived with their books and pieces of paper and started to discuss among themselves which member of the cast they should approach first.

'Look, there's Arthur Lowe,' said one. 'Shall I go and ask him?'

'I wouldn't!' said one of the morning fans. 'He's a miserable old toad, he is!'

Bill Pertwee overheard this, and at The Bell that night,

recounted the story at dinner. Arthur Lowe's wife leant over and said, 'There you are Arthur. That's the impression you give to people. A miserable old toad!' He had the good grace to join in the laugh at his expense.

Of course he wasn't being miserable at all, but just trying to remember his lines for the next scene. Indeed filming did require concentration. We were filming different bits, from half a dozen episodes, and all out of sequence. One moment I would be talking to the verger who was dressed as a sea scout and the next be riding my bike shouting lines from a totally different episode, as I chased after Jones's van.

One of my favourite episodes was 'The Day the Balloon Went Up'. It was about a large barrage balloon that had broken loose. The platoon is told to march the balloon to safety in the woods. There were a dozen or so ropes hanging down from the balloon, enough for each one of us to grab hold of. The vicar and verger were commandeered to help with the exercise. We were given strict instructions not to wrap the rope around our hands in case it took off and we were carried up with it! This inspired David to suggest that I should clasp my rope in between my hands in an attitude of prayer, which got quite a good laugh. Once in the woods, the platoon ties the balloon to a fallen tree, which Mainwaring sits astride. Unfortunately, when they let go the tree is not strong enough to hold the balloon and it breaks away carrying Mainwaring with it. We spent most of that day looking up at Captain Mainwaring dangling helplessly from the rope.

'The Royal Train' was filmed on a little private railway line near Sheringham and a small station at Weybourne. The amateur enthusiasts who had restored and kept the old line going seemed to be mainly professional men such as solicitors and bank managers when out of their engine driver's boiler suits. At the end of one day's filming, the train driver, alias the local bank manager, asked Bill, Teddy and I if we would like a trip back to the other end of the line on the footplate. We accepted with alacrity like schoolboys being given a treat, and watched him shovelling coal in a way in which any real train driver would have been proud. I was involved in a sequence with the verger, the warden and the mayor as we struggle to stay on a tiny pump-trolley trying to catch up with a runaway train. Our vehicle was a truck used by people to go up and down the line when doing repairs. It was propelled by means of a double-sided lever which had to be pulled up and down like a pump. It was quite hard work pulling and pushing the pump but between the four of us it was easy to get up a pretty good speed. At the beginning we chase the train, and then to our horror we find that the train has reversed and is now chasing us on our little platform with wheels. As we were filming this bit we had a frightening moment. We suddenly realized that the train seemed to be gaining on us. As we pushed and pulled, up and down, Bill glanced behind us and suddenly shouted, 'The driver can't see us, you know!'

It was true. The plot required that it was Ian Lavender who was driving the train, but talented though he is, train driving is not one of his accomplishments. He stood on the footplate for the camera while the real driver kept out of sight crouching on the floor and was therefore unable to see what was ahead on the line. What was ahead on the line was us! We were desperately trying to keep ahead. By this time we seemed to be travelling about 60 miles an hour, and gathering speed. 'We'll all have to jump!' Bill bellowed.

'But we'll kill ourselves!' I shouted back.

'If the train crashes into us we'll all be killed, but if we jump it'll be just a few broken bones,' replied Bill.

'Not at this speed!' I yelled.

As the train grew ever closer, I noticed that Bill now had a piece of his jacket caught in the pump-truck mechanism. We felt as if the train was nearly upon us when it suddenly stopped, and we breathed an enormous sigh of relief, and sank down exhausted from our efforts.

Of course we need not have worried, it was all in hand. A member of the crew had a walkie-talkie and was in constant touch with the train. It had been a worrying few minutes, and if you look at that episode now, I can vouch that the look of terror on our faces is very much for real!

At the end of the episode, having managed to clear the line of the runaway train, the platoon has no time to get back to the platform, but lines up to honour the King beside the track. They are joined by the vicar, the verger and warden who are determined to be in on the act. As the express train goes by, it throws up the contents of the water trough all over the platoon and the three of us. This sequence was filmed right at the very end of the day as we were told we would get wet. We all stood there, fully clothed waiting for the cold water to arrive. As David shouted 'Action!' the crew had enormous fun as they threw buckets of freezing water at us. Despite our sodden clothes, we all sat on the coach on the way back to the hotel, happily joking and making the best of things. Even a saturated Arthur was quite cheery now that the prospect of a hot bath and a stiff whiskey was in sight.

Reading one script, I saw that I was to be involved in a motorbike sequence. My heart sank as my mind flashed back to my *Inn for Trouble* problems and anything to do with an engine. To my relief I saw that I was only required to be a pillion passenger. Bill Pertwee would be the one who had to cope with the temperamental quirks of a vintage motorbike. We were supposed to be chasing something at great speed, but for some reason there was little time to rehearse the shot. It was an original bike of the period, and Bill looked at it doubtfully, then mounted and tried a few short practice runs. He seemed quite confident that all would be well. The cameras were placed a couple of hundred yards down the road. I sat on the pillion and Teddy got in the sidecar. My arms were firmly around Bill's waist, as David called for 'Action!' Bill kicked the starter and the engine roared into life, and we were off. We only had to cover a short distance and I could see the smile on the cameraman's face as we approached. He was obviously getting the shot David wanted. Suddenly I saw the smile turn to total panic as it became absolutely clear that Bill had no idea how to stop the thing. The camera went one way and everyone else shot in all directions, the bike ploughed on, narrowly missing everyone, and we ended up in a ditch. Miraculously, no one was hurt, and as soon as we had recovered from the shock, we began to laugh. My view that I should avoid all things mechanical was confirmed. Even when I wasn't in charge, it was clear that it could still go wrong.

'All Is Safely Gathered In' ends with the vicar's arrival to take an open-air service of thanksgiving for the harvest, in a field. It is accompanied by a lady organist playing 'We plough the fields, and scatter' on her portable harmonium. She was a real organist from one of the local churches and had had her hair done especially for the occasion, so was not too pleased to find that it was concealed under the severe 1940s hat provided by the wardrobe department. To my mind, she ended up as the star of the whole scene. All those that helped with the harvest, including Mainwaring and his men, are invited to the service. Unfortunately they have all got very drunk on homemade wine. As they all try to stay upright and sing the first hymn someone inadvertently staggers into the vicar. The verger attempts to protect him. 'Don't you push his reverence!' This causes a scuffle which eventually becomes a general free for all. The lady organist sits there stolidly playing away and totally ignoring the pandemonium that is breaking out all around her. David's expert editing comes into its own. As the fight develops he keeps cutting away to a close-up of this wonderful lady still playing away and oblivious to it all. The whole scene is a wonderful ending to the episode which was recently voted as one of the top favourites by members of the '*Dads Army* Appreciation Society'. This episode prompted a letter from a viewer who had read in a newspaper that I was a churchgoer in real life. The writer asked how I thought I could appear as a vicar in robes, in this disgusting scene of a drunken orgy, and still call myself a Christian. As far as I know, she was the only one who was worried.

In the early days we did not have the luxury of the portable lavatories, or honey-wagon as it was called. Teddy Sinclair, a very modest person, would go wandering off into the woods as far as he could to ensure privacy. He seemed to forget that we were filming on army property that was still used for training. There were restricted areas that were known to be dangerous. On one occasion he went off so far and disappeared for such a long time that Bill Pertwee turned to me and said, 'If he's not careful he'll get himself blown up by an unexploded bomb one of these days!'

The battle area was a fascinating place. When we filmed near some stables, John Le Mesurier turned to me and said, 'Do you know, this is where the big manor house was? I can remember being brought here as a small boy for tea.'

The area contained several villages that had been evacuated during the start of World War II. This was because the army wanted to use the area for training purposes. It must have been very difficult for the residents to leave the homes in which they had been born, and the villages in which they had lived all their lives. They were told that they could return after the war, but in point of fact they never did. The army hung on to the area, which became more and more like a ghost town, and by the time we were filming there many of the buildings had been reduced to rubble.

A few years ago, Pamela Cundell and I were invited up to the area for a very moving occasion. The army had invited those that had lived there to re-visit what was left of their childhood homes. There were several coachloads of people, and one or two of them had even come from the United States of America. In talking to the commanding officer, I mentioned how sad it seemed that these people were forcibly moved out. He said that most of the houses had not had any modern facilities, and that the residents were billeted in places where they could at last enjoy hot and cold running water, heating and other amenities. By the time this visit took place, there were pretty well no buildings left whatsoever because the army had used them as target practice.

As I sat next to one elderly man on the coach he pointed to what was now an empty space and said, 'I remember when I used to cycle down this road. That's where my school was. There was a pub on that corner, you know.' Pamela told me that on her coach a woman said, 'Can we stop the coach because I'm sure that was my house?' All Pamela could see was a small pile of rubble, but the woman climbed out and collected a single brick to take back with her as a keepsake. Pamela and I found it all very moving and their reminiscences of interrupted childhood were fascinating.

The only buildings that had remained unscathed were the village churches. The war department had agreed that these would be preserved, and they had been as good as their word. A few years ago, one of these churches was fully restored and all the interior furnishings replaced. One of the couples on our coach party recognized it as the church where they had been married, many years ago. Every year a carol service is held there. We had used one of these as the exterior of St Aldhelm's, the parish church of Walmington-on-Sea.

Meeting back in The Bell Hotel bar after a hard day's work was always enjoyable. After dinner at The Bell or, if we fancied a change, at The Anchor down the road, we would sit around talking for hours about everything under the sun. This was the point at which Arnold Ridley, who was not as young as some, usually retired early. His wife Althea would always go with him to make sure he was all right, although she would probably rather had stayed chatting with the rest of us. 'Althea is a saint,' said Arthur's wife, Joan. She and Arthur were not early to bed and were always happy when it came to staying up late chitchatting over a round or two, and it was wonderful to see Arthur slowly unwind. I certainly enjoyed our late nights. I have always been one who comes alive at night, and when I was writing one of my plays would often sit at my desk until three or four in the morning.

One visiting actor, who shall remain nameless, was famous for getting rather the worst for wear after a day's filming. His party piece was to say goodnight to everybody rather loudly before making a very determined if rather wobbly exit, only to return moments later having decided to have another tipple. This performance would often be repeated several times. We wondered whether he ever did his re-entrance after everyone had gone to bed and couldn't understand why the place was empty.

Some evenings after dinner we would go to the local cinema to view the 'rushes' of the previous day's work, after the public had gone home. I never really enjoyed seeing 'rushes' and when working on feature films quite often avoided them. I think my problem is that I am so busy concentrating on myself that I don't see the scene as a whole. I spend my time thinking 'I shouldn't have scratched my nose at that moment!' or 'What was that facial expression meant to convey?' However, on *Dad's Army*, in the cinema at Thetford after a few glasses of wine, the whole thing didn't seem quite so bad.

Watching sequences that I hadn't been involved in was always fun. The shots of Jack Haig clipping the hedge as Arthur swoops by hanging from the barrage balloon in 'The Day the Balloon Went Up' actually got a round of applause from those of us seeing it for the first time.

I look back on our days spent at The Bell Hotel and on location in Norfolk with enormous affection. When eventually we knew that *Dad's Army* was coming to an end it was Ian who summed up our feelings when he said, 'So what are we going to do about our fortnight's holiday every year in Thetford?'

In an episode recorded in July 1973, the vicar and the verger are allowed to join the platoon while Captain Mainwaring is temporarily absent. When we arrived for rehearsal, we learned that Jimmy Beck had been taken ill and rushed into hospital. Some hasty rewriting was done to explain Walker's absence and when the platoon line up, there is a gap in the ranks with a note explaining that Walker is in London attending to some business. The audience knows that this business will be concerned with his usual dealings in the black market, and the discovery of the note and Mainwaring's reaction to it get the expected laugh. However, we knew the real reason for his absence, and it was far from funny. At first, we had no idea that his illness was serious, but as the week went by it became clear that it was.

We arranged that Arthur would be in contact with the hospital and with Jimmy's wife Kay and he would relay the news to the rest of us. Each day we would wait anxiously for the bulletin. 'The Recruit' was the last episode of that particular series, and when we broke up Jimmy was still in hospital. By this time we knew that he was very seriously ill indeed. In spite of this, the news of his death came as a great shock. Apart from Ian, he was the youngest member of the platoon and only a year or so older than I was.

As we were not working together when the news came through, each of us had to cope with it in our own way. Jimmy had a great talent and had he lived would, I believe, have become one of those stalwart character actors who have always been such an essential part of the British film and television industry. It was perhaps as well that there had been a break at this time, but even so when we re-assembled for the next series we were all aware of the loss. The character of the spiv had been an integral part of the programme from the beginning and Jimmy's cheerful personality had contributed much to the enjoyment of rehearsals. Very wisely the writers had decided that there could be no question of recasting the role or even of writing in another similar character.

In 'A Man of Action' we were re-introduced to Mr Cheeseman, a reporter on the local paper who had first appeared in 'My British Buddy'. He was splendidly played by Talfryn Thomas. I thought the character was a wonderful creation and excellent foil for Mainwaring's pomposity. It has been suggested that John Laurie was worried that Mr Cheeseman was getting more laughs then Private Frazer. I have no idea whether this was true or whether John ever said it. It sounds unlike him and if he did comment, I think it would have been in the tongue-in-cheek manner in which he was so adept. In true Welsh style, Talfryn would often add 'Oh yes indeed' or some such phrase to the end of a scripted line and I think Arthur, who was probably struggling to remember his own line, found this somewhat disconcerting. For whatever reason, Mr Cheeseman did not last beyond that particular series.

It is something of an irony that a number of my own favourite episodes are ones in which I did not appear. I hasten to add that this is not cause and effect, but just the way things turned out. I was sad not to be in the episode that contains the famous line voted in a recent survey as one of the funniest of all time: when the U-Boat commander asks Pike for his name, Mainwaring replies, 'Don't tell him, Pike!'

I think I would also have rather enjoyed the moment on location when Arthur realized that the script called for him to have a grenade down his trousers, decided this was an affront to Mainwaring's dignity and demanded a script change. It is a tribute to David and Jimmy that apparently they re-wrote the scene on the spot, so that Corporal Jones had the indignity instead.

'Mums' Army' was a wonderful episode clearly based on that great film *Brief Encounter*. Carmen Silvera gave a very moving performance and the delicacy with which the relationship between Mainwaring and Mrs Gray develops is beautifully handled. Of course there are laughs in the script but the poignancy which Arthur brings to his scenes enables us to see a new aspect of his character. This episode shows that all great comedy, including *Dad's Army*, is not that far away from tragedy as it gives us the ability to laugh and cry all at the same time.

9

WALMINGTON COMES
TO TOWN

In the 1970s it was fairly common to make a feature film of any successful television series.

In August 1970 I did a week on *The Worker* with Charlie Drake at Elstree Studios. We recorded the episode on the Thursday evening. On the Friday morning the car picked me up and took me off for my first day's location for the *Dad's Army* feature film.

Columbia Pictures had decided to transfer us all to the big screen quite early on in the show's career. The television cast were all in it, with one exception. In my opinion, it was a mistake to replace Janet Davies who played Mrs Pike in the TV series. Liz Fraser gave a lovely performance as Pike's mother, and she was a 'known' name, but to the viewer, Janet was Mrs Pike. It was an unnecessary and unhelpful confusion and was very sad for Janet.

It was to be a film that matched the series in looks and feel. The outside location was at the idyllic Buckinghamshire village of Chalfont St Giles, which was posing as Walmington-on-Sea for the purposes of the film. As I had to be there for the early call of eight o'clock, I had difficulty keeping awake as the car rolled along the country lanes. There was so little traffic on the road that the car dropped me off a lot earlier than had been arranged. Thanking the driver, I decided to kill some time by having a look around the village itself. As usual,

'Croft's Weather' prevailed and it was a beautiful day, already quite warm despite the early hour. As I wandered down the High Street I felt that the location manager had certainly excelled himself in choosing this place. It seemed absolutely perfect, and had hardly changed since the war. Peering into the shop windows I saw that some of the goods on sale were the same as I had seen in my childhood. Then I was astonished to see a 'Craven A' advert, and a 'stop me and buy one' bicycle, things I hadn't seen for years and years. Turning a corner I suddenly came across an upturned boat with a notice pinned on it: 'To the Sea'. Then it dawned on me. The entire High Street had been dressed for the film.

Every morning someone would climb onto the roof of any houses that would be in shot, and remove the television aerials. Every evening, he would climb back up and replace them so the residents could switch on and perhaps watch *Dad's Army* in peace.

Clearly people in modern dress had to be kept out of the shot, even though the High Street was officially open for business. This meant that the director would ask all those in the shops to stay there until the sequence had been completed. The assistant director would stand out of sight holding up the traffic while the cameras rolled. We would complete the scene as quickly as possible and allow the good citizens of Chalfont St Giles to resume their normal business. They were extraordinarily patient with us and it amazes me how co-operative the British public are on occasions like this, even when it involved having the criss-cross wartime anti-blast tape stuck to their windows.

One person who was not so forbearing was someone who had been a friend of my parents, who was now living in the village. As I entered the shop in which she was entrapped she took one look and instantly recognized me.

'You're very unpopular here, you know,' she said. 'You're causing absolute chaos in this village.'

I was relieved to find that the other shoppers did not seem to share her view.

My location filming over, I was off for a couple of days before joining the film back at Shepperton Studios. Here the church hall set seemed identical to the regular television version we used each week, and we all felt very much at home working within it. The church near the entrance to the studio was used as the exterior for St Aldhelm's this time, and the front door of my vicarage was a building in the studio grounds. It was strange at first being directed by someone other than David Croft, but Norman Cohen knew his job and everything seemed to go smoothly. Jimmy Perry, enthusiastic as always, was there to cheer us along. Even when there was the odd problem his positive approach never failed.

The film premiere was at a cinema in Shaftesbury Avenue, and received mixed notices. The *Times* said it was a wonderful film in the great tradition of British farce, while one of the tabloids complained that it was too episodic and slow. I have since learnt that David Croft was disappointed too. He said that it lacked the cut-away reaction shots that were so much a part of the television series. Whatever other people thought, I had an enormously enjoyable time doing it.

It was well known that Jimmy Perry could sell you anything. It was one night while on location in Thetford that we assembled to hear Jimmy tell some of us about the planned stage show. Ian, Teddy, Bill and myself were there and one or two of the others. Jimmy was at his most expansive, his characteristic enthusiasm well to the fore. We learned that it would be a musical, and a slight feeling of consternation descended as most of us didn't see ourselves as singers. The scenes of the Home Guard on duty would be similar to the television series but there would also be war-time songs and a nostalgic look at the popular music hall 'turns' of the day. This was not surprising given Jimmy's long-term fascination with the music hall. Once he got going he was unstoppable and at a climax of his enthusiastic description he told us about the dream sequence. For Jimmy, this was clearly the highlight of the show. Ian was going to fall asleep and dream about having a banana. These were not available during the war. He would not only dream about a banana but actually turn into one, and end up wearing a banana costume. Carmen Miranda would be involved and there would be a chorus of boys and girls all singing about bananas. Well,' he said. 'What do you think of it?'

There was a stunned silence. Ian looked bemused. The thought of having to be a banana was obviously obliterating everything else. Bill stared in amazement and I was speechless. It was Teddy who broke the silence. 'Well, that all sounds very interesting,' he said. It was the understatement of the century.

As the weeks progressed we all became excited by the idea of a stage show. Jimmy Perry continued to regale us with wonderful stories of how the script of the show was taking shape. We were all in the show except for John Laurie, who said that he could think of better things to do with his time than travelling up to the West End every night. He was coming up to 80 years of age, and he decided that he preferred to be at home with his wife. Hamish Roughead played Private Frazer. Hamish was very good, but we still missed John's dry Scottish humour.

When James Beck died it was felt that it would be wrong to recast his character and so Private Walker had disappeared from the series. In the stage show, however, Jimmy and David felt he should be re-introduced. The 'spiv' was such a central part of life in wartime and John Bardon was cast in this role. He was later to become well known to viewers as Jim Branning in *Eastenders*. The stage show also introduced Jeffrey Holland. He played the part of a German inventor and understudied Ian Lavender, and actually went on in Ian's place one matinee. Replacing one of the stars that everybody has come to see is always a difficult thing to do. When the announcement is made before the show that someone well known is being replaced, the sighs of disappointment coming from the auditorium don't exactly encourage the understudy! Jeffrey did a great job, however, and his comic talents were eventually fully recognized in *Hi-de-Hi!*.

The show's young director, Roger Redfarn, had been the artistic director at the Belgrade Theatre in Coventry. The first rehearsals took place in the Presbyterian Church Hall in Richmond. Our worst fears about being in a musical were confirmed when the American musical director Ed Coleman lined us all up and announced that he wanted each of us to sing the first line of 'Somewhere over the Rainbow'. I looked at Bill, and he looked back at me and we both raised our eyebrows. Apparently the first two notes of this particular song are a very good way of judging a singer's range. From 'Some' to 'where' is an octave. Most of the cast were very nervous. When I had given my version I received a wan smile before Ed moved quickly on to the next in line. Having heard my effort he wisely decided not to use me in the more difficult numbers, although I was allowed to join in some of the good old wartime songs.

There was a sequence at the beginning of the show when the warden, vicar and the verger proclaimed the blackout regulations to an Anglican chant. The government suggested that in order for pedestrians to avoid being run over in the blackout they should not tuck their shirt tails into their trousers but should let them dangle out from behind. All three of us were to sing 'Let it dangle!' in the deepest voices we could manage. I asked why the writers hadn't used a real Anglican chant. 'Because we've written this, and if it's performed we get a royalty.' A very sound reason, I thought.

The out-of-town tryout in Billingham was designed to iron out any problems before the show came into the West End. There was a large orchestra in the pit, and arriving to do a band-call was something quite new to a lot of us. Most of us had never worked with a live orchestra before and it was somewhat nerve-wracking. Despite all the first-night nerves, it got a good reception from the audience, and I rang Betty straight afterwards to tell her how well it had gone. With a mixture of relief, exhilaration and exhaustion I made my way to the first night party where we all celebrated what we hoped was to be a big success. Once we had opened, the main problems seemed to be concerned with the famous banana sequence and the cast were called in almost every day to rehearse it. This was good news for Bill, Teddy and me as we were not in it, and so spent many happy days enjoying outings in the surrounding countryside. Quite often we were accompanied by John Le Mesurier. In fact none of the main platoon was in the Banana sequence apart from Ian. So while the rest of us enjoyed ourselves Ian practised being a banana all day and did the show each evening. Perhaps he had been right to look so worried when Jimmy first mentioned the idea to him.

2 October 1975 was opening night in the West End, and the Shaftesbury Theatre was to be our home for the next six months. We were all nervous, and I decided that it was a rather good idea to pop across the road to St Giles-in-the-Fields. They had an Evening Eucharist, which would enable me to get back to my dressing room in plenty of time before the first performance. I said some prayers about the show and the people in it and made my way back across the road ready for the first night. Fortunately the show went like a bomb, and we expected to be in for a good run.

In the music hall sequence, various stars of the time were represented. Bill Pertwee played Max Miller; Pamela Cundell and Joan Lowe were Elsie and Doris Waters – Gert and Daisy; Arthur, Michael Bevis and Ian sang 'We Three in Happidrome'; while Arthur also did Robb Wilton. The climax was Flanagan and Allen doing their famous wartime hit, 'Hometown'. The sequence started out with Arthur and John as the two famous comics, with the entire cast joining

14. Niall Buggy deciding whether to murder me in *Stage Struck*

15. With David John in *The Winslow Boy*

16. Caught in the middle with Arthur Lowe and Teddy Sinclair

17. Risking our lives in *The Royal Train*

18. *Knights of Madness*

19. In the blackout with Bill and Teddy on stage with
Dad's Army

20. Preferment at last in *You Rang M'Lord*

21. With Betty on the Yorkshire Moors

22. One sausage or two? Efficient service from a
    Prime Minister

23. You're never alone with an Ugly Sister! Tony Bateman
and me in *Cinderella* at Birmingham, 1977

24. My two lovely sons James Crossley (Hunter) as Aladdin and Jon Clegg as Wishey Washey, Torquay 2001

25. Eric Longworth, Pamela Cundell and Bill Pertwee enjoy a laugh on a *Dad's Army* personal appearance, 2002

26. My father and me

27. Tring Festival Company revive *Dad's Army* on stage, 2002. Philip Madoc and other members of the real cast join them at the curtain call

them as the song built. On the first night, towards the end of the song, John slipped off stage and was replaced by Chesney Allen himself which was a wonderful moment.

Several weeks later the show, which included the sound of bombs, had its own bomb scare. During World War II it was the famous Windmill Theatre that boasted 'We never close'. Other theatres, too, carried on in spite of air-raid warnings, although an announcement was always made and the audience were invited to leave if they wished to. Few people did. In wartime, the actual show was never interrupted, but now in peace time one night our show was brought to a halt. It was a bomb scare from the IRA. Right in the middle of Act One the front-of-house manager came on stage with the announcement that the theatre had to be evacuated as quickly as possible. I don't know where the audience went, but most of the cast went over to the pub opposite the theatre. The staff behind the bar couldn't believe their eyes as Captain Mainwaring, Sergeant Wilson, Corporal Jones and Private Godfrey came in for a quick pint. True to form, Arnold Ridley got there first. He might have been a bit slow in other areas, but when the pub was the destination, he was off the mark quicker than anyone. We were enjoying our drinks when the company manager, knowing instinctively where he would find the group of actors, came to tell us that the bomb scare had been a hoax. We all went back to the theatre and carried on with the show.

Once we were relaxed into the run, I soon got into the actor's routine of going to work when most people are going home. This is always a bonus as the rush hour is going in the opposite direction. I would arrive at the theatre, do the show (two on matinee days), usually go out for dinner, arrive home in the early hours, and rise late the following morning to start the whole process all over again. Pamela Cundell and I often enjoyed a meal together after the show, and Luigi's in Covent Garden was our usual haunt. Other members of the cast sometimes joined us, but performers from other shows in town also frequented it. It was a well-known theatrical restaurant and there were people such as Andre Previn, Mia Farrow or Michael Crawford at an adjacent table. Most of the *Dad's Army* cast had played in the West End before, especially Arnold Ridley. Arnold was a prolific writer and several of his scripts were made into films. He had written *The Ghost Train* in the early 1920s when he was a young man, and it had a very long and successful run at the St Martin's Theatre. Even today, not a week goes by without *The Ghost Train* being produced somewhere in the world, and a recent touring production had Ian Lavender in the part which I had played at school. Fortunately the character's age is not important to the plot!

Arnold told me that he had sold the amateur rights for *The Ghost Train* for just £200. 'But Arnold,' I said. 'That would have been worth hundreds of thousands of pounds over the years. Don't you feel bitter about that?' 'No,' came the reply. 'I was a young and struggling actor/playwright in those days, so £200 meant a great deal to me.' It was a wonderfully philosophical way of looking at it.

His character of Godfrey in *Dad's Army* often reminisced about the past when it was easy to have a night on the town and still have change from a ten-bob note. Here was yet another example of the writers using the actor's background in creating the character. Apparently *The Ghost Train* had been produced in Germany several times during the war. With typical German thoroughness, the producers had kept their financial accounts meticulously and, at the end of the war, sent Arnold a lump sum for all the performances that had taken place. Sadly, with all the bureaucracy and red tape surrounding the act of getting money out of Germany at that period, by the time it arrived there was not a lot left.

When Arnold came to *Dad's Army* he was in his seventies and had enjoyed a long and successful career as a playwright

and actor. He was a very gentle man unless anyone called him
'Arthur' by mistake. He would correct them forcefully and
with great vehemence. Apparently there was another actor
who was called Arthur Ridley and Arnold had once lost a
lucrative film contract because the casting director had booked
the wrong person.

The producers were all a little worried whether the oldest
member of the cast would be able to cope with the strenuous
nature of a West End run. They needn't have been concerned
because he often seemed stronger than the rest of us put
together. He arrived one evening with Althea and we saw she
was looking somewhat anxious. 'Arnold's got a temperature
of 101 and he's still insisted on coming in,' she said. Despite
pleas from other members of the cast, Arnold refused to go
home. 'I've never missed a performance in 60 years,' he said,
'and I don't intend to start now!' He played the performance
perfectly, but the next day he was forced to retire to bed and
his understudy was on for the next week.

The custom of playing the National Anthem at the end of
the show had largely disappeared from the theatre at this
time. However, whether to reflect the war-time practice or
because *Dad's Army* had a patriotic content, we defied the
trend and always ended with it. It was fascinating that it
was our American musical director who pointed out that we
Britons were singing the words inaccurately. He listened each
night, and woe betide anyone who sang the word 'our' instead
of 'the' in the third line.

It was while we were in the West End that Arnold Ridley
celebrated his eightieth birthday. On that night the National
Anthem was omitted as we all turned to Arnold and sang
'Happy Birthday' instead. The curtain call seemed to go on
for ever but when the tabs finally dropped a birthday cake in
the shape of a large '80' was wheeled on stage and we all
applauded as the press cameras flashed away.

Actors are accustomed to working together, sometimes

over quite a long period, but once the show is over you're on to the next thing and working with a new set of people. However, sometimes lasting friendships are made and this was certainly the case in *Dad's Army*.

Pamela Cundell and I went out for dinner with Arthur and Joan Lowe for years after *Dad's Army* had finished. Bill Pertwee also kept in touch and Betty and I would often visit Teddy and Gladys Sinclair. For me, a long lasting friendship that came from the stage show was Ronnie Grainge. He was a singer and dancer and played a number of small parts in the various sketches and we shared a number of interests in common. When the show eventually went on tour Ronnie was often part of the daily outings with Bill, Teddy and me.

We were all very excited when we were told that we had been invited to be part of the Royal Variety Performance. As this was to be on a Monday night, the performance at the Shaftesbury Theatre would have to be cancelled that evening and we would be appearing at the London Palladium. Mounting a huge show in a busy theatre, with stars from around the globe, and with a massive company who barely fit on the stage, must take months of meticulous planning and I was lost in admiration for the way in which this was achieved.

There was no room for us to have dressing room facilities backstage, so we got into costume at the Shaftesbury and were taken by coach to the upstairs room of a pub behind the Palladium. At the appropriate time we were summoned to stand in the wings of one of the most famous theatres in the world, and await our entrance. We did our version of the Floral Dance and it seemed to go well, getting some good laughs. It all seemed slightly unreal and before we knew it, it was over, and we found ourselves back in the pub with our sandwich boxes and coffee flasks. Quite a time elapsed before we were called back to line up for the finale. It was a moving moment when we all turned to face Her Majesty to sing the National Anthem. I had sung 'God Save the Queen' on hundreds of occasions in many different places and circumstances. Now the Queen was standing there and we were singing it to her.

For the presentation we were arranged all the way from the stage and up a flight of stairs. One poor man had the unenviable job of arranging us into the correct pre-arranged order. There was Harry Secombe, Dame Vera Lynn, Michael Crawford, Count Basie, Charles Aznavour, Dukes and Lee, Telly Savalas, Bruce Forsyth, The Kwa Zulu Dancers, not to mention the contingent from Walmington-on-Sea. By some miracle, when the Queen appeared, we were all in place. As I stood waiting, my mind flashed back to *The Army Game* when only one member of the cast had been presented to the Queen Mother. Tonight it was the entire *Dad's Army* team standing there. I glanced at Teddy standing next to me, and saw that he was still wearing the famous cap. Of course it was an integral part of the costume, but was it right when one was meeting the Sovereign? I need not have worried for as she approached, he swept it off in a way that would have done credit to a courtier of Elizabeth I. You had to hand it to Teddy – he always worked out any business he was going to do, well in advance.

When the Queen got to me, she smiled and shook my hand. As I made my bow, the Duke of Edinburgh following behind made some comment to Teddy, but I couldn't hear what it was, I was far too busy savouring my own special moment. The Queen, whose Coronation I had watched on television, who over the years I had come to revere as someone who symbolized all that was best in the British nation, was standing there in front of me and shaking my hand. Betty had, of course, been in the audience with Bill's wife Marion and Teddy's wife Gladys. Bill, Teddy and I met with them afterwards and talked excitedly about the evening's events. With my memories of the *The Army Game* Royal Variety Show, I had not expected to meet the Queen, and I think I had put this doubt in the minds of the others, so we were full of the fact that we had all been presented. Eventually we went for a celebratory meal and enjoyed ourselves into the early hours of the morning.

After six months of playing eight times a week we were told that the West End run of the *Dad's Army* stage show would come to an end. However, this was not to be the end of our time on stage. A national tour had been planned. While the cast enjoyed a short break, some script adjustments were made. Re-casting had to take place as some of the cast had other commitments. Pamela Cundell went into *Liza of Lambeth* which followed us into the Shaftesbury Theatre, so Mrs Fox was played by Peggy Ashby on the tour.

Veteran actor Jack Haig had already made several cameo appearances in the TV series, and was signed to take over the role of Corporal Jones halfway through the tour when Clive Dunn left. There had also been some changes in the chorus and those who were playing small parts, so it was a slightly different company when we regrouped for the touring show. We were to open at the beautiful old Opera House in Manchester, a large theatre seating over 2000 people. It would be a grand start to the tour.

Teddy had invited me to travel in his car. Some of my favourite moments during the stage show were with him. He created a wonderful character as the verger and we were already good friends, but on the tour our friendship was to be greatly strengthened as we travelled from one town to the next in his little old banger. The problem was that neither of us was good at reading maps, and we consistently got lost. Our journey to Manchester was no exception. When we eventually arrived at that great city, our troubles were by no means over. We had to find the digs. 'Well, I really can't find this place at all!' said Teddy sounding more and more like the verger as we drove round and round in circles for what seemed like miles. 'Don't worry about it!' I said in my best vicar's voice. 'I'm sure we'll get there in the end.' Somehow we suddenly seemed to be getting into character even before we had arrived. 'Well, it's all very worrying,' said the verger.

'Yes, and what's even more worrying,' replied the vicar, 'is that we've driven all round Manchester and we haven't seen a single poster for the show.'

Since the days when I had put on *The Substitute* at Watford, I had known the importance of good publicity. In some places, it seemed almost as if the theatre had forgotten we were coming. *Dad's Army* was enormously popular and audiences wanted to see us, but they needed to know we were there. As we toured the country we noticed that when the theatre had made an effort and really marketed the show, we were sold out with people queuing for returns. When publicity was lacking there were seats to spare for the first few days until word of mouth got round.

On the first day in Blackpool I was on a tram, and a woman sitting opposite stared at me for a while and then leant across and said, 'Excuse me, but aren't you that vicar off that *Dad's Army*?' 'That's right,' I replied with my best smile. 'So what are you doing up here then, luv?' she asked. 'Well actually, we're appearing at the theatre just round the corner,' I said. 'Oh, I thought that was just the film,' she said. When I went to look at the front of the theatre I felt the mistake was understandable. There were huge advertisements for the forthcoming summer season. They totally dwarfed the small announcement over the door that said merely 'Arthur Lowe and John Le Mesurier in *Dads' Army*'. This notice had been put there using the glass capital letters so popular at the time for cinemas advertising a film, and I could appreciate why the lady on the tram was so surprised to see me in the flesh. Fortunately our company manager was Pamela's brother Tony Cundell, a man who had years of experience in dealing with theatres. As soon as he saw the front of house, he demanded that the huge hoardings for the summer show were taken down until after we had left and were replaced by a proper advertisement for *Dad's Army*. It worked but it took time and it was only towards the end of our run in Blackpool that we began to get the audiences that the show deserved.

The second week of the tour was in Nottingham and we arrived on Palm Sunday. The Actors Church Union Chaplain came round to see us on opening night, and did everything he could to make us feel welcome in his town. I was particularly grateful to be given a Palm Cross as I had attended a church that day that did not go in for such things. A good chaplain is a valuable asset to the theatre and can be of great help to a visiting company in all sorts of ways. Besides telling you about the local church services, they can tell you the best places to eat, where to find the cheapest laundry and probably the best pubs.

I was in Nottingham at the beginning of the most important week of the Christian year. John Keble Mill Hill and All Saints' Margaret Street were out of reach. I asked the chaplain what services were available and it was not very promising. Maundy Thursday traditionally has only one Mass and that is celebrated in the evening and we would be performing. It looked as if I could manage something on Good Friday, but the Paschal Vigil with the lighting of the new fire would be on Saturday evening when again we would be performing. I felt very deprived but knew there was little I could do about it.

Bill, a Roman Catholic, suggested that we might go and keep a short watch before the Blessed Sacrament on Maundy Thursday night after the performance, and this we did. Easter Day itself was no problem as there were no performances on Sundays, although we were due to be travelling on to the next date. I got up early and went to the said 8 o'clock at the nearest Anglican church. As I turned the corner I saw masses of yellow daffodils. I might have been deprived of the lighting of the new fire and the other ceremonies attached to the Paschal Vigil, but here was a sign of new life that could become my symbol of the Resurrection for that year, and I was very thankful.

10

THE WRITER'S MUSE

On the tour, many of the company took the easy option of travelling on the company coach. It was quite a sight for the locals to see the bus load or unload their favourite television characters. As many of the cast were not in the first flush of youth, it took some while for everybody to climb aboard, and we were quite often waved off by a collection of little old ladies who had stood for ages watching the whole procedure. Once inside, the coach was very modern and comfortable, and we would all settle down for the long journey. Joan Lowe would play cards around the four-seater table with some of the dancers. Ian would busy himself with the *Times* crossword. Teddy and I would comment on anything and everything. And what of Arthur? The moment he sat down, he fell asleep and he did not wake up until we reached our destination. Once he was off, nothing would rouse him. If the coach had been struck by lightning, he would have slept through it. When it was time to disembark, Joan would give him a gentle shake and after a momentary pause while he wondered where he was and why, he would be fully awake, refreshed and ready for anything.

John Le Mesurier was a past master of vagueness both on and off screen, and one day on the bus he asked Teddy Sinclair and me what we did about our dirty washing. I said I found a laundry and Teddy said he always used a laundrette. John stared at him in disbelief. 'You mean you sit there and watch it going round and round?' he said, shaking his head in amazement.

'So, what do you do, John?', I asked.

'Well,' he confided, 'I just leave the washing lying around and some kind person always does it for me.' Such carefully created helplessness, seemingly so innocent when combined with John's natural charm was, of course, irresistible. Later in the tour John and I were both working on the film *Jabberwocky* and we would be whisked off from Brighton after the evening show, stay overnight in an hotel near Shepperton film studios, shoot some scenes the following day, and be driven back in time for the evening performance of *Dad's Army* on stage. John would stand around on the set, looking rather helpless and would say, 'You know, it would be awfully nice if one could sit down.' People would immediately rush to find him a chair and he would sit back with a grin on his face.

One of the problems when touring is sorting out where you are going to stay. Sometimes digs have been recommended but there are other occasions when you have to take pot luck using the list provided by the theatre. It was in this area that John made two big mistakes. The first was when he booked himself into a temperance hotel. I am not sure that he lasted the week there. On the second occasion, he found himself in a gay hotel. It was certainly not his scene, but it didn't seem to faze him at all. He invited a number of us around to the hotel after the show one night. While we were sitting around having a drink, his wicked sense of humour got the better of him and he suddenly placed his hand on Teddy's knee while gazing soulfully into his eyes. We all began to laugh and in the end even Teddy joined in, but only John could get away with something like that. This wicked sense of humour showed itself again one day when we were out in Bill Pertwee's car. Teddy and I were sitting in the back and John was in the front passenger seat. Suddenly, he wound down the window and started to sing a bawdy parody version of one of the songs from the show. Teddy, ever respectable, spluttered incoherently next to me and then finally came out with, 'Stop it, John. Stop it, you'll get us all arrested!'

It was our days out that cemented what we came to see as the 'unholy trio' of Teddy, Bill and myself. We enjoyed each other's company off stage as well as on. It was a very hot summer, so 'works outings', as we called them, often took the form of outdoor exploration and sightseeing. One day this included the famous Longleat Wildlife Park. I still have cine film of Bill in his car banging on the windscreen in an attempt to stop a baboon ripping the rubber from his wipers. Much to Bill's annoyance, the baboon totally ignored him and began to pull at the washer tubes to try to get some drinking water.

The 8-mm cine camera was a new toy for me. I had bought it so that I would have a permanent record of our life on tour. Naturally, I had consulted Arthur before making the purchase. One always did consult Arthur, somehow, it seemed the natural thing to do. He pondered the matter for a moment and then said, 'Well, if you're going to operate it, Frank, you'd better get something simple. Don't get anything complicated, whatever you do.' It was surprising how well he knew me!

Unfortunately, he did not teach me the virtue of economy when using it. He probably realized I would need to learn this for myself. The first opportunity I had to use the camera was in Blackpool and I filmed its famous tower from every possible angle. I panned slowly up and then I panned slowly down. I took shots from the ground looking at the top and then I took shots from the top looking at the ground. I filmed as we were going up in the lift and I filmed as we came down. If you want to be bored by views of the Blackpool tower, I am your man. Actually, there are some quite good shots taken at the top of Ronnie, Bill and me. The shots of Ronnie and Bill taken by me are rather shaky; those of Bill and me taken by Ronnie are as steady as a rock.

I also took the camera backstage at the theatre, and the footage I took there is probably the only moving record of being backstage with the *Dad's Army* tour that exists. Seen from the wings, there is a snatch of the famous 'banana number' and a view of the cast in the opening of the second half before I had to put the camera down and go on stage myself. A shot of a half-naked Teddy washing his make-up off after the show makes interesting viewing. The shots of the dressing-room drinks for Bill Pertwee's birthday show us all enjoying ourselves. His birthday cake was in the shape of a white ARP helmet, with one solitary candle on the top. It's a silent film, of course, which is probably just as well!

Visits to the coast were a regular feature of our days out. My cine film of the seaside shows Teddy and Bill stripped to the waist, then shows me with shirt firmly in place, sitting elegantly on a rock, gazing at them from beneath my favourite white panama. On an outing to see Hadrian's Wall, Teddy suddenly appeared with a bright yellow hat to protect him from the sun. 'Why did you choose that colour?' I asked. 'Well, the man in the shop said it could be easily seen from a helicopter,' was his reply. 'Why on earth would you want to be seen from a helicopter?' I asked. He gave me one of his looks as if to say that the answer was obvious. Teddy always believed in being prepared for any eventuality.

One Sunday he took me to meet a friend of his and after tea we were both invited to attend a special service for the British Legion in the city's cathedral. The building was packed, and with so many old soldiers attending, the singing was splendid. As we left I was listening to the voluntary and was suddenly stopped in my tracks.

'Did you hear that?' I said to Teddy.

He listened and recognized it too. The organist must have known we were there and kept introducing bits of the *Dad's Army* signature tune into the piece he was playing.

Teddy had been baptized as a baby by a chaplain of the

local Actors Church Union while on tour with his parents. He knew where this had taken place and when we arrived in that particular town, went off and found the entry in the parish records.

When we played a date near Arthur's home village of Mayfield, many of the cast took part in a charity cricket match one Sunday. Afterwards we repaired to the local pub before boarding the coach, with some of us a little worse for wear. It was not far into the journey before a number of people were regretting not having used the pub lavatory before they left. When the situation got desperate they persuaded the coach driver to stop. We were in a small country lane and there was no other traffic about. Gratefully, they all got off the coach and lined up behind it. Arthur waited until they were all in place and then leant out of his seat and told the driver to pull away. Those of us still in the coach scrambled to peer through the back window, and the looks of surprise, dismay and sheer panic were wonderful to behold. Arthur did not even bother to get up and look, he just sat there quietly enjoying the joke.

Sometimes the works outings would take a different form. A lace-making factory was on the agenda one day, and I bought a shawl for Betty. At another famous factory, we learned how toothpaste was put into the metal tubes from the bottom so one could squeeze it out from the other end. Fascinating stuff! In Bath we were invited to lunch by Neville Chamberlain's daughter-in-law. It was a wonderful and very happy occasion. We saw the original table that had been in the Cabinet Office, and the famous umbrella that the Prime Minister had taken with him on his foreign visits.

Bath was our final date and our six-month tour was now drawing to a close. We were due back in the studio for another series of the television programme, but it was sad to say goodbye to those members of the stage cast who would not be involved in that. As the coach deposited us for the last time, outside the Shaftesbury Theatre, where *Liza of Lambeth* was now playing, we looked at the place where the whole thing began. With the run at the Shaftesbury and then the tour, we had been together for a whole year and enjoyed some great times.

Whether in the theatre, studio or on location the social life of the company was always important. We enjoyed being with each other and there were many occasions when we were able to do this. During our times in Thetford, we would be invited to David and Anne Croft's lovely country house, Honiton Hall. It was a great opportunity to relax together, in the company of our very fine hosts. David always made sure he chose an evening when we didn't have an early call the next day! The gatherings on Arthur Lowe's steam yacht *Amazon* were splendid affairs. Arthur was truly proud of his boat, which he had restored, having rescued it from rusting in an old shipyard. We were shown round on many occasions and admired the hours of work Arthur had put in lovingly bringing it back to its former glory.

Arthur always welcomed us aboard with his captain's hat on and made us feel very much at home, while Joan would run around making sure everybody had a drink and something to eat. Perhaps it was a good job the boat was moored, as we might have lost some of the old boys over the side! Arthur's tipple was gin and ginger with a slice of cucumber in it. I was always handed one of these whenever I visited his dressing room after the show, and very quickly acquired the taste.

Dad's Army was eventually adapted for radio by Michael Knowles and Harold Snoad. Michael had appeared in several of the television episodes, and Harold had directed some of them. The recordings were made in front of a live audience at the BBC's Paris Studios in Regent Street or the old Playhouse theatre down on the Embankment. The programmes were very well adapted and even the most visual elements of the television series were somehow conveyed to the listening audience. We would do two, or even three, episodes in each session. Arthur kept a strict eye on the scripts and if there was anything remotely questionable, it had to go. In a scene in which we were putting a fire out by handing buckets of water to each other, Arthur suddenly noticed that I had the line 'Mr Yateman, will you pass water through the window?'

'Oh, no, no, no!' said Arthur. 'That won't do at all. You can't say that, Frank. It will have to be changed.'

And it was.

Working on the *Dad's Army* television and radio series only occupied a small portion of the year and between times I worked fairly solidly in other programmes. I played a number of characters in various episodes of *The Dick Emery Show*. I was also lucky enough to appear in a sketch with the great Morecambe and Wise. In this, I played the proprietor of a healthfood store and stood behind the counter while Eric delivered the wonderful gag lines as only he could. These kept coming in a constant stream whether the camera was watching or not.

Monty Python's Flying Circus was a bizarre experience but great fun. They were an extraordinary group of people. John Cleese, Eric Idle and the others were all tremendously inventive during rehearsals. The sketch in which I was involved was set in a courtroom and as the clerk of the court my main function was to keep asking Michael Palin, playing a policeman giving evidence, to refrain from addressing me as 'Darling'. The jury consisted of the wives and girlfriends of the cast, but for some reason it was decided that they should all be men so they sat there in pinstripe business suits complete with moustaches to add the final touch. At the end of the sketch they decided I should appear as a heavily bandaged policeman. My head was knocked off accidentally and the cast all looked down the hole in my neck to see one of those wonderful animated cartoon sequences for which the programme was so famous. It all seemed quite crazy but there is no doubt that it worked.

Being asked to play Pastor Manders in Ibsen's *Ghosts* at Birmingham Repertory Theatre was a great challenge, but also a great opportunity. I always wanted to be taken seriously, and this was my chance. It was done in the studio theatre. Performing in such close proximity to the audience, one could use a style of acting normally reserved for the intimacy of a television studio. We performed in the round and there were only three or four rows. The people sitting in the front were so close that I could have reached out and touched them. Once on stage, immersed in the character and playing scenes with Mrs Alving, (a brilliant performance from Clare Kelly) it was amazing to find how little I was distracted by the people seated only a couple of feet away. We even survived the evening when a young girl sitting in the front row constantly moved her hand to fiddle with her hair causing the numerous metal bracelets on her arm to jangle loudly. Rehearsals went well and I enjoyed working with the director Robert Knights who helped me find some of the depths of the character and the motivation. By the time we opened, I felt I knew Pastor Manders almost as well as I knew myself. We went for the reality and truth of the play and I think we found it. I had done so much comedy in recent years, and indeed had just finished playing Frank Foster in Alan Ayckbourn's *How the Other Half Loves* in the main house, that I was quite nervous whether I would be accepted in a straight role. In the event, the production was very well received and I got some good notices, one even comparing me favourably with the great Donald Wolfit. Perhaps because it was such a departure from my normal work, I am probably more proud of being part of this production than many of my commercial television roles.

Finding that I was to play a small cameo role in *The Human Factor*, a film directed by the great Otto Preminger, was a challenge of a different sort. I knew he had a reputation for being something of a bully. My fears were made even worse when I received my call for the day's filming. Having told me the time at which the car would arrive to take me to the studio, the assistant added a message from Nicol Williamson with whom I would be playing the scene. He had asked the assistant to tell me that I must not arrive on set without knowing my lines perfectly, or Mr Preminger would go mad. I had learned them, of course, but throughout the evening, I went over them again and again to make doubly sure. When I finally arrived on set, Mr Preminger was in a rage because of some technical problems that had occurred. To relieve his fury, he walked on to the set and kicked a cupboard door. The door broke and everything on top of the cupboard fell off. We all had to wait while the continuity people got the photographs out to match the positions of the ornaments with the previous shot. It made the great man seem a little ridiculous and I found that I was not nearly as worried as I had been.

My scene took place in a Russian apartment in the middle of winter, with snow drifting down artistically outside the window. We filmed it in the middle of an unusually hot British summer and I had the thickest costume I have ever worn. The poor make-up girl spent most of the time wiping the sweat from my brow as the props man dusted artificial snow on to my shoulders. Even the coffee breaks afforded little relief as it was almost as hot outside as it was in the studio. However, I survived and completed the scene without incurring Mr Preminger's wrath.

When I was asked to play the part of a make-up man in the series *Rock Follies* it was my lack of technical ability that let me down once again. I managed the scene perfectly until it came to making up Rula Lenska's lips in bright red gloss. This was a separate close-up shot and was filmed last. The camera was focused on Miss Lenska's face and my hand was to come into shot and apply the lipstick. Simple you would think, but not for Williams. Every time I tried to outline her lips, I made a complete mess of it. After several unsuccessful attempts and the embarrassment of covering half of her face with red blotches they gave up on me. The director decided to use a genuine make-up artist to double for my hand. Unfortunately there was no male available so I watched while the girl who had made me up earlier that day, patiently removed the varnish from her finger nails, donned my jacket and did the take in one.

The film *O Heavenly Dog* was set in London but the star was American. Benji had already become famous with audiences all over the world. The whole film revolved around him. However, there was a problem: he could not come to England for the location shooting as he was a dog and, despite his star status, he would be subject to our strict quarantine laws. The answer, of course, was simple. He could travel to Canada, and Montreal could stand in for London. All the English actors would be absolutely delighted to go out there to work with him.

I had a small part in a short scene with Jane Seymour, one of the human stars of *O Heavenly Dog*. Omar Sharif was also in the film and was staying in the same hotel but I never met him. I waited in my luxurious room for the call, but day after day they were not ready for me and, after a leisurely breakfast, I was free to go sightseeing in the beautiful city of Montreal. When I finally got to the studio and was introduced to Benji, he seemed quite charming and very friendly. I noticed that he tended to tire rather easily and his double would be brought in to do the scene. I think he was a little unwise to allow the understudy to shine so brightly, but I suppose he knew what he was doing. I do not think the film has ever been released in this country but I believe it was quite successful in the States. For me it was one of those actor's perks, a chance to see somewhere new, and of course a chance to work with probably the most famous canine star since Lassie.

Between acting jobs, I continued to write. *No Traveller* at the Gateway, *The TV Murders* and *The Substitute* at Watford had not been masterpieces, but they had demonstrated that I could write dialogue that actors could speak, that I could construct a plot which audiences found interesting and that I had a reasonably good idea of what did and did not work on stage.

Plays by Agatha Christie had for many years been a staple part of the diet in repertory theatres. Actors usually hated them but audiences loved them. I have never really totally understood why performers regard her work with such suspicion. The characters are no more cardboard than in many other commercial plays and, at her best, she is a superb craftswoman. I had played two small roles in *Witness for the Prosecution* at Watford, and it always fascinated me to hear the gasps from the audience at the end of the play as she produces one unexpected twist after another. Whatever else it demonstrates, her popularity with audiences shows that there is nothing they like better than a good thriller. It was said by those who knew about such things that the word 'Murder' in the title was always guaranteed to boost the sale of seats at the box office.

Conscious of this, I embarked on writing *Murder by Appointment*. I wrote in long hand in an exercise book and once I really got going, I found it difficult to put the work aside. As the play progressed, I would sometimes realize that I needed to plant a clue in an earlier scene. I would go back, find an appropriate place and mark it 'insert 1', write the extra dialogue on a small piece of paper and then attach it with a paper clip to the appropriate page. Sometimes a page would have more than one insert and there were scraps of paper with 'insert 2' and 'insert 3' and so on. By the time I got to the end of the script, it seemed that almost every page in the early part had more inserts than original dialogue. As I struggled to decipher my handwriting (my enthusiasm and anxiety to get the words down before I forgot them sometimes made it illegible) I tried to polish it before laboriously turning it into a typescript. When it was finished, I started submitting it to various managements, but with monotonous regularity it came back. In the end it was through a personal contact, a management for whom I was doing pantomime, that I finally achieved some success. They agreed to produce it for a provincial tour. A director was chosen and he and I discussed possible casting with the management. Box-office names were important and it was the fashion to choose actors who were well known on television. This could cause problems as some of them, although excellent on the small screen, were lost when they had to perform in a large theatre. We were lucky enough to get Margaret Ashcroft and Nigel Rathbone. Both of them had been on television recently but they were also highly experienced stage actors.

Some managements and directors feel the author should keep out of the way at rehearsals, but I was very anxious to be there. Once I had made it clear that I did not regard my script as Holy Writ and that I was always happy to make any necessary changes, I think the cast welcomed my presence. They would come over and say that a line was not working and between us we would find something better. Sometimes if a longer sequence was causing problems, I would go away and try to re-write it for rehearsal the next day. It became a truly collaborative effort and I think it worked. The play was a straightforward 'whodunnit' and the plot concerned a murder in which the editor of the local newspaper and his family become involved.

It opened in the lovely theatre at Bury St Edmunds and I stayed with Donald and Violet Smith – he was now an archdeacon in that diocese. Betty came with them to the first night, and they all metaphorically held my hand. In many ways it was a frightening experience. Once the curtain had gone up, there was nothing further I could do; it was now all down to the actors. It was exciting to see Margaret, Nigel and the other members of the cast bring the play to life and to sense for the first time the audience's reaction. It went well and at the end of the performance the producer came over to me and said, 'I think this has real potential and I shall be keeping an eye on it.'

During the tour I occasionally went to see how it was getting on in the different venues. I always enjoyed listening to the audience in the interval as they discussed which of the characters would turn out to be the murderer and I was pleased that they nearly always seemed to get it wrong. On one particular occasion, perhaps fortunately I have forgotten where it was, I watched things go badly awry. In the final moments of the play, Margaret Ashcroft had a long speech to the murderer. He was in the shadows and all the audience should have seen was an unidentifiable figure in a belted mackintosh with his back to the audience. Only at the end of Margaret's speech did we see who this was. On this particular occasion, the lights suddenly came full up. Despite the fact that the actor had his back to the audience and the upturned collar of his mackintosh concealed his face, it was quite clear who it was. Remembering my time doing stage management at the Gateway, I waited for the mistake to be rectified. If the correct lighting could be achieved fairly quickly, perhaps some of the audience might have had insufficient time to make the identification. I waited in vain. Nothing happened. The lights remained obstinately full on for the rest of the performance.

I went round backstage, asked for the stage manager and demanded to know what had happened. He was deeply apologetic but explained that the lighting plot was worked by a computer and for some reason it had jumped a cue and gone straight to the full-stage lighting intended for the curtain call. He also explained that once this had happened, it was well nigh impossible to override it. So even in the theatre, computers can be blamed. Bring back human beings, I say. They are much more reliable.

The tour went well and copies of the notices which I received from the company manager through the post were all good. Of course, if there were any bad notices, he could have kept them from me, but there were enough good ones to show that it was something of a success. My weekly royalties – a percentage based on the box-office takings – suggested that it was also playing to good houses. Sadly, the producer did not keep an eye on the play as he had promised, and as far as I know, did not see the production again after the first night. He was a busy touring producer and once my play had opened, he was on to other things. The cast certainly expected that the tour would be extended and if the producer had really kept his eye on it, I am fairly sure it would have been. As it was, the tour ended once it had completed its original schedule, but I was not too depressed. It had gone well, I had some money in the bank to prove it, I had some good notices and I had enjoyed the experience of seeing my play brought to life.

Samuel French published an acting edition which made the play available for any amateur company who wished to venture their luck with it. I have to be honest and say that although I have received occasional royalties from amateur productions, it has not been popular in that area. Perhaps the fact that there is only one good part for a woman and that the cast requires two young men has not helped. Perhaps some of the content is considered unsuitable. I don't know, but it is still there if anyone wants to do it.

Alibi for Murder was a 'will he get away with it' rather than a 'whodunnit'. We know who the murderer is from the beginning and we watch him arranging an elaborate alibi so that he can kill his wife.

It was a different management who decided to take a risk with this play. Brian Rawlinson, who I had known as an actor, was chosen to direct it. Before rehearsals began we spent many days together at his flat, talking through the script. It was a very stimulating experience. He would question something and I would seek to justify it. We would argue about it in a friendly way, sometimes I would agree to make some changes, sometimes he would agree that I had probably got it right in the first place. It was a very productive time and meant that we went into rehearsals with the script in much better shape than with my previous play. During this time we developed a rapport and came to trust each other, so that he was happy to welcome me to the rehearsals.

The casting of the leading man, the murderer, was crucial to the success of the piece. We discussed several possibilities and eventually came up with Paul Darrow. He had something of a cult following from the successful series *Blake's 7* and he was an experienced stage actor.

Once again the rehearsals were exciting, not only working with the actors but also discussing the set, props, costumes and everything that goes to make a successful production.

Costumes were important as the play was set in 1951, the year of the Festival of Britain, and I was delighted that the young designer, who was certainly not old enough to have been around at that time, seemed to know the period as well as I did.

We opened in Peterborough and I attended the first night with Betty. It went well except for one unwanted laugh. When it came, I was taken aback but the cast carried on as though they had not noticed. Brian and I both agreed afterwards that it was amazing that neither of us had noticed the danger. The young couple were dancing when the sound of a door banging was heard. The sound effect had echoed through the theatre so loudly and clearly that no one could have missed it. 'What was that?' asked the girl. 'I didn't hear anything,' said the boy. The boy was neither deaf nor stupid so the audience found his reaction laughable. The sound effect was removed from that time on, and the problem was solved.

I stayed in Peterborough for the entire week and worked with the cast and director making other changes to improve the script and by the time the play went on to its next date we were all reasonably satisfied with it. Once again it did well and I received a number of good notices from the company manager. This time the management maintained their interest in the play, visiting it in a number of different venues. Well before the tour was due to end, the management said they intended to finish the tour as planned, store the set and costumes, think about some re-casting and then send it out again later in the year with the idea of bringing it into the West End. Sadly, shortly afterwards, they had a couple of disastrous productions which lost a great deal of money and as a result, they went out of business. So the second tour did not take place and *Alibi for Murder* went back on the shelf.

The idea for my next play, *Mask for Murder*, came from reading about a famous Victorian murder case. The play was not an account of the case but it was referred to in the script. Simon Barry, for whom I worked in pantomime, read it and agreed to produce it for a week's try-out. This was one of those occasions when timing did not work. The dates for the production were fixed well in advance, but when they arrived I was away on tour and unable to attend rehearsals or even to see a performance. Simon sent me a spoof photograph showing the entire cast slumped dead over a table with a bottle of poison and the message saying, 'I hope you don't mind, but we have rewritten the ending.'

Simon did several later productions which I was able to see and indeed co-directed with him. In one of these, Bernadette Nolan, one of the famous Nolan Sisters, played the lead. It was the first time she had done a straight play and she gave a great performance, so I was not surprised when I saw her magnificent and deeply moving portrayal in the musical *Blood Brothers*.

People had often asked me why I had never written a part for myself in any of my plays, so I decided that I would try to do so. I wrote *Murder Weekend*, a play in which an eccentric group of people arrive at a country house hotel in order to play a game in which they re-enact a famous murder from the past. For myself, I wrote the most eccentric character of the lot, the one who organizes the event and in the play within the play doubles as the murder victim in the first part and the detective investigating the crime in the second part. If I was going to write something for myself I would make sure I had a chance to demonstrate my versatility!

Simon Barry agreed to give this a try-out as well. He was happy that I would play the lead and he would direct. It would be a return to the past as we would only have one week's rehearsal. It was a long time since I had learnt and rehearsed a play in one week, but remembering my early days I was sure I could still do it. The detective was a bit of a problem. These parts are always difficult to learn as they usually have to lead the dialogue by asking questions. I got round this by jotting the odd line down in my policeman's notebook. There was a slight hiatus one day at rehearsal, when Mark Burgess and I had an attack of the dreaded corpsing virus. I think in this case it was excusable. He produced a photograph album, and showed it to me with the line which identified the murderer, 'I think you'll probably recognize this man.' He opened the album and we both found ourselves gazing at a large picture of a bride in her wedding dress. We dissolved into hysterics and the company had a tea break while we pulled ourselves together. After this, the stage manager ensured that the album only contained suitable photographs and the danger was passed. That first try-out went well with the audience, and Simon revived the play from time to time doing an odd week here and odd week there.

We were doing the play in Horsham and Simon and I were in the same digs, together with the stage manager. One morning at breakfast the landlady arrived with the toast, looking very severe.

'Which one of you three gentlemen had a young lady in his room last night?' she asked, sounding like a headmistress.

We looked at each other in amazement. Then suddenly it dawned. 'I think I might have been the culprit,' I said.

The other two looked even more astonished. After all, I was supposed to be the good churchman.

'She came in, jumped into my suitcase and curled up in the corner,' I explained. 'I did not have the heart to throw her out.'

Yes, you've guessed right. It was the landlady's cat.

Most people seem to think that *Murder Weekend* is the best of my thrillers and I think they are probably right. While at Horsham I sold an option on the play to a new management and had hopes of another commercial tour. They felt, probably rightly, that my name would not be big enough to carry the show and tried to find someone else to play the lead. The reluctance of actors to be away from home for too long and the fear of losing a lucrative television or film part proved to be a real obstacle and they were unable to cast it, so the option lapsed and *Murder Weekend* still awaits a full-scale commercial production.

I have on occasions departed from the murder theme and written more serious plays, but so far I have been unable to interest managements in them. *Two Children on a See-Saw* which I had written for the Good Companions, despite the extra two acts, still languishes on my shelves. *The Boating Lake*, set in 1938, shows an orderly family on a seaside holiday in a world that is about to change for ever. It had a rehearsed reading at the Theatre Museum but went no further. One problem with this might be that I was unwise enough to write two young children into the play and that could create difficulty in casting.

The Playing Fields, set in a minor public school during World War II, examines the way in which two prefects in their last year at school come to terms with their feelings and emotions, knowing that when they leave they will go into the Armed Forces and may have only a short while to live.

My serious plays are all set in a more innocent age and it may be that this is the real problem. Perhaps I am out of tune with modern trends but I would find it difficult to write in any other way.

11

NOTHING LIKE A DAME

When my agent telephoned me to say that I had been asked to audition for a part in the West End, I was thrilled. The play, *Donkey's Years*, had been running for some time and the management was looking for a new cast to take over. I had seen the play, and the part for which I was being considered seemed totally right for me. I arrived for the audition at the appointed time and read a couple of scenes with the assistant stage manager. For once in my life I felt I had not done too badly and returned home quite hopeful that I would be successful in securing the role. When my agent rang me the following day, my hopes were quickly dashed. 'I'm sorry Frank, but you didn't get the part,' she said.

It was Ash Wednesday, the beginning of Lent, and the news added to the sombre character of the day. I was quite prepared to try to be penitential for the next six weeks but this was going too far. I went for a very long walk and tried to bring God into my thoughts. I had sometimes questioned the continued use in church of those psalms in which the psalmist seems to rail against God. Now I understood why they were there. 'What on earth do you think you're doing, God?' I said. 'Don't you realize I was absolutely right for the part, so why didn't I get it?' Not surprisingly, I did not receive an answer.

Looking back, I realise this was actually a case of all things working together for good. Preparations were already being made for the final episodes of *Dad's Army*. It was 1977 and although no official statement was made, when I arrived in the rehearsal room there was a feeling that season nine would be our last. I realized that had I been working in the West End, not only would I have been unable to do the location filming, but also I would probably not have been able to do the final season at all.

While drawing the programme to a satisfactory conclusion the writers did not want to make this series of *Dad's Army* too final. They left it sufficiently open for the series to be revived at a later date. None of us was killed off, nor was the Home Guard to be disbanded. Many of the cast's partners were invited to be in the last episode. Joan Lowe, Marion Pertwee and Althea Ridley were all there as guests at the wedding reception when Corporal Jones and Mrs Fox finally tied the knot. The ceremony itself was not shown but I was there in festive cope ready to perform the marriage even if it did not take place in front of the camera. The final shot in which the platoon toasted all the men of the Home Guard was a poignant moment and a moving tribute to the men of the real *Dad's Army*. It was a mark of the series that *Dad's Army* was able to take an affectionate look at, and pay homage to, the original Home Guard.

Although the programme is a comedy, there is always in the background that underlying determination to win through which was so much a part of the thinking of ordinary people during the war. The characters may be comic but they are also heroic. They care about King and Country, and they really are going to save Britain from the Nazi hordes. Quite often, Captain Mainwaring, in the face of danger and of common sense, behaves with great bravery. He is the one who will do something about an unexploded grenade or will take over when something is about to demolish a power station, for example, even at his own personal risk. All the characters on *Dad's Army* were not cardboard cut-outs, but men with a purpose. There was never anything malicious in the comedy, which is perhaps why it has remained so endearing to viewers of every generation.

When the last episode had been recorded we met for the usual drinks and I think we probably all went off for a meal together. We were sad that such an enjoyable experience had come to an end but we felt it was good to finish while we were still on top. I knew I would miss the friendships which I had made but felt that we would continue to meet socially. This rarely happens at the end of a TV programme but after such a long time together I felt sure *Dad's Army* would be the exception to the rule, and so it was. Over the years we have continued to meet from time to time on various occasions. The continued popularity of the programme has given birth to the '*Dad's Army* Appreciation Society', which does a wonderful job calling the survivors together from time to time.

My introduction to pantomime had been in 1968, the year before my first appearance in *Dad's Army*. It was at the Palace Watford, which had by now become a civic theatre. As such it was concerned that the pantomime should be artistic. It was all very tasteful and not as rumbustuous as commercial productions.

Even the subject was an unusual one. It was *Beauty and the Beast* and I played Beauty's father. My first scene involved rushing on stage to nail a notice to a prop tree. Needless to say, once again my technical inadequacy came to the fore. There was a piece of comedy business in which I was supposed to hit my thumb by mistake. On the first night, I did it for real and spent the whole of the panto season with a black thumbnail.

My first pantomime dame was in *Sleeping Beauty*. It was an interesting production and taught me a lot, although more about pitfalls to be avoided than the positive aspects of the genre. The musical director and the choreographer were both extremely indulgent. The fairy ballet which ended the first half went on for ever. I was playing the Queen, and at each performance I sat on stage with the court around me, all of us asleep while the fairies clomped around. At every performance, we could hear the audience becoming restive. 'Mum, how much longer is this going on?' 'Mum, when can I have an ice cream?' 'Mum, I want to go to the toilet.' Even for small girls with ambitions to be ballerinas, a pantomime ballet can go on for far too long. The star of the show was in a highly popular television series. He was a very good stage performer, but he also got carried away. Every night he came on to tumultuous applause at his first entrance, but by the time he had completed his opening routine which lasted 20 to 25 minutes, he had lost the audience and exited to the sound of his own footsteps.

Meanwhile, I had my own problems. Being a straight actor and completely unversed in the ways of a pantomime dame, I relied totally on the writer and director. I was given a little song to sing, 'I'm a little teapot, short and stout. Here's my handle, here's my spout. When the tea is ready, hear me shout, Tip me up and pour me out.' There were actions to go with this and I was to encourage the children to join in. It was a great success with small children at matinee performances, but not so good in the evenings. My invitation to be a little teapot to an audience consisting of sophisticated 11- to 14-year-olds was greeted with a look of incredulous blank amazement. A presenter from a popular children's television programme who had a spot in which he built a cot for the baby princess did not fare much better. My protest to the director fell on deaf ears. 'Don't worry, Frank, it's fine,' he said. But he did not have to get up and do it every night. It was on New Year's Eve, with a largely adult audience, some of whom were mildly inebriated, that I finally snapped. I knew that in a less polite area or in a previous age, my invitation to be a teapot would have been the cue for a barrage of rotten tomatoes and other missiles. The next day I went to the director and insisted that something had to be done.

Reluctantly, he agreed and the little teapot was consigned to matinees, and Gracie Field's 'Little Bottom Drawer', which I happened to know, was substituted in the evenings.

Playing one of the robbers in *Babes in the Wood* at Richmond was a much happier experience and one from which I learned some positive lessons. The great Arthur Askey was the Dame. At an early rehearsal, Arthur had done his opening routine and the director said, 'Arthur, you've only done seven minutes.'

'I know,' he replied. 'That means when I go off, they will want more.'

How right he was. Every entrance was brilliantly timed and every exit left the audience wanting more. If only our *Sleeping Beauty* star had learned that lesson. Once we opened, Arthur would always spend the interval between the matinee and evening performances having a nap in his dressing room. At that time, I always went out for tea with other members of the cast, but as I have got older, I have found the value of following Arthur's example.

By now *Dad's Army* had become extremely popular on television and my fellow robber in *Babes in the Wood* was Ian Lavender. It was a good script, and for most of it we could invent business without too much trouble. However, the scene in which the two robbers, having abducted the children, quarrel with each other and eventually get into a fight was something of a problem. At this point the script, obviously intended for a double act that had their own routine, said simply 'comedy business for robbers'. It was here that Arthur was a great help to us. Drawing on his years of experience working with some of the great double acts, he suggested all kinds of business we could do. Thanks to him, we had a really good routine and it worked brilliantly every night. That passing on of knowledge to a younger generation is invaluable. It keeps pantomime tradition alive and helps to ensure its continued popularity.

However, almost every pantomime has its problems and this one was no exception. Richmond had originally planned to do *Mother Goose* that year. By the time the decision was made to change the subject to *Babes in the Wood*, the Goose had already been booked. In pantomime, anything goes, so a goose in *Babes in the Wood* should be quite acceptable. After all it was common knowledge that a well-known comic, having had a great success with a sentimental scene in which he sold the cow in *Jack and the Beanstalk*, had demanded that a cow be written into Cinderella the following year.

Ed 'Stewpot' Stewart, who was playing Idle Jack, was, for some reason, not present for the first read through. As we read, every now and then the director would mutter, 'What am I going to do with this goose?' Each time, Arthur Askey would say, 'Well, give him a scene with Stewpot!' Ed, not being able to defend himself, arrived next day to find he had been lumbered with the goose in almost every scene. He soon found that this was no picnic. Geese are very demanding and this one was no exception. She had a routine and it had to be followed and woe betide the poor human being who was acting with her if he got it wrong. We almost pitied Ed as he stood there trying to obey her imperious commands: 'Now, at this point, you walk round me, straighten my hat, and then I lay an egg.'

If a goose falls over, with no arms to help, it cannot get up. It happened one night when it was on stage alone. We stood around in the wings debating which of us would go and get it back on its feet. No one seemed keen and I have a feeling that the faithful Ed was summoned from his dressing room. After all, by now, he understood its funny ways.

Over the years I was to play in many more pantomimes: some large productions, some rather more modest. I did the occasional squire or baron, but soon found that more often than not, I was playing the Dame. One production, by a management who shall remain nameless, had pretensions to being a lavish and spectacular show. Unfortunately, the budget did not match these ambitions and this was reflected not only in the salaries paid to the actors but also in other aspects. I was Sarah the Cook and had some quite good costumes – which they had purchased from a well-known Dame who had his own wardrobe and had recently retired. The one thing that was missing was a wig. I expressed concern about this but was assured something spectacular would be coming from the costume store any day. The opening night was fast approaching and still there was no sign of a wig, spectacular or not. I was now getting really worried.

On my way to rehearsal one day, I saw a wig in the window of an Oxfam shop. For a moment, I toyed with the idea of going in and making a purchase. After all, it would be better than nothing. However, I dismissed the thought, naively trusting that even this management would not allow the Dame to appear without any hair. I carried on with rehearsals and awaited the arrival of the promised wig. It was just before the dress rehearsal that the senior partner of the management himself came into my dressing room. He had a look of triumph on his face. 'You didn't believe me, did you Frank?' he said. 'I told you we had a spectacular wig for you in the store and here it is.' With the air of one displaying the crown jewels, he opened a plastic bag and reverently produced the wig. I recognized it at once. It was the one I had seen in the Oxfam shop window.

One year, not having been offered a big pantomime, I accepted a quite modest production at the theatre in Luton. This had no pretensions to grandeur, the facilities at the venue would not have allowed anything on a big scale, but it was a good workmanlike production and gave good value to the audiences who came to see it. Luton was sufficiently near to allow me to travel from home each day, so I had no expenses living in digs. It was a happy company and I enjoyed the experience. When it was over, I thought no more about it.

Some years later, I found myself without a pantomime at all. Knowing that most shows would now be fully cast, I had more or less resigned myself to being out of work over Christmas, when someone showed me a leaflet for the pantomime in which they were appearing. The name of the management was not familiar and I rang my agent to ask if she had approached them. She had not but said she would do so straightaway. Her phone call was answered by Simon Barry who had directed me at Luton. The Dame at the Theatre Royal Hanley was still uncast and I found myself playing Widow Twankey. It was the start of 12 happy years working for the same management. Widow Twankey was followed by even more dames. Having mounted a pantomime, New Pantomime Productions tend to repeat it over a number of years moving it to a different venue. Working with the same nucleus of people for several seasons creates a real company feeling, and as we meet for rehearsals each year, we know how the chemistry between us works. It makes for a good production and also a happy one.

There are those who deplore the use of Australian soap stars in pantomime, but they are good for the box office and if they can turn in a good performance on stage, I see no problem. Ian Williams from *Neighbours* had a great stage presence and all the girls swooned over him as Prince Charming. Lynne McGranger from *Home and Away* is a real ball of fire and would be a great asset to any pantomime even if she were not a star.

Another controversial practice is the use of sports stars, presenters and other celebrities in pantomime. Once again, if they can turn in a good performance, I have no objection. In recent years, stars from *Gladiators* have been making regular pantomime appearances. Clearly some of them can do little more than stand centre stage and look good. However, recently I have worked with James Crossley (Hunter) who certainly does know what he is doing on stage and was a splendid Prince Charming in *Snow White and the Seven Dwarfs* over a number of years. As Sarah the Cook, determined to get a man, I flirted with him outrageously. One night – I think we were in York – I rushed at him with perhaps more than my usual vigour and flung my arms around him. We both lost our balance and landed on the floor. My wig and my glasses flew off and the two other characters on stage dissolved into hysterics. The audience thought it was hilarious and a few people even cheered. Someone gave me my glasses, and James rescued my wig. My attempt to put it on without the aid of a mirror resulted in its being back to front, which set everyone off again. When eventually I got it right and order was restored we all attempted the song with which we usually made our exit. James and I were more or less all right at first, but we had not seen the vision of six foot of Gladiator entangled with a bald man in a long yellow dress trying to maintain a semblance of dignity. The other two could not get a single line out, and soon their hysteria spread to us and by the end none of us was singing. We staggered off stage, still completely helpless, and we got the biggest exit round we had ever had. We were almost tempted to keep the routine in.

The Christmas following the final series of *Dad's Army*, Teddy and I had been booked to play Ugly Sisters in *Cinderella*. The production had been at the London Palladium the previous year with Brian Murphy and Yootha Joyce playing our parts, and we were to take the production to the Birmingham Hippodrome. We were both looking forward to it and we spent quite a lot of time together talking about the various bits of businesses we could get up to. It would be a wonderful extension of the partnership – the vicar and the verger being nasty to Cinderella instead of Captain Mainwaring!

I was at home when I got a telephone call from Teddy's son to say that he had suffered a sudden heart attack and had died. 'I'm ringing you because I didn't want you to switch on the television and hear the news,' he said. I was stunned. It just did not seem possible. I replaced the receiver and sat down to collect my thoughts. When I recovered from the shock, I rang Betty, I was still feeling numb. She was as shocked as I was.

As Teddy had been baptized by an Actors Church Union chaplain it was appropriate that his funeral should be taken by one of the ACU's senior chaplains. After talking to Teddy's wife Gladys, it was arranged that Father Michael Hurst-Bannister would take the funeral. He was chaplain to several West End Theatres and he was a familiar figure backstage going round the various dressing rooms.

All the members of the *Dad's Army* cast were there, including Arthur who gave the address. He referred to the great friendship that Teddy and I had enjoyed together, and commented how much this had spilled over into the series. At the end, he said, 'With the loss of Teddy, it is now quite clear that there will be no more *Dad's Army*.' It was not really news to any of us, but hearing Arthur say it so directly made it seem final. He was right of course. Teddy was a unique person, a brilliant character actor who had made the part of the Verger so much his own. He would have been totally irreplaceable, and so his death seemed to mark the end of an era.

With Teddy now gone, I was unsure what was going to happen to the pantomime. I was still contracted to appear as an Ugly Sister, and my agent confirmed that they still wanted me and were looking for a new partner. They suggested Tony Bateman. I did not know him, but I learned that he had done a lot of work at the famous Players Theatre. We met for the first time over lunch in a pub, and seemed to get on quite well together. Rehearsals were due to start within a few weeks and we both agreed to go for it.

Before I could start thinking about pantomime properly, I had another engagement to fulfil with the English Theatre in Vienna. I was to play a cameo part in *Otherwise Engaged*. I had seen the play in the West End and thought it was a very fine piece of work. Understandably, *Dad's Army* had not been seen in Austria, so they had no preconceived ideas about me and would be prepared to take me seriously. The leading role was played by David Cameron, an English actor who had lived in Vienna for many years. He had been married to the film actress Hildegard Knef but they were now separated. The rehearsals in London went well and after three weeks we set off by boat and train to Vienna. Our company manager who had done many other plays out there roused us early in the morning so that we could see the great monastery at Melk from the train window. We all grumbled a bit, but I have to say it was worth it.

We found that the theatre was a small but beautiful building in the Josefsgasse, a side street off the main ring road around the city. I fell in love with Vienna and the whole thing was a wonderful experience. I would have not been able to do it if I had got the part in the play in the West End. For me it really was a case of all things working together for good and I had to admit that God had managed to get it right after all!

At the end of the play I had a long speech off-stage which consisted of a telephone message heard on the answerphone. I say that I have a gun in my mouth, and am about to commit suicide. I am not quite sure why, but I did it live every night. It is a powerful speech and I found it emotionally draining, and it always took me a few moments to get back to normal at the end of it.

As an instinctive actor, rather than a technical one, I try to get inside the character and actually feel the emotions which I am trying to express.

I was to do two other plays in Vienna: *Stage Struck*, also by Simon Gray, and Terence Rattigan's *The Winslow Boy*, in which I played the father. In the first of these I had another quite long and hysterical speech, on stage this time. In *The Winslow Boy*, when the father's campaign to win justice for his son is finally successful it is clearly an emotional moment.

So my memories of Vienna always include those times in the dressing room in which I got myself back to some semblance of normality before going on stage for the curtain call.

When one member of the cast of *Otherwise Engaged* was reading my biography in the programme, he came up to say how delighted he was to be working with another churchgoer. Nicholas Courtney is best known for his appearances as the Brigadier in the BBC's *Dr Who,* and that first play in Vienna began a friendship with him that has lasted to this day.

Apart from all the usual sightseeing, Nicholas and I did the local church-hunt together. Although I am an Anglican and he is a member of the United Reform Church, we both became good Roman Catholics in Vienna. Most Sundays we went to the Augustinekirche, and the worship was enhanced by the marvellous music there. On some occasions other members of the cast joined us to experience it. Mozart, Haydn, Schubert. I was used to hearing them at Margaret Street but in this vast church with the orchestra and a choir drawn largely from those who normally sang at the Opera House, the experience was stunning. Of course the services were in German, but it really did not seem to matter. The drama of the liturgy transcends language and even when one does not understand the words it is perfectly clear what is going on. When the priest holds up the Host, you know that God is there and language is totally irrelevant. After a time, I found that by listening to the inflections, I could even make good guesses at the readings. I listened to the Gospel one day and I thought I recognized it. Thomas was putting his fingers on the crucified hands of the risen Christ and saying 'My Lord and my God.' When I got back to my hotel room, I checked up the reference, and sure enough, it was right. I would not want to deny the importance of preaching but I really do believe that we also need to recognize that the liturgy can speak for itself. I was amazed one day in Vienna when the priest came in to celebrate Mass, and apologized profusely that he did not speak German so the service would have to be in English. I did not have to guess at the readings on that occasion!

The passing of the peace during Mass has now become an integral part of the service. The priest says 'The Peace of the Lord be always with you', and we reply, 'And also with you.' Then he invites us to offer one another a sign of peace and we turn to greet our neighbour. There are still some people who dislike the practice. Donald Smith, when he was visiting a church as Archdeacon, would usually go down and give the peace to those in the front row. On one occasion he was confronted by a woman who said pointedly, 'No, thank you. I don't take it.' For me, it is a meaningful action emphasizing that we are members one of another, and that it is the Lord's peace that we are sharing. If you are a stranger in the church, it is a form of welcome and makes it clear that you belong. When I was in Vienna, at this point someone would greet me in German and I would reply in English. We both knew what the moment meant and it gave us a sense of one-ness with each other. I do not like those churches where the whole thing goes on for hours while everyone mills around exchanging the latest gossip, creating a fair imitation of Waterloo station in the rush hour. Fortunately, they are few and far between.

On that first visit to Vienna, Nicholas and I visited the art galleries, the palaces and the churches. We went to the cinemas and it was fascinating to see an American film with German subtitles. A long line of dialogue was often translated by a single word. A character would be asked if he was going out that night and reply, 'I've got a lot of work to do so I think I'll stay in.' At the bottom of the screen would appear, 'Nein.'

We had the usual company outings and we walked in the Vienna woods. We were entertained royally by Counts and Countesses. We all went to the Opera and to the Spanish Riding School. Taking a break from the Augustinekirche one Sunday, we went to hear Mass sung by the Vienna Boys' Choir in the chapel of the Hofburg Palace. Wonderful stuff.

Then there were the cakes. I found the famous sachertorte a bit dry, but there were so many other wonderful confections. Each day I would visit a patisserie to sample a new one. By coincidence our company manager, James Gill was also to be company manager for *Cinderella* in Birmingham. Before leaving I had costume fittings for the pantomime and James said to me one day, 'I've just sent a telegram to the panto management telling them that I can't keep you off the cream cakes, so they had better let all your costumes out by at least three inches.' The costume fittings had been quite an experience. For some reason it had not occurred to anyone that the costumes made for the slim Yootha Joyce would not even go on, let alone meet anywhere, so the first session was something of a disaster. After that, however, all was great efficiency. I stood for hours while crinolines, riding habits and ballgowns were fitted. It was my first experience of a really major pantomime and I was very impressed by the attention to detail and the final result was certainly worth all the effort.

The cast of *Otherwise Engaged* was to return from Vienna by boat and train the day after the final performance. I had to be back for pantomime rehearsals in London, so having enjoyed the last night party, I went straight to the airport and flew home. The following morning I set off for rehearsals. Once again I was impressed by the organization of it all. We were rehearsing in one place, the dancers and chorus in another, there was a room where we could go through numbers with the musical director and when necessary we were whisked off for final costume fittings.

We arrived in Birmingham and began rehearsing on stage. Tony Bateman and I got on and we seemed to work well together. I was the dominant sister and he was the weak one who always follows my lead in being nasty to Cinderella.

In the final scene, I had a line, 'I'm so ashamed I could sink through the floor.' The stage direction then said, 'She disappears through the trap'. I suggested that it would be more in character for Tony to say it and anyway the crinoline I was wearing would be far too wide to go through the trap, and that Tony who was wearing a slim fitting skirt would do it much more easily. He was not deceived by my arguments, but he was a good-natured man and agreed to do the disappearing trick, so my well-known inability to deal with all things technical was not put to the test.

I found I enjoyed playing Ugly Sister much more than a straightforward Dame. I am not a natural solo performer and always having someone with me was a great support. As Tony said when we were doing a radio interview together, 'You're never alone with an Ugly Sister.' Richard O'Sullivan played Buttons to Tessa Wyatt's Cinderella. They were both big stars from the television series *Robin's Nest* and were a big box office draw. After the show one afternoon I was in my dressing room when I heard Tessa take her small child to see Tony Bateman in the dressing room next door in order to meet one of the Ugly Sisters.

'Would you like to meet the other Ugly Sister now?' she said to him afterwards outside my room.

'No I would not!' he said emphatically. He obviously did not want anything to do with two people who had spent the last couple of hours being absolutely horrid to his mother. I always think it must be rather disconcerting for a small child to meet the Dame after the show. It is particularly worrying if the actor appears to be half and half – still wearing his bosom but suddenly having no hair. I always try to ensure that I am one thing or the other, wearing the lot or in a dressing gown with wig, bosom and costume all safely stowed away.

The following year we took the production to Bristol with Harry Worth in the lead. This was a bit of a problem as Buttons and Cinderella make natural leading characters, but Baron Hardup is normally quite a small part. Harry's script had to be developed beyond the natural storyline and it did not quite work despite Harry's great talent.

We went to a radio interview together. It was an early morning programme transmitted live from Cardiff and we were picked up from our hotels by the BBC driver very early. We both fell asleep in the car and I awoke to hear Harry say, 'I do like the civic buildings in Cardiff.' I agreed that they were indeed very elegant and then suddenly wondered why I was seeing them. I knew we should have turned off the motorway before we actually got into the city. I mentioned this to the driver and it became quite clear that he was hopelessly lost. The car radio was playing and we heard our programme begin. Wyn Calvin told the listening audience that he would be talking to us later in the show. He managed to sound quite confident. The driver stopped the car, went into a shop to ask for directions and a moment later we were speeding back the way we had just come. When we arrived, the studio manager greeted us with open arms. The other pantomime guest who was expected had not arrived either and was delayed in traffic. We were rushed into the studio and the look of relief on Wyn's face was wonderful to behold. The other star did not manage to make it at all, so we had a much longer interview than expected and got some very good publicity for the Bristol pantomime.

Teddy Sinclair's passing was soon to be followed by the death of other members of *Dad's Army*. Arnold Ridley's funeral was at his local church in Highgate, where he and his wife Althea had been regular worshippers. John Laurie had a memorial service at the Actors Church of St Paul, Covent Garden. They were both in their eighties when they died, but the loss of John Le Mesurier and Arthur Lowe who were still comparatively young came as a great shock. When the series was over Arthur Lowe and his wife, Joan, did a number of provincial tours of popular plays. The fame of Captain Mainwaring meant that he was a good box office draw and they were all very successful. Pamela Cundell, Betty and I managed to see most of these productions when they were at a theatre near London. We would go out to dinner with Arthur and Joan afterwards. As I reached for my notecase at the end of the meal Arthur would wave it aside. 'No no, I've just done a rather nice little voiceover. It's on me tonight.' He was a most kind and generous man. He clearly enjoyed the opportunity to work with Joan and they even went on a tour of New Zealand where the programme was very popular and they received a wonderful reception wherever they appeared. It was on one of these tours that, while appearing in Birmingham, Arthur suddenly died in his dressing room. It was completely un-expected and we were all shocked. The memorial service was held at St Martin-in-the-Fields and the church was packed. I realized that although Captain Mainwaring had been an important part of his life there had been so much else. He was a wonderfully talented actor, not only in comedy but also in serious roles.

Memorial services are rarely gloomy and sombre affairs. People have gathered to give thanks for, and to celebrate, a life. At Arthur's service someone suggested that he was probably in heaven complaining about the fact that his kippers were overcooked and that the toast was too crispy just as he always did at The Bell Hotel. Well, why not?

John Le Mesurier had been unwell during the recording of the last series and when it was shown a number of people remarked on how ill he looked. When he died, it was typical of him to have arranged that the notice in the *Times* should say that he had 'conked out'. One of the last things he uttered summed his life up beautifully. Apparently he turned to his wife Joan and said, 'You know, it's all been rather lovely.'

12

THE EPISCOPAL BENCH

Now that *Dad's Army* was well and truly in the past, I turned to the theatre once more.

For many years I had enjoyed seeing the plays of William Douglas Home and had directed an amateur production of one of them, *Master of Arts* for the Good Companions. So I was delighted to be offered the chance to appear in a production of his new play *The Editor Regrets*. I had worked with Anthony Roye in the past, and he had apparently been responsible for a number of try-out productions of some of William Douglas Home's earlier successes. In this new play, Anthony was not only producing it but was also going to play the lead. The production was presented at the charming little Kenton Theatre in Henley-on-Thames. Following rehearsals, we played for two and a half weeks; when it was over, we all waited to see what, if anything, would happen.

A few weeks later we were summoned to rehearse for a short four-week tour. There had been some cast changes, but the script, which had worked well at Kenton, remained basically the same. We played four extremely pleasant dates: Eastbourne, Brighton, Bournemouth and Bath. It was during the run at Eastbourne that Anthony Roye was told he would have to go into hospital. The author, who had been an actor in his youth, agreed to take over the leading part, but there was a problem. He was no longer a member of Equity and in those days of the closed shop, only members were allowed to perform in a professional production. I had been elected the

Equity deputy, the one who has to liaise with the union if there are any problems. I contacted them and after a number of phone calls, they tracked down William's original membership and agreed to renew it, so all was well. He played it with an effortless charm which made you wonder why he had given up being an actor. While he was with us, he had a horse running in the Derby. The racing correspondents clearly did not think much of the animal and one or two even questioned whether it should be in the race at all. However, the whole company decided to have an outing to Epsom and we all loyally put a bet on William's horse. It did not win, so we all lost, but we were pleased that it did not disgrace itself either as the pundits had predicted. Those who were natural gamblers bet on other races and some of them actually managed to find some winners. The rest of us just relaxed and had an enjoyable day's outing.

Another highlight of this short tour was lunch at Arundel Castle with the Duke of Norfolk, whose daughter Marsha Fitzalan was in the cast. Betty was down on a visit and was invited to join the lunch party. She was staying with Anna Turner who had a house in Worthing, and when Anna heard where Betty was going, she insisted that Betty took a hat with her as Anna felt it might be one of those occasions where all the ladies wore them. It was not and the hat remained neatly rolled up in Betty's pocket.

In Bournemouth, we all went to one of Mrs Yorke-Batley's tea parties. This splendid lady was the widow of an Actors Church Union chaplain and her tea parties were famous throughout the profession. They had started when her husband was alive. He had come home one day after visiting the theatre and told her that he had invited the entire cast of the play for tea. She provided boiled eggs for everyone as well as the usual tea-time fare. On that first occasion, she learned that the food was really important. In those days members of the chorus were very poorly paid and she realized that her tea party was probably the best meal some of them would get in the entire week. Thereafter, these events became an institution and after her husband's death she carried on with the tradition. Every company visiting Bournemouth was invited. This was my second visit, as the *Dad's Army* cast had all been there when we were touring. In the summer you played croquet on the lawn, and in winter you sat around the fire in the drawing room and played a card game called, I believe, 'Oh Hell'. As both my visits were in summer I never experienced the latter. Mrs Yorke-Batley had mountains of photograph albums dating back over the years showing all the many people who had been there and her housekeeper told us that she had now lost count of how many thousands of eggs she had cooked in that time.

At the end of the short tour, we all dispersed once again, but a few weeks later we were summoned once more. This time we would do a five-week run at the Greenwich Theatre. Again there was quite a bit of recasting. Anthony Roye was now back in harness in the leading role but Marsha Fitzalan who had moved on to something else was replaced by David Croft's daughter Penny. When we went our separate ways at the end of our time in Greenwich, we all wondered if there would be another call to present the play somewhere else but it never came. There were a few enquiries at one point when it seemed that a West End management was interested but it did not come to anything. I was not too disappointed. With rehearsals of the different companies, the two-and-a-half-week try-out had ended by providing what amounted to several months' work in total. I had created a role in a new play, worked with very pleasant people and thoroughly enjoyed myself.

Soon television beckoned once more. Working with Jimmy Tarbuck gave me the opportunity to experience a revue type show. *It's Tarbuck!* consisted of sketches in which I played a variety of different parts. There were some regular characters as well as Jimmy himself but at other times we fitted into a sketch playing anything that came along. The other members of the cast included Kenny Lynch, Josephine Tewson and Hugh Paddick. The atmosphere was very relaxed and rehearsals were enormously enjoyable. In one sketch neither Hugh nor I could get to terms with the character we were supposed to play, so we asked the director if we could swap roles; he agreed and it worked perfectly. There were musical items in each show and sometimes I even got to sing with the others. I have a feeling that on one programme we found ourselves singing with the great Tom Jones.

Jimmy is a very relaxed performer and enjoys practical jokes. He decided to try to make me corpse one day by placing a rude picture in the bottom of a box that I had to open. I found to my surprise that it had no effect on me. When I caught Jimmy's eye, he started to go instead. I have a feeling that it probably never works if you deliberately try to make someone corpse. There is a story that a company once tried to make the great actress Yvonne Arnaud corpse by placing fruit salts, a substance that would fizz, in the bowl from which she was going to put sugar in her coffee. When it frothed, they were all waiting for her to start laughing, but she simply turned and said 'Tonight the coffee is espresso.'

Meanwhile my television career was advancing apace, and I was summoned to Scotland. On the way to the hotel I learnt from my taxi driver that *Grey Granite*, which we were filming, was considered to be a modern Scottish classic. I was one of the boarders in an Aberdeen lodging house and rejoiced in the name of George Piddle. The book had been adapted into four episodes and although the theme was a deeply serious one, and the story very moving, my character of a local newspaper reporter brought some light relief. I rode a bicycle, my mackintosh billowing behind me in the wind; I got drunk and was mixed up in a riot, hiding behind a cart while all hell broke loose around me. So, the Scottish classic turned out to be quite a lot of fun as far as I was concerned. As we were not residents of the city the director said that I did not necessarily have to have a Scottish accent, but suggested I tried doing one at rehearsal. I enjoy trying to use different dialects and I assumed a refined Edinburgh tone in rehearsal and he seemed very happy with it. There were several breaks in filming when I returned home for a few days and got myself into something of a panic when I found my carefully cultivated accent seemed to have disappeared. Fortunately it always returned once I crossed back over the border.

In 1983 I found myself appearing each night at the London Palladium. I was not actually in *Singing in the Rain* but featured in a filmed insert as a slightly eccentric character explaining how moving pictures worked. The scene was filmed one cold morning and directed by the star of the show, Tommy Steele. I was a little miffed that I was only paid for the one morning's filming and received no royalties, especially as the sequence was used throughout the long run and in the subsequent tour. I recently met someone who said that he had appeared with this piece of film every night and sometimes had to paraphrase my dialogue. When the projector broke down he had to explain to the audience what the missing piece of film would have said. However, it was no longer my problem, especially as I was not being paid for it. I needed to move on.

My career was beginning to drag its feet a bit, and I wondered if a change of image would be helpful, and so I decided to grow a beard. It was a very splendid beard and made me look like an Old Testament prophet, so I rather hoped that I might be whisked off to some exotic location as part of a biblical epic. However, it only got me as far as Jersey. I went to have lunch with Nicholas Courtney who was working at the BBC and he introduced me to the director of the programme on which he was working. Two or three weeks later my agent received a call.

'Has Frank still got that beard?' he enquired.

She reassured him that I had.

'In that case,' he said, 'I'd like him for an episode of *Bergerac*.'

When I got the script, there seemed no reason why the character could not have been clean-shaven. Clearly the director liked the beard and realized that if he wanted it, he had to have me as well. So growing it had got me at least one job. Now that it had served its purpose, I decided to get rid of it. It made me look older than Methuselah and I was still comparatively young. In any case, I was just about to play a Dame and bearded ladies may be fine in the circus but are not acceptable in pantomime. Hastings was the venue this year, and I was Sarah the Cook in *Dick Whittington*. I was just about to have my customary nap between the matinee and evening performances, when there was a knock at the dressing-room door. I opened it and there stood Nicholas Courtney. He explained that he was staying with friends, had seen my name outside the theatre and decided to pop in for a chat. It is always good to see Nicholas and I was happy to postpone my proposed nap. During the course of conversation, he mentioned the Equity Council and asked if I had ever thought about standing for election. I had to admit that apart from attending the Annual General Meeting I had taken little interest in the affairs of the union. He suggested that perhaps I ought to think about becoming more involved, and I promised to do so.

Equity, the actors' trade union, was founded in the early 1930s by some of the leading players of the day. They realized that the conditions under which most ordinary actors worked were far from satisfactory. Those who were not star names could easily be exploited, particularly if they were young and inexperienced. The stars met together and decided that performers should have a union. They were able to use their influence to ensure that West End managements had to take the idea seriously, and so the British Actors Equity Association was born. Since then it has become a powerful force in negotiating contracts not only for the theatre but also in television, radio, films and many other areas. Working conditions and rates of pay have been established in contracts, the terms of which have been agreed between Equity and the various management organizations. The Council is the governing body of the union and is elected by a vote of the whole membership. It debates a wide range of subjects concerning things that affect an actor's life.

I had always stood on the sidelines, happily accepting the improvements in the terms of employment which Equity had negotiated. I had never become really involved. As I thought about what Nicholas had suggested, I realized that I probably needed to change my attitude, so when I returned from pantomime I contacted him and agreed to stand for election. I was somewhat surprised to find that I got sufficient votes to become a member of the Council and I have been there more or less ever since. I was unable to be there at the beginning of my first Equity Council meeting as I was filming a sketch for *The Two Ronnies*. I was playing a wig-maker who had created a hairpiece for Ronnie Barker which the script demanded should blow away in a gust of wind. The enormous fan normally used to create hurricane conditions failed to dislodge it, and I was interested to see how eager Ronnie Barker was to offer alternative suggestions. In the end we resorted to the old device of an invisible thread attached to the back of the wig and on cue it disappeared from the top of his head as if by magic. The studio car drove me back to Harley Street where Equity had its headquarters and I arrived at the morning coffee break in time to be introduced to my fellow councillors.

It was through my membership of the Council of Equity that I was invited to be on the panel for the Olivier Awards. The panel is made up of members of the public, together with some representatives of the theatrical profession. As an avid theatre-goer, I enjoyed the prospect of having two of the best seats free for every new production in the West End as well as those taking place at the Barbican and the National Theatre.

Betty usually accompanied me on these occasions, and we enjoyed most of the productions we saw. I found that we often had a rewarding evening when we went to see a play that normally I would not have touched with a bargepole. There were times when Betty declined the offer of a free seat if the play was obviously not going to be her cup of tea. I usually found someone else on these occasions but there were times when I had to go on my own. No one seemed to want to see a five-hour play in the Pit at the Barbican and I sat there on my own watching the audience diminish every time there was an interval, but feeling I had to stay in case there was a stunning performance right in the last act.

At the end of each year the panel would meet and we would conduct a secret ballot for the various categories. Only the chairman knew the result of this and when Betty and I attended the awards ceremony the winners sometimes came as a surprise to me. It was a satisfying experience to see some great performances honoured in this way.

Whether it was my debating skills on the Council or for some other reason, I was now called to appear in the High Court of Parliament. In Granada's serialization of *First Among Equals* I became the speaker of the House of Commons. My script was largely ad-libbed and I had a wonderful time shouting 'Order! Order!' It gave me a real sense of power to call the Prime Minister to speak and then sternly quell the riot and the clamour that greeted Mrs Thatcher's words.

While all this was going on, my career acting as a clergyman was far from over. I found that, like many vicars, I had to serve in a number of other parishes before I could hope for preferment. After serving my time during the war at Walmington-on-Sea, I had clearly moved to a parish near the famous *Hi-de-Hi!* holiday camp and it was there that I was called upon to marry the lovely Gladys Pugh (Ruth Madoc) to her man.

Here, the hilarity was in the difficulty of getting the previous group of people out of the church before the *Hi-de-Hi!* wedding party came in. It was complete bedlam, although I was assisted by my verger, played by Colin Bean who had been Private Sponge in a number of the *Dad's Army* episodes. The producers wanted to keep the wedding a secret until the episode was shown, but news that we were filming something important had got out and there were reporters behind every tree around the church in which we were shooting the scene. I was smuggled in with my dog collar duly hidden and Ruth Madoc's wedding outfit was concealed under a coat. We all refused to satisfy the reporters' curiosity about what was going on inside the building and I think the secret was successfully kept.

The vicar had some more parish work to do before he could move on and I appeared as an elegantly bearded clergyman with the wonderful Thora Hird in *Hallelujah!*, the Yorkshire television comedy about the Salvation Army. I had one more posting as a vicar in an episode of the children's series *Bad Boyes*, but after that came the preferment for which I had waited so long. I became an Archdeacon, delivering one of the final speeches in the last episode of the television adaptation of *Vanity Fair*. It was filmed in the small seaside town of Sidmouth which had been miraculously transformed into the correct era. Artificial cobblestones covered the modern roads and pavements, families in colourful dress clustered around the Punch and Judy show on the sands and children bowled their hoops along the promenade. I was very impressed that all the background artists were professionals. The BBC had cast the net far and wide in order to give the work to proper performers and some had travelled long distances to appear. I spent most of the day enjoying the sunshine and it was getting towards evening when, in an elegant drawing-room, I delivered my speech extolling the virtues of Becky Sharp. As I did so, I reflected that my days as a vicar were now over. I had taken a step up the ladder of ecclesiastical hierarchy and who could tell where it might lead. From serving as an archdeacon, clearly the next step had to be into the episcopate. Finally the call I had been waiting for came from my good friends David and Jimmy. They had seen the inevitability of the progression and had made me a bishop, in the series *You Rang, M'Lord?*.

Mary Husband, the costume designer whom I had known from *Dad's Army* days, met me in Whippell's, the famous ecclesiastical outfitters who supply real clergy with everything from cassocks to cloaks as well as all the vestments worn in church. I had a wonderful time trying on various items, and although it was not needed in the first series, I persuaded them to let me try a mitre just in case it was required in the future. I was given a splendid episcopal ring and a large pectoral cross and left the shop feeling quite ready to assume my role as a dignified but kindly prince of the Church.

You Rang, M'Lord? could be seen as a comedy version of the popular *Upstairs Downstairs*. Many old friends were in the cast: Michael Knowles, Donald Hewlett, Catherine Rabett and Susie Brann were the family upstairs; Mavis Pugh, who as well as being in episodes of *Dad's Army* had been in my *TV Murders* at Watford, played the wonderfully dotty aunt who had eccentric conversations with a parrot in her bedroom; downstairs, the kitchen was presided over by the cook, Mrs Lipton, played by Brenda Cowling (who had been the farmer's widow in the *Dad's Army* episode 'All is Safely Gathered In'); Paul Shane and Jeffrey Holland were the male servants; the splendid Barbara New appeared as the downtrodden char; and my good friend Bill Pertwee as PC Wilson popped into the kitchen from time to time to pay court to Mrs Lipton.

Then there was the unbelievable Su Pollard. Her larger-than-life personality made rehearsals enormously enjoyable. If you were sitting in the BBC canteen with your back to the door, you would always know when Su entered because there would be a sudden outburst of noise. Everyone was always delighted to see her and called out greetings. Her flamboyant dress style suits her down to the ground and she has a lovely spontaneous sense of humour. At the party following the end of one series, she suddenly jumped on a chair, gave a piercing whistle to silence everyone and said, 'Listen everybody, I've got an announcement. Frank and Betty are going to elope tonight and they are off to the Caribbean.' Everyone laughed including Betty, and Su came over to make sure Betty had not minded the joke. 'I get a bit carried away sometimes,' said Su. When Betty assured her that she had found it hilarious, Su suddenly said, 'Mind you, it's not a bad idea. Why don't you elope, you could be back in plenty of time for the next lot of filming?'

The programme ran to four series and I had a great time. I got to sing 'The foggy foggy dew' in the drawing room. I got to ride in a two-seater aeroplane with Catherine Rabett. I preached a splendid sermon which Jimmy and David had written for me and I appeared in cope and mitre in order to perform the wedding ceremony for Mrs Lipton when she finally married her policeman. I believe the series was much underrated. The fact that the episodes were longer than the usual half-hour normally allowed for situation comedy may have had something to do with it, but I felt Jimmy and David created a wonderful set of characters that were absolutely true to the period.

Now that I had reached the episcopal bench, perhaps my ecclesiastical career had gone as far as possible? Or had it? I was at a party to celebrate the sixtieth birthday of George Austin, then Archdeacon of York. He told me that he saw two of his guests pointing at me and heard one say, 'I'm sure I know that man over there.'

'Of course you do,' replied her friend. 'His photograph is always in the papers. It's the Archbishop of Canterbury.'

So perhaps I could go one step higher. Who knows?

Promotion came in another area when I found myself back in army uniform in two television plays for the acclaimed director, Moira Armstrong. I was no longer a captain; I had now reached the rank of Major. In *How Many Miles to Babylon?* I had one small cameo scene. This very moving play was filmed in Ireland and the period was World War I. This was one of those occasions when the weather decided that I should have a double contract. I arrived in brilliant sunshine but when next day we were due to film my scene, the heavens opened and as it had to match a previous shot, we were not able to do it. The weather conditions continued for several days and the worried production manager asked if I could stay on beyond my contracted time. As this meant a second contract, and a second payment, I happily assured him that I could.

My second play for Moira, *The Mountain and the Mole Hill*, was set in World War II, and although I was playing a schoolmaster this time I was still in uniform as the master ran the school cadet corps. As I strode through the woods commanding my troops with thunder flashes exploding all around me I was taken back to my experience of field days at Ardingly.

Another scene did not bring back memories of my own time at school. I was teaching the boys to waltz, and being an all-male establishment, they had to dance with each other. This was something that had certainly not been on the curriculum at Ardingly. We were filming at a real school which in these modern days had become co-educational. The boys were acting as extras and the girls were watching out of shot from a gallery above the hall floor. They found it difficult to suppress their giggles as they watched their friends stumbling around awkwardly holding each other at arm's length. The

huge embarrassment that the boys displayed contributed
greatly to the reality of the scene.

My friendship with Betty had strengthened over the years.
She now had a flat in Finchley which was only a 20-minute
bus ride from Edgware and we saw each other several times a
week. When I had first known her, she had been a Crusader
leader, and as such had to agree not to wear make-up, go to
the cinema or theatre and generally avoid those things which
were felt in those days to be something of a snare and delusion
to young people. I think even then she had felt that these pro-
hibitions were not a necessary part of leading the Christian
life, but had gone along with them because they were required.
Those days were now long past and we greatly enjoyed going
to the cinema or theatre together. On special occasions she
would come over and worship at John Keble with me or
I would go over and worship with her at St Mary at Finchley.
She would also come to All Saints' Margaret Street with me
although she was slightly suspicious of it at first. She soon
found that the gospel was proclaimed as faithfully there as in
any evangelical church and came to value the services as much
as I did. She never quite came to terms with the Blessed Virgin
Mary but did not find this an insuperable problem. We always
went to the evenings said Mass on my birthday before going
on to the theatre and a celebration dinner, and from her point
of view it was somewhat unfortunate that in those days it was
a feast of the Visitation. So Our Lady featured rather promin-
ently! Betty's birthday was the day after mine so we always
tried to make sure that we were still together at midnight
when hers began.

She took a great interest in my work and would come and
see anything I was doing. On each of the occasions when I was
in Vienna, she came out to visit for a few days and we had
some very happy times exploring the city together. We visited
the Prater with other members of the company. She went on
the terrifying big dipper with them, but I chickened out and

said I would look after their candyfloss while they risked life and limb. I did agree to go on the famous wheel with everyone else as this was much more sedate and I felt relatively secure in the closed cars. Betty often came as a member of the audience to the various television recordings. In *Dad's Army* and *You Rang, M'Lord?* she was accepted as part of the family in the same way as the wives of the married members of the cast. She once said to me that she thought that actors often put church-goers to shame in the way they made people feel welcome.

In October 1992, the deacon who had been working at John Keble moved to another church. Quite a large group including Betty went to her institution. Various people who had cars gave others a lift and Betty and I sat in the back of our car while the driver got himself hopelessly lost. We refrained from comment as he conferred with his other pas-senger, consulted maps and retraced the route for several miles. Eventually we ended up in a very quiet country lane but found, somewhat to our surprise, that he had got it right and the church was at the end of it. In spite of the delay we were in good time for the service. It was much more informal than John Keble or St Mary at Finchley but Betty and I both liked experiencing different types of worship and we enjoyed it. The bun fight afterwards was very friendly and we felt the parishioners would make their new deacon feel very much at home. It was quite late when we left and as Betty was going back to Finchley and I was going to Edgware, it was decided that one of the cars which was going in Betty's direction would take her and I would travel with our original driver. Betty and I said our goodbyes and went off in our separate cars.

Betty was the leader of the Women's Fellowship at St Mary's and she had a meeting the following day. I was at the Equity Council all morning and when I returned home after lunch, there was a telephone call from a friend of Betty's.

'Frank?' said the shaky voice. 'This is Huguette. I went to Betty's flat this morning and found her unconscious.'

I stood listening in silence.

'The neighbours helped to break in, and we sat by Betty while we waited for the ambulance. They've taken her to hospital, but I don't know which one.'

I asked how serious it was, but she didn't know. The paramedics had only said that they needed to get Betty to hospital as soon as possible. I replaced the receiver and stood there for a moment frozen and I felt a knot tightening in my stomach. I could not think what to do. Then I realized I needed to find out where Betty was. I picked up the phone and started ringing round all the hospitals in the area. No one had a record of a Betty Camkin having been admitted. I decided to try the ambulance service but they too were unable to help. I was by now quite frantic with worry. I felt totally helpless.

A few moments later the phone rang. Huguette, who always described herself as an atheist, had taken the trouble to go down to St Mary's and tell the Women's Fellowship what had happened, and the call was from a member of the group wanting to make sure that I knew about Betty. I was grateful to have someone to talk to and told her about the frustration of not being able to find out where Betty had been taken. She said that as soon as I knew, I must ring her and she would drive me to hospital.

While I was trying to think what to do next, the telephone rang again. This time a more formal voice was on the other end.

'Mr Williams?'

'Yes.'

'I'm a consultant at the Whittington Hospital in Highgate. We have admitted a Betty Camkin and looking in her diary we see that you are the person to be informed in case of an accident.'

The Whittington was one of the hospitals I had rung earlier but this did not seem important now. I waited for what was coming next.

'Your friend has suffered a massive brain haemorrhage,' he said.

'What does that mean?' I asked.

'I'm sorry,' he said. 'I'm afraid it means that there is really nothing we can do.'

I rang my friend, and she and her husband drove me to the Whittington. I found out where Betty was and within minutes I was at her side, but she was lying in a coma, her bed surrounded by curtains. I felt totally lost and did not know what to do.

'Just sit there and chat to her,' suggested the nurse. 'She can probably hear you, even if she can't speak.'

I sat down next to her and thought of all the laughter and tears we had shared. I held her hand and tried to talk naturally about our plans for Christmas. I was doing pantomime in Preston that year, and a few weeks earlier we had been up there sorting out where I was going to stay. We had found a very good hotel, and had booked a room for Betty so that she could spend Christmas with me. I tried to sound confident and positive, but it was very difficult because I knew it was never going to happen. After a while it all became too difficult. I knew that there were other people who needed to be told what had happened, so I decided to leave.

'I will come back in the morning,' I said to the nurse as I left.

I went back to Betty's flat and phoned her goddaughter Frances. She said that she too would come to the hospital the next day. By the time I got there the next morning, Betty had died.

It was just so sudden, so unexpected. Two nights ago, we had been laughing as we said goodbye after that church service. Now she was gone. I just could not take it in. The next few days seemed somehow unreal. Frances and I went back to Betty's flat from the hospital to telephone friends who needed to know. I was due to start rehearsing in a couple of days for an episode of *You Rang, M'Lord?* and I rang Roy Gould who was directing it to see which day I could have off to attend the funeral. He was extremely understanding and said he would work around me on any day that was chosen. We arranged the funeral, put the notices in the *Times* and the *Daily Telegraph* and tried to make sure that all Betty's friends knew the details.

When I arrived for the first day's rehearsal of the episode of *You Rang, M'Lord?*, Roy had told everyone what had happened and the cast were very supportive. Su Pollard, with whom Betty had always got on rather well, was particularly kind. Many of the cast were unsure what to say, but their few words of sympathy were deeply appreciated. Su, in her uninhibited way, was able to talk about Betty quite naturally and she was genuinely upset that rehearsals would prevent her being at the funeral. I was moved that she wanted to be there.

Betty loved flowers, so Frances and I had decided that the funeral would not be a 'family flowers only' occasion. I was deeply touched to see that among the many flowers, even Joe Allen, the theatrical restaurant where Betty and I often dined after a play, had sent some. The church was packed and I was very grateful to Betty's family for suggesting that I should sit in the front pew with them. The Rector of St Mary's, John Barnett, spoke of the importance that Betty attached to her friendship with me. He quoted the hymn 'Jerusalem the Golden'.

'In some hymnbooks,' he said, 'you will find the line, "I know not, O I know not, what joys await us there". In the original version the line is "What social joys are there". The Victorians did not feel that "social joys" were an appropriate thing for heaven but Betty certainly would have approved of the phrase. She was very much a social person, always enjoying being with other people and she would certainly expect to find that in heaven. Betty didn't just shine, she sparkled,' he concluded.

John Barnett got it right. Betty was certainly an enthusiast for life. Although our relationship had never been anything more than a very deep friendship, many people wrote letters of condolence to me. I was particularly moved to receive one from a consultant at the Mildmay Hospital where Betty had worked. He said that he noticed that a great change had taken place in Betty when I came into her life. He implied that she had blossomed in some way. I hoped this was true. She had certainly made a great difference to my life and I knew I was going to find it very difficult to be without her. Richard Buck, Edward Holland, Ronnie Grainge and Pamela Cundell were all immensely helpful. They allowed me to grieve in my own way, but they were always there for me when I needed them.

Betty died on 22 October 1992, which was my mother's birthday. Just over a week later I was able to remember Betty at the All Souls' Requiem Mass. Her name together with that of my parents has been remembered on All Souls' Day ever since. On the Sunday following All Saints' Day, I attended the High Mass at Margaret Street. David Hope, then Bishop of London, was visiting the church where he had been vicar and was celebrating and preaching. In the courtyard afterwards he said to me, 'I felt she was here with us this morning.' I knew he was right.

On that particular Sunday it is our custom to sing the hymn 'In our day of thanksgiving' at the end of the service. It is sung very quietly except for the final two lines, which are sung with a great swell of sound. It is always deeply moving and I do not think that I am the only member of the congregation who finds it difficult to remain dry eyed. On that day, it had a particular poignancy for me and I thought of Betty as we sang the last verse:

> Sing praise, then, for all who here sought and here found him,
> Whose journey is ended whose perils are past:
> They believed in the Light and its glory is round them,
> Where the clouds of earth's sorrow are lifted at last.

13

NEVER TOO OLD

As always, work was a help in the healing process, although pantomime in Preston that year seemed very strange. I wanted to ring Betty to tell her how things were going and I found it difficult to accept that she was no longer there. It was obvious that Betty was sorely missed in other areas too. She was a great Conservative in London's Finchley ward, and I attended a reception there a short while after Betty's death. All of a sudden I turned to see Margaret Thatcher standing beside me. 'I'm really sorry to hear about Betty,' she said looking very concerned. We stood chatting for a moment and I realized that the popular conception of the iron lady without a heart simply wasn't true. It was moments like these that helped me forward.

When Betty had retired from the Mildmay Hospital, she had decided to see something of the world. She went to the Holy Land, visited a cousin in Australia, and went to see friends in Zimbabwe and the United States, where she took the opportunity to stay with an actor friend of mine in New York. She also took holidays nearer home. One evening the phone rang and when I picked it up she said, 'I thought you might like to have a phone call from inside the Arctic Circle!' She tried to persuade me to accompany her on some of these trips, but I have never been a great one for going on holiday, so I always declined. After she died, I think she must have pulled some heavenly strings to ensure that I saw something of the world beyond England. I was asked to go on one of the Derek Nimmo tours which visited various locations in the Far and Middle East.

My first acquaintance with Derek had been in the BBC's comedy series *All Gas and Gaiters*. It was great working with him and he could wriggle, bumble and stutter to great comic effect. His timing was superb, and the creation of his ineffectual, nervous young Reverend Mervyn Noote was so good that he played various clergy roles for many years afterwards. Derek's touring productions had been going for some years and he specialized in presenting popular English plays in various exotic locations. I was in William Douglas Home territory once again as the play was *Lloyd George Knew my Father*. Needless to say, I was to play the inevitable vicar. The glamorous Moira Lister played the lead role and Derek himself played opposite her as the dotty old general. I soon found that playing a scene with him on stage was even more rewarding than working with him on television. At every performance, the lines were brilliantly timed and the laughs never failed to come.

We opened in Hong Kong and I soon became used to the routine which was to be part of my life for the next few months. We stayed in one of the best hotels in each location. The ballroom had been converted into a dinner theatre venue with a stage constructed at one end. Each evening the audience, having dined well, would see the play. There were dressing rooms backstage, but those of us who did not have an elaborate make-up would get ready in our hotel room and go down by the service lift to the backstage area. As I did not appear until the second act, the stage manager phoned the half-hour call to my room and I knew that I had plenty of time to have a bath, get into costume and perhaps even write a few cards to friends back home before I was needed. In some of the locations, the sight of a strange man all in black with a collar back to front caused much giggling among the chambermaids and others with whom I sometimes shared the lift. The audience consisted mainly of expatriates, although when we were in China we gave a special matinee perform-ance to a large group of students who were studying English. I think the play probably convinced them that the English were as mad as they had been led to believe!

Having Derek with us in the company was a great bonus as he was well known wherever we went. The local royal family would lend us their yacht so that the cast could have a day out. We were entertained by Sultans in their palaces. Derek was anxious that we should experience real life in the various places, and as well as taking us to some exotic restaurants, he would sometimes lead an expedition to sample the food in an open-air street market. Wherever we went, if Derek had not arranged something, most of us would go sightseeing and Donald Sinden's son Jeremy who was in the company with his wife Delia, soon emerged as the natural leader. He had a guidebook and would take his band of intrepid explorers all over the place. There were occasions when he got himself and the rest of us hopelessly lost but somehow we always found our way back even if it meant hailing a friendly taxi. In Muscat, a friend of Derek's took us far away from the usual tourist routes. We went to a remote village high up in the hills where the way of life seemed not to have changed for cen-turies. It had exactly the feel of being back in biblical times. That same day we went even further up into the hills and met a group of people who lived in very primitive one-room build-ings during the summer and in caves during the winter. It was fascinating to know that, despite their simple lifestyle, modern ideas had reached them in some ways, for a bus would call every day to collect all the children and take them to school and would bring them back again each evening.

In the middle of the run, we all returned to the UK to present the play for a three-week season at the lovely theatre in Windsor. When we resumed the tour, the props and

costumes were unpacked at our first date and it was discovered that my clerical collar had been left behind. Clearly in an
Arab state there was no ecclesiastical outfitters from which
one could be purchased. Various suggestions were offered.
Someone had heard that the clergy sometimes resorted to a
piece of plastic cut from a washing-up liquid container. This
was certainly true but I did not have the kind of clerical shirt
with which this would work. Remembering my improvisation
while doing *Make Believe* at Hendon County, I suggested
folding stiff paper, and the stage manager agreed to experi-
ment. Derek had other ideas and we went off together to find
an Arab tailor. The sight of Derek trying to explain what
was required with sundry drawings and diagrams would have
made a splendid sketch in a television programme. His attempt
to demonstrate by winding a tie around my neck had the poor
man decidedly worried as he clearly thought Derek was about
to throttle me. Eventually, Derek seemed to think that he had
conveyed the requirements satisfactorily and he paid in
advance. We left the shop, Derek quietly confident that when
we returned later in the day we would be presented with a
collar which any clergyman would be proud to own. I had my
doubts. When we arrived back at the hotel, someone had
found out where the Anglican church was and had borrowed
a collar from the priest. Derek, Moira and I were all church-
goers, so why had none of us thought of that? The collar
arrived and fortunately the clergy neck was approximately the
same size as mine so the problem was solved. When I went
to church later in the week, the reverend gentleman seemed to
be quite pleased that his collar was appearing on stage with
Derek Nimmo and Moira Lister. I don't think Derek ever
went back to see the tailor, so he is probably still waiting for
the two mad Englishmen to collect the curious piece of clothing which they had ordered and for which he had been paid.

In one state, the Crown Prince came to see the production
and at the end we were all lined up to be presented to the royal

party. He came down the line followed by his entourage and we all bowed and shook his hand. Unfortunately no one had closed the door after him and we soon realized that the entire audience had joined on the end and thought shaking hands with the cast was all part of the entertainment. We smiled and made appreciative remarks as about 300 people passed by making polite comments about the show. When the last hand had been shaken, those of us who had not eaten before the performance made a beeline for the restaurant hoping that it was still open. It was and we felt we had really earned our dinner that night.

Our time in Beijing was particularly fascinating. We visited the Summer Palace, the Forbidden City and, of course, the Great Wall. We were taken by cable car to one of the higher points and then walked downward for which I was very grateful. I had heard about it and seen pictures but nothing prepared me for the reality. From some angles you can see it stretching far into the distance on both sides and we realized what a remarkable feat of building it was. That day was quite unforgettable.

Opportunities for churchgoing varied from place to place, but I always managed to find somewhere. Westernized cities such as Hong Kong, Singapore and Kuala Lumpur were no problem, since there was a strong and visible Anglican presence. In some of the Arab States, it was more difficult. Christianity was tolerated but had to be kept out of sight and the places of worship were often concealed behind high fences. Somehow, there was always someone who seemed to be able to tell me how to find them. I wondered if China was going to be the one place where I would be unable to get to church. I decided to try anyway, and asked the receptionist at the hotel if she could help. She wrote some Chinese characters on a piece of paper and told me that was the location of the Catholic church, and if I showed the paper to a taxi driver, he would take me there. Fortunately I remembered to ask for a similar piece of paper with the name of the hotel in Chinese on it so that I would be able to get back. The taxi dropped me outside a heavily secured fenced compound and the driver pointed to the entrance. I was viewed with some suspicion by the young Chinese man at the door but after a moment he decided to let me in. Despite the Communist repression, there were clearly many devout Catholics who maintained their faith, and the buildings seemed very full. I was delighted as the congregation rose to sing the first hymn to recognize the tune of 'What a friend we have in Jesus'. I have no idea whether the words were a Chinese translation of the ones which were so well known to me, but hearing them singing the familiar tune made me feel quite at home. As always the action of the Mass transcended the language barrier and as the priest held up the Host I knew that here in the centre of Beijing, this was the same Lamb of God who takes away the sin of the world, once more being presented to His faithful people.

In England my religious life had taken on a new dimension. James Gill, who had been our company manager in Vienna and also of *Cinderella*, invited me to a small dinner party one day. 'There's someone I'd like you to meet,' he said. Knowing that I was a churchman he wanted to introduce me to Derek Pattinson, who was a friend of his. Derek was the secretary-general of the General Synod. We got on well together and became good friends. One day he suggested that I might like to stand for election to the Synod. I was a bit taken aback. 'Why would anyone vote for me?' I asked. 'I'm not really very well known in the diocese as a whole.'

He was nothing if not honest. 'You've got a face that people will recognize,' he said. 'I think you might just scrape in at the last place.'

Like most other people I had sat around and criticized some of the decisions that were being made in the Church, and when I thought about it I felt that maybe Derek was right and I ought to try to get more involved. I wrote my election address with a suitable photograph at the top and managed to get in a bit about having been the Vicar in *Dad's Army* for anyone who might not have recognized me. I had the required 500 or 600 copies printed and delivered them to the diocesan office who would send them out with all the other election addresses and the voting paper. The voting method used was the single transferable vote which ensures that no one group or faction can sweep the board. The voter marks his or her paper, not with a cross but with a number placing the candidates in order of preference.

On the appointed day I attended the count and watched in fascination as the proceedings got underway. In those days, it was all done by hand and the first count had already been completed. The ballot papers were set out on a long table with a pile for each candidate. Each pile consisted of those papers which had a number one against the candidate concerned. Some of the piles were quite thick and others seemed to have very few papers. They were arranged in alphabetical order, so I could easily identify mine at the very end of the row. It was not very thick but was not painfully thin either. The returning officer announced the quota: the number of votes a candidate has to achieve in order to be elected. This figure is worked out by a complicated equation involving the number of valid ballot papers received and the number of places available. The Diocese of London, for which I was standing, had eight. He announced that one candidate had already achieved the required number of votes and he was declared elected. Thereafter the complicated process began. The candidate with the least number of first votes was eliminated and his votes transferred to the candidate who had a number two against his name. As it was done by physically moving the papers on to another pile we could see how each person was progressing. This went on until another candidate was found to have achieved the quota and she was declared elected. There were other complications involving sharing out any surplus votes which a successful candidate had achieved. At each point as a candidate was eliminated we looked anxiously to see where his or her votes would go. When the seventh candidate was declared elected, my pile was still there but so were a number of others. None of us had achieved the target and the returning officer redistributed the smallest pile. Again, no one had made it, so the next smallest pile was dealt with. It was nail-biting stuff. Eventually I saw him place a number of papers on my pile and he declared that I had been elected. Derek had been right and I had scraped in on the last count.

I stood for Synod on two subsequent occasions. On the first of these I was once again elected towards the end of the count. At my last election I made it on the first count with a substantial number of spare votes. However, by then the counting had been computerized and was not nearly so exciting.

My first experience of the Synod was the inaugural service held in Westminster Abbey in the presence of Her Majesty the Queen. On a cold November morning we all assembled in the cloisters. Each diocese had its allotted place. The eight of us who had been chosen as lay representatives for the Diocese of London joined our clergy who had been elected in a separate vote. The dioceses were lined up around the cloisters in alphabetical order so London was roughly in the middle. We had each received a ticket for a guest to attend the service and naturally I had given mine to Betty. As I processed into the Abbey wearing my dark grey suit, along with the 500 or 600 other members of the Synod, it was an amazing feeling. After the service we went into the circular chamber of Church House in which the Synod always meets in London. We were addressed by Her Majesty and then the first session began.

When he was Archbishop of Canterbury, I once heard Robert Runcie say in a sermon, 'I sometimes think Synods have stolen away my Lord and I know not where they have laid Him.' It got a good laugh and clearly expressed the suspicion many people have about the Synod and all its works.

I soon came to find that it was a remarkable body. The elected lay members had come from so many different areas of life that whatever subject was being debated, there would always be a number of people with expert knowledge. The clergy came from a wide variety of parishes – some from deprived inner-city areas, and others from leafy suburbia. There were clergy serving in rural areas where they would have charge of several parishes, and there were those who served in the big industrial towns. There were those who ministered to affluent congregations and there were those who worked in parishes where the majority of people were unemployed.

The standard of debate was very high, indeed there were those who suggested that our debates were often better than those taking place in the building just down the road, the House of Commons! People seemed surprised that I was clearly nervous whenever I spoke. They thought that an actor should have no worries when speaking in public. I tried to explain that when I was on stage, I was using words that had been written by someone else and in a character other than my own. Here, I was trying to make a point in my own words, which was a very different thing. I also knew that those who were listening included some very erudite clergy and lay people and senior bishops, not to mention the two Archbishops. With an audience like that, I think my nervousness was under-standable.

The fact that the debating chamber was circular clearly demonstrated one very important difference from Parliament. There was no sense of a government and an opposition. We were all working together for a common purpose. Clearly there were different viewpoints and groupings within the Synod. The three main groups were: the Open Synod Group, who tended to be those with a fairly liberal attitude; the Evangelical Group, in General Synod affectionately known as 'EGGS'; and the Catholic Group, which stood for traditional

Catholic understanding of doctrine. It was this last group that I was invited to join. I agreed to do so with some misgivings. At the first meeting of the group I confessed to one of my fellow members from London that I did not accept the rather rigid Catholic views on remarriage after divorce. I explained that while I believed in the sanctity of marriage, I felt there were cases when the relationship had irretrievably broken down and it was unhelpful if the Church refused to recognize a subsequent marriage. She was a very senior member of the group and had been on the Synod for a number of years and I was greatly relieved when she said that she shared my views. From then on, I happily remained as a member of the Catholic Group throughout my time on the Synod.

There were three sessions a year, each lasting three or four days. In February and November we met in London, and in the summer we had a residential meeting over a weekend on the university campus in York. These summer sessions had a much more informal and relaxed atmosphere, although one or two of the more elderly members seemed somewhat scandalized to see a bishop walking around in shorts! Eating meals together and relaxing in the bar at lunchtime and after the evening session gave everyone an opportunity to get to know each other better. I was highly amused to hear the barmaid say to a very senior and dignified bishop, 'What can I get you, flower?' This northern term of endearment had not come his way before and I think he rather enjoyed it.

There was an early morning Eucharist each day and a stream of people from the different colleges would be seen crossing the road to Heslington Church; and it was usually full to overflowing. During my first five years, Donald Smith was also on the Synod as the Archdeacon from the diocese of St Edmundsbury and Ipswich, so he usually stayed with me and we went to the meetings together.

When I joined the Synod one of the key questions being addressed was the thorny issue of the ordination of women.

The Catholic Group took the lead in opposing the measure and I spoke in several debates. I had examined my conscience carefully to be sure that I was not just giving way to prejudice. I had always valued and continued to value the ministry of women, but ordination to the priesthood was a very different matter. I believed there were many arguments against it, but for me the most important one was that it would be very divisive within the Church. My speeches in Synod were designed to make that point.

The final vote on the matter came in November 1992. I was actually working at the time and had negotiated a day off rehearsals in order to be present at the debate. The importance of the matter was demonstrated by the fact that an entire day had been given over to it and the debate would be chaired by the two Archbishops: the Archbishop of York in the morning and the Archbishop of Canterbury in the afternoon. To be called to speak in a debate, members had to stand at the end of the previous speech and wait for the chairman to call them. I stood throughout the morning and again throughout the afternoon but neither Archbishop called my name. In matters as important as this, the standing orders stated that the debate could not close while anyone still wished to speak. As the hours moved on, His Grace of Canterbury imposed a speech limit of two minutes and then reduced it to one minute. At this point I gave up, feeling that a one-minute intervention would probably make little difference.

We knew that the majority of the bishops were in favour of it and that there would be a sufficient majority in the house of clergy for it to go through, so the outcome rested on the votes of the house of laity. I was one of the last people to go to the Noes door and a senior member of the Catholic Group who had been standing near the tellers told me that she did not think we had achieved sufficient votes to defeat the measure. She was right: when the figures were announced, the motion had been passed in all three houses, the house of laity receiving the necessary majority by only two or three votes.

Clearly the result was an occasion of great rejoicing for the many women who had worked and prayed for this for years. For some of us, at that moment, it seemed like the end of the Church of England. As we left Church House through the throng of people cheering the result, I was near to tears.

The reality of what had happened hit me the following Sunday. Our woman deacon preached a sermon which was eirenic and understanding of those who were unhappy with the decision and I was grateful to her for that. Then came the creed. We came to the line 'I believe in one Holy Catholic and Apostolic Church'. I did believe in it but I felt that what the Synod had done had divorced us from it. Of course it was an over-reaction and I have now come to terms with the decision. It is typical of the Church of England that it made every effort to make it possible for those of my persuasion to stay within the fold. Many good friends, clergy and laity left the Church of England but I have remained, though I still cannot accept the priesthood of women. I deeply value their ministry in all other ways and I have found that with goodwill on both sides it is possible to work things out.

On many issues, opinion went right across group boundaries. It was the time of the Bishop of Durham's questioning whether a number of events recorded in the Gospels were historic fact. His famous 'conjuring trick with bones' speech on the resurrection made headlines in many newspapers. When I spoke of my own firm belief in the Virgin Birth and the resurrection appearances of Christ as historical events, it won the approval of the evangelicals as well as the Catholics. My plea in another debate that the Church should show greater understanding and compassion when discussing the subject of homosexuality was less popular in some quarters.

Throughout my time on Synod, the liturgy was going through a period of great change and the Church was moving towards the publication of *Common Worship*. As someone who spent his life speaking words and even trying to write them on occasions, I felt I had something to offer in this area. I spoke in a number of debates on liturgical matters usually defending traditional texts. When I was growing up, there was one commonly accepted version of the Lord's Prayer and even those who never went to church were able to say it.

Now, when a group of people from different churches meet together and say this prayer, the leader has to make it clear which form is to be used. I am sad when I see that those who are not regular churchgoers find that the one thing they thought they knew has somehow been changed. New translations of the Bible or new words for worship may make the Church more accessible, although I sometimes doubt it. In any case, there is certainly a down side. In my youth, the Authorized version of the Bible and the *Book of Common Prayer* were used by almost all Anglican churches. As a result, my generation had the words of these two books deeply ingrained. My dying soldier in *Shield of Faith* was able to use the words of the twenty-third Psalm because they had become part of his very being. The Authorized Version of the Bible was so well known that the titles of many films were taken from it: *Our Vines Have Tender Grapes*, *East of Eden*, *The Little Foxes* and so on. The titles of many plays were also taken from it: *Rain on the Just*, *The Silver Cord*, *Now Barabbas*, for example. Now few people know any biblical quotations because there are so many different versions to read. I believe this is a real loss. Maybe in 50 years time, phrases from *Common Worship* will be as well known as those magnificent resonances from the *Book of Common Prayer*, but somehow I rather doubt it.

Common Worship was introduced to the Church on Advent Sunday 2000. I was not there to see its inauguration at John Keble or All Saints'. I was away in pantomime and attended the church where the Actors Church Union chaplain was the vicar. The church was part of a team ministry, and they had decided to use the many variations allowed in the new book, to change almost everything in sight. The vicar, who knew his congregation, obviously felt this was unwise. He was a jolly and extrovert man, who had been on the stage before he was ordained. Some of his comic theatrical style was still very evident and he had a great rapport with his congregation. He introduced the new service and told them they could follow it on the printed cards which they had been given. He then pointed at me and said, 'and if you don't like it, you can blame him, because he was on the General Synod when it was written.' I joined in the laughter, but after the service I found that a number of the congregation were indeed not happy with it and wanted to know why they had wasted £10 on buying the book if the whole thing was going to be on a card anyway. The next Sunday, the vicar told his congregation, 'The cards have been binned and you can use the books for which you have paid £10.' The service then proceeded keeping it as near to what had gone before as possible, and everyone seemed happy.

During my time on Synod, I served for five years on the Crown Appointments Commission. This is the body which is concerned with the appointment of diocesan bishops. It meets and after considering the needs of the diocese concerned, sends two names to the Prime Minister. He is then free to choose either. The commission is made up of 12 people: three lay members elected from the house of laity in the Synod; three clerical members elected from the house of clergy; the two archbishops; and four people elected by the vacant diocese. For obvious reasons, the meetings were highly confidential and even the time and location were not supposed to be divulged. As a bachelor, this was no problem for me, but I often wondered how married people explained their absence to their spouses.

We always met within a framework of worship. The daily

offices were said and we attended a celebration of the Eucharist in the morning. Sometimes we met in a retreat house, and the worship was organized within the group, one of the clergy members celebrating the Eucharist. On one of these occasions, I was asked to read the lesson at Evensong. I looked in the lectionary and turned to the appointed passage. I found myself reading the account of the apostles choosing the one who was to replace Judas by casting lots. I wondered if God was trying to tell us something! More usually we met within a religious community and joined them in their worship.

There has been much criticism of the system but I have to say I think it works. The secrecy surrounding the process is necessary if confidentiality is to be preserved. This confidentiality was so necessary to the process that I tried to forget everything that had taken place as soon as the meeting was over. I found I usually succeeded so well that when the appointment was announced, more often than not I had forgotten the names we had put forward. People would come up to me and tell me with great confidence that they knew who the second name had been. I always refused to make any comment, but on the rare occasions when I remembered myself, I can say now that people nearly always got it wrong.

14

A FUTURE IN SIGHT

The invitation to appear in *A Midsummer Night's Dream* at the Almeida Theatre came out of the blue. It was to be directed by Jonathan Miller, who saw the mechanicals as a group not dissimilar from the *Dad's Army* troop. I had played Flute back in my days at the Gateway Theatre and now I was to play Quince. It was, in some ways, a controversial production, set in the 1930s with a set made up largely of mirrors. Rehearsals were enormously enjoyable and I found Jonathan Miller a stimulating director. He was also an extremely interesting man. In rehearsal breaks his knowledge and ability to talk on almost any subject was quite amazing.

We opened to mixed notices but most of them were favourable, and I was particularly pleased that one paper described my performance as 'Betjmanesque'. The production certainly found the humour in parts of the play which can sometimes be a bit heavy. Jonathan decided that Quince was a cut above the rest of the troop, a bank manager perhaps, and at the beginning I wore a business suit, a trilby hat and a slightly shabby riding mac for the rehearsal scene in the forest, and a rather flamboyant flowing cravat when we presented our play before the Duke. The dressing-room space at the Almeida is very limited and several of us were crowded into one room. Peter Bayliss, who was a wonderful Bottom, was as entertai off-stage as he was on. He was a great computer turned up one day having very convincingly c

paper column from one of the tabloids saying that a close
nd of mine had got very drunk in the Green Room club,
d been arrested for damaging the portrait of its founder.
he prose style was a little too flamboyant, so I was only
momentarily taken in.

The run at the Almeida was followed by a rather unusual
mini-tour. We did a week in Glasgow, and a week in Brussels
where Neil Kinnock came to see us, as well as a week in
Lisbon. It was a good way to end the run and it was certainly
different!

So what of the future? Actors never retire, and I certainly
haven't. Pantomime still beckons every year and other odd
jobs crop up from time to time. However, bearing in mind
that some of the *Dad's Army* cast were over 70 years old when
they started their career in the Home Guard, I am sure there is
something new out there waiting for me. Over the years, as
Dad's Army has become a classic in the annals of television
comedy, I have found myself spending more and more time
making personal appearances associated with it. Interviews
on radio and television covering various aspects of the series
have become the norm. The on-going tour of 'A Night with
the Stars', in which I am interviewed about my life and career,
has been great fun. I even get to perform on stage as a vicar
again.

I often tell the story of the elderly actress who was visited by
an old schoolfriend backstage after her performance one day.

'Do sit down, darling,' she said. 'It's been 20 years since
we've seen each other and we've got a lot of catching up to do.'

The actress proceeds to give her life story and bring her
friend up to date with all that she has been doing. After about
30 minutes of non-stop talking, she finishes. 'Well, now dear.
That's quite enough about me, we must talk about you. So
what did you think of my performance?'

It just illustrates how much actors love talking about
themselves, and I am no exception.

Although I sometimes get mildly frustrated that people on think of me in terms of my role in *Dad's Army*, I am immense ly proud to be associated with it.

Not far from Thetford lies the Bressingham Theme Park. It is here that they have a *Dad's Army* exhibition which contains, among other things, a replica of the church hall, and a street area from Walmington-on-Sea. There is Jones's butcher's shop and the Swallow Bank, but Bill Pertwee has to put up with a portable barrow for his greengrocery. Some of the vehicles used on the series are displayed as are a number of uniforms. In the year 2000, 23 years after the final series, the survivors of the show were invited to open this new exhibition. Wallowing in nostalgia, we all stayed at The Bell Hotel once more where a plaque was placed commemorating the spot on which the actors first gathered to begin the location filming.

The weekend began with a dinner at the hotel. The following day we were given a civic reception by the mayor. It was a glorious summer's day, and the reception took the form of drinks on the lawn behind the Town Hall with various civic dignitaries in attendance. After socializing we were escorted by the police through a big crowd outside the town hall and took our places on a wonderful period fire engine. This took us on a triumphant ride through Thetford, and we were amazed that all along the route people lined up to give us a cheer. Every now and then I was allowed to clang the fire engine bell. We were told that we would disembark at the town square and sit at a table in the centre so that we could sign autographs. As we reached the square, the scene that met our gaze was unbelievable. On all four sides, people stood several deep, and a path had to be cleared for our fire engine to reach the middle. As we climbed off the engine, the crowd showed how greatly loved the series actually was, as smiles, cheers and autograph books came in every direction. 'My children and my grandchildren love your show!' shouted one lady.

All thoughts of letting a few autograph hunters in

re abandoned and we went on a royal walkabout to greet
s many people as possible as hands were thrust towards us to
shake. Autograph books, scraps of paper, copies of the various
books about the show were passed over the heads of the crowd
for us to sign. It was quite, quite amazing to see so many people
there, and the excitement they displayed was overwhelming.
We were delighted that over 20 years on, *Dad's Army* was still
commanding such an enormous following.

The next day I got up early and went to the service at
Thetford Parish Church and had fond memories of my visits
there some 20 years earlier. Then it was up to Bressingham for
the grand opening. The fire engine was parked in the courtyard of a nearby pub and we mounted it once again. Pamela
Cundell rashly agreed to wear a fireman's helmet which was
solid brass and weighed a ton. It was worth it, as she arrived
triumphantly looking like Britannia. We were astonished to
see that the crowds here easily matched those of the previous
day. When David and Jimmy cut the tape to declare the *Dad's
Army* exhibition open, there was an immense cheer. Another
session of autograph signing took place in the replica church
hall, but this was much easier than the day before as we could
actually sit down.

The day ended with a magnificent dinner given by David
and Ann Croft at Honiton Hall for the cast and some of the
members of the *Dad's Army* Appreciation Society.

On the anniversary of the opening, we went to Bressingham
again, and still there were crowds waiting to welcome us. It
seems this may well become an annual event.

'Do you still get money for all those repeats?' is one of the
most common questions I am asked. The answer is that I most
certainly do. I had done two Shakespeare plays for the BBC
and at the time everyone assured me that I would receive a
nice little pension. They have not seen the light of day again,
so it is *Dad's Army* that has provided my pension. I get more
now for the repeats than I did for the original series. These

repeat fees are negotiated by Equity and take into account what an actor might be earning if they were doing the programme today.

The invitation to be part of the Queen Mother's one-hundredth birthday parade was a great honour. The procession was made up of individual displays and floats, each marking a decade in her life. We were in the group representing the war years. As Bill Pertwee, Pamela Cundell and I walked round Horse Guards' Parade leading the Home Guard contingent and hundreds of others in various uniforms and costumes, we were proud to be part of such a great occasion. Walking was quite difficult, especially for Pam who was wearing the very high heels fashionable in the 1940s. The ground was covered in several inches of sand to make it easy for the horses and camels that were part of the procession. It certainly did not make it easy for human beings, but on passing the Royal Box, I was able to bow to the Queen Mother, while Pamela waved in true Mrs Fox style. Bill raised his arm towards his famous tin hat, in salute.

Looking at this gracious lady who had served this country throughout my lifetime, I was moved to be wishing her a happy one-hundredth birthday. In spite of the advice to be seated, she often insisted on standing, especially when her regiments marched past. At the end of the parade, when Sir John Mills wished her a 'Very Happy Birthday Ma'am', he was expressing the sentiments that we all felt.

Although she was of a great age, the news of her death came as a shock, as I think we all felt she would be there for ever. I sat watching her funeral on television and remembered that day on Horse Guards' Parade.

Apparently *Dad's Army* was one of her favourite programmes. I was very touched that on the day of the Queen Mother's funeral, the BBC showed *The Royal Train*, which was apparently her favourite episode. She particularly liked the fact that it referred to her late husband.

Being one of the surviving members of the cast, I still get fan letters from viewers all over England and some from foreign parts as well. Most of these simply say that they love the show and could they have a photograph, though some want to know all sorts of details and technicalities about the show. I usually have no idea of the answer but I can often find it in one of the many reference books. Failing that, I can always put them on to the *Dad's Army* Appreciation Society, who all seem to know a great deal more about the series than I do. I also get some fan letters that make me chuckle. 'Can I have three photographs please? One for myself and the other two for swaps.' I often wonder who I get swapped for. 'I'll give you my vicar if you give me your Dot Cotton.'

Occasionally I get some rather peculiar ones: 'Dear Mr Williams, I have got Ian Lavender, Clive Dunn and Bill Pertwee. I've also got Pamela Cundell, but I haven't got John Le Mesurier – can you get it for me, please?' When a letter asks for cast members who are no longer with us, I feel it's somewhat bizarre. Perhaps they think I have a secret stock of Arthur Lowe's signature hidden away in a drawer.

I also get many fan letters wishing my team good luck in the coming season. This puzzled me at first until I discovered they are intended for the Formula One racing driver who shares my name. I get these letters with remarkable frequency and have learned that a website has published my private address as belonging to him. I write back to say that they have got the wrong Frank Williams, and sometimes have to return compli-cated drawings and sketches of engines which the writer has designed. These correspondents are not the first to make this mistake. My agent once phoned me in a state of bewilderment saying that a television company had asked if I would be will-ing to drive round the circuit at Le Mans. After explaining about my technical inability, I declined the offer! Anxious that I should not turn down work, my agent tried to persuade me otherwise, but I took pity on him and explained the mistake.

The continuing popularity of *Dad's Army* over the years is amazing. It goes right across the age range, as grandparents watch it with their grandchildren. A friend of mine once introduced me to someone he felt was my youngest fan. It was his three-year-old granddaughter. 'She prefers your programme to *Postman Pat*,' he said. I was a bit sceptical but smiled benignly. The BBC had recently shown an episode in which I had an argument with Captain Mainwaring over the use of the office. Suddenly the little girl looked up at me and said very solemnly, 'Tell me. That desk, is it yours or Captain Mainwaring's?' It seemed she not only preferred it to *Postman Pat* but also followed the plot!

People often wonder why *Dad's Army* has stood the test of time. Pamela Cundell once asked a twelve-year-old boy why he enjoyed the programme. He thought for a minute and then said, 'Because it's funny and not rude.' He was right, of course – it *is* a programme that a family can sit down and watch together knowing that there is going to be nothing which will embarrass or offend anyone.

The plots are all wonderfully simple. A group of men in extraordinary circumstances, doing their best against the odds, and occasionally even managing to get it right. For me some of the adventures are reminiscent of *Just William and the Outlaws*, but instead of twelve-year-old boys we have grown men. The characters are wonderfully drawn and are very funny in themselves. People laugh at them in the same way that I laughed at George Formby, Gert and Daisy and Old Mother Riley, but in their own way, they are also very real and the audience has a great affection for them.

Looking back on my career I realize that I was fortunate to be part of the golden age of television. I started in the pioneering days when everything was new and exciting. I worked for great directors such as Rudolph Cartier and for great comedy writers such as Perry and Croft. I worked with many of the great comics, and in the early days had good opportunities to play in many straight dramas. Undoubtedly there is some marvellous television being made now, but to my mind there is much that is less worthy. Too often directors seem to vie with each other to see who can push the barriers the furthest. Nothing is left to the imagination and sex and violence are shown in graphic detail. Often these scenes add nothing to one's understanding of the plot or character. I am not asking for bland television, since programmes with a cutting edge are nothing new. Ken Loach and directors like him were producing them years ago.

When I was a young actor, starting out in the theatre, we still had censorship, and we were all very opposed to it. We believed that if the censorship laws were abolished everyone concerned would exercise self-censorship which would avoid any problems. I am still opposed to censorship but I fear that unless we get our house in order, there may be a backlash which will impose it once again from above. The censor basically dealt with the theatre. He did not allow serious plays to be performed if they dealt with certain subjects, thus depriving the theatre of one of its most important functions in encouraging debate and thought on a range of important moral questions. Ironically he did allow cheap innuendo which treated the same serious subjects as a joke.

One of the things that incensed us as young actors was the fact that the censor would not allow certain words to be used in any circumstances. We couldn't see the problem and used to chat about the absurdity of it whenever we met. We were young and, of course, we knew it all. How wrong we were. We were actors dealing with words all the time, and we of all people should have known their power. I am saddened when I sit on the bus and hear four-letter words coming from children aged six and seven. What I notice when I hear this sort of thing is the aggression that nearly always seems to accompany it. I accept that there are situations where realism demands the use of language which would have been taboo 20 years ago, but all too often these words are just thrown in merely in order to shock.

When I watch television I do sometimes wonder what's happened to our ideas about humour. Of course, there has always been in England a great tradition of anarchic, disrespectful bawdy humour from Chaucer onwards, but in the past it had some style, some wit and some purpose. Now all too often what we get is the kind of sniggering smut that I might have thought funny when I was still at my prep school. By the time I got to Ardingly, such humour would have been considered utterly juvenile. We need to understand that television not only reflects life, but is a powerful medium, which also has a strong influence in forming the culture in which we live.

So what do I want from television? I want the comedy to be witty and amusing with good characters and funny situations. I want the drama to entertain but I also want it to stimulate my mind and make me think about the problems which people face. I want it to help me to understand situations which I will probably never experience for myself. I want it to help me to be compassionate. I want it to help me laugh, and I want it to make me weep. I want it to be responsible and have ideals. At its best it should enrich the spirit and deepen our understanding of what it means to be a human being made in the image of God. I suppose for me the prayer of the Actors Church Union says it all:

O God, the King of Glory, who in the making of man didst bestow upon him the gift of tears and the sense of joy, and didst implant in his nature, the need for recreation of mind and body give to those who minister to that need through drama and music in the calling of the theatrical profession, a high ideal, a pure intention and the sense of great responsibility. And both to them and to those who accept their ministry give the will so to use it that it may be for the enrichment of human character and for thy greater glory.